Making Never-Never Land

LATINX HISTORIES

Lori Flores and Michael Innis-Jiménez, editors

Series Advisory Board

Llana Barber
Adrian Burgos Jr.
Geraldo Cadava
Julio Capó Jr.
Miroslava Chavez-Garcia
Kaysha Corinealdi
María Cristina García
Ramón Gutierréz
Paul Ortiz

This series features innovative historical works that push boundaries in the study of race, ethnicity, sexuality, gender, migration, and nationalism within and around Latinx communities, premised on the view that Latinx histories are essential to understanding the full sweep of history in the United States, the Americas, and the world.

A complete list of books published in Latinx Histories is available at https://uncpress.org/series/latinx-histories-2/.

Making Never-Never Land

Race and Law in the Creation
of Puerto Rico

Mónica A. Jiménez

The University of North Carolina Press CHAPEL HILL

Set in Merope Basic by Westchester Publishing Services
Manufactured in the United States of America

Library of Congress Cataloging-in-Publication Data
Names: Jiménez, Mónica A., author.
Title: Making never-never land : race and law in the creation of Puerto Rico /
    Mónica A. Jiménez.
Other titles: Race and law in the creation of Puerto Rico | Latinx histories.
Description: Chapel Hill : The University of North Carolina Press, [2024] |
    Series: Latinx histories | Includes bibliographical references and index.
Identifiers: LCCN 2023048938 | ISBN 9781469678443 (cloth ; alk. paper) |
    ISBN 9781469678450 (paperback ; alk. paper) | ISBN 9781469678467 (epub) |
    ISBN 9798890887306 (pdf)
Subjects: LCSH: Race discrimination—Law and legislation—United States—
    History. | Constitutional law—United States—Territories and possessions. |
    Constitutional law—Political aspects—Puerto Rico. | Constitutional law—
    Social aspects—Puerto Rico. | Puerto Rico—Colonial influence. | Puerto
    Rico—Politics and government—20th century. | Puerto Rico—Politics and
    government—21st century. | United States—Relations—Puerto Rico. |
    Puerto Rico—Relations—United States. | BISAC: SOCIAL SCIENCE /
    Ethnic Studies / Caribbean & Latin American Studies | HISTORY /
    United States / General
Classification: LCC F1971 .J55 2024 | DDC 972.9505—dc23/eng/20231103
LC record available at https://lccn.loc.gov/2023048938

Cover art: Detail of Bemba PR, *Puerto Rico before Profit* (2020).

For
Germain Jiménez
August 24, 1977–October 2, 2010
&
Patricia Navarro Vélez
October 11, 1984–December 6, 2023

Contents

Acknowledgments

As I sit down to write these acknowledgments and put the final touches on nearly two decades of work, the state of Texas, where I currently live, is attempting to pass legislation that would make this type of inquiry and the teaching of it unlawful. For the past several months, I have been engaged in work to push back against the forces of ignorance and the fascist turn that would limit what can be taught and therefore what can be known. To my comrades in this struggle, who have been with me at the state capital, in meetings with lawyers and activists, in drafting and disseminating petitions and talking points, in refusing to accept that knowledge should be censored or limited, I am buoyed by your commitment and grateful for your friendship and community. *Seguimos pa'lante siempre.*

My time at the University of Texas at Austin has spanned two decades and various departments and institutions. The research that would eventually lead to *Making Never-Never Land* began during my time as a law student and developed over the subsequent decade while I worked as an attorney and then returned to graduate school to pursue a PhD in history. As with any endeavor of such duration, the list of people who helped care for and shape this project, and my spirit along with it, is long.

At the University of Texas School of Law, I'd like to thank Sanford Levinson, for sharing my interest in the Insular Cases, and Karen Engle, once my professor, now a mentor and friend. My advisers and committee members in the History Department and the Teresa Lozano Long Institute for Latin American Studies helped guide the first searching drafts of this project with patience and care. Thank you to Frank Guridy, Jossianna Arroyo-Martinez, Benjamin Brower, and Virginia Garrard. My eventual transition to faculty in the African and African Diaspora Studies Department was smoothed by the many friends and colleagues who make this community truly special. My gratitude to Minkah Makalani, Christen Smith, Cherise Smith, Ted Gordon, Omi Jones, Yasmiyn Irizarry, Eric Tang, and Lyndon Gil.

Funding for this project was provided by many institutions and organizations. At the University of Texas at Austin, I am grateful to have received research support from the Department of History, the Graduate School, the Teresa Lozano Long Institute for Latin American Studies, the John L. Warfield

Center for African American Studies, and the African and African Diaspora Studies Department. Fellowships from the Ford Foundation, the Mellon Foundation, the Center for Puerto Rican Studies at Hunter College, and Duke University's Summer Institute on Tenure and Professional Advancement provided not only research funds but also mentorship and guidance. Some of the chapters that developed into this book were first workshopped at Harvard Law School's Institute for Global Law and Policy Global Workshop, which provided a rich environment to think through nascent ideas.

This book would not have been written without the time and space provided by a Career Enhancement Fellowship from the Institute for Citizens and Scholars. When the COVID-19 pandemic began, I was on my one semester of research leave provided by the University of Texas. When my then four-year-old daughter's day care closed, my leave effectively ended, and I worried that so too had my career. Amid the upheaval of the early days of the pandemic and the disorientation and depression that came with it, my writing came to a full stop. The Career Enhancement Fellowship could not have arrived at a more opportune moment—when I desperately needed leave from teaching and mental space to write this book. I cannot thank the Institute enough for buying me both.

I am incredibly fortunate to have a wide network of colleagues and interlocutors in Puerto Rican and Caribbean studies who challenge and push my thinking and who have helped make me a better scholar and thinker. Thank you for the intellectual camaraderie, care, and friendship: Joaquin Villanueva, Sarah Molinari, Jorell Melendez Badillo, Aurora Santiago, Pedro LeBrón, Marie Cruz Soto, Daniel Nevarez, Karianne Soto Vega, José Atiles, Margaret Power, Michael Staudenmeir, Yarimar Bonilla and the members of the Bridging the Divides study group.

The network of friends and family who helped make this project possible is wide and far-flung. My graduate school friends, Ava Purkiss, Blake Scott, and Adrienne Sockwell, held me up during a most difficult time and have continued to provide encouragement ever since. In Washington, D.C., the Trepel and Strauss families have housed me, fed me, entertained me, and cheered me on over many years. My law school buddies, John Tustin and Jeremy Freeman, kept me laughing and dancing through months of archival research. In Chicago, during cold months of doubt and sunny ones of play, Judy Razo, Yinka Owolabi, Kyle Churney, Cristina Correa, Anthony Martinez, Sam Goldberg, and Larissa Brewer-Garcia were family.

In Puerto Rico, my cousins Glorymar Maldonado and Hector Galarza opened up their home to me and helped me navigate various archives. Nicolle

Diaz and Paquito Cruz became fast friends and confidants. My aunts Gloria and Cecilia del Valle are the original storytellers who set me on this path. The home of my grandparents Josefina Santos and Efrain Jiménez in Puerto Viejo has always been a place of respite and of care. I cherish the quiet times I spent there while researching and writing this book. Finally, I am grateful to the extended Jiménez, del Valle, and Navarro clans for the love, loyalty, and celebrations.

My closest friends and confidants have held and buoyed me and been my greatest cheerleaders and coconspirators. My heart is fuller for having them in my life. Thank you to Christopher Loperena, Bianca Flores, Courtney Morris, Martín Perna, and Eddie Campos for being *hermanes*. Thank you to the Turn Up Crew—Nicole Burrowes, Ashley Farmer, Ashanté Reese, Ana Schwartz, Chelsi West-Ohueri, Marisol LeBrón, Jenny Kelly, Traci Ann Wint, Tyrone Hayles, Amira Rose Davis, Bedour Alagraa, Ade Adamson, Pavithra Vasudevan, Snehal Patel, and Ashley Coleman-Taylor—for the friendship, the many hangs, and the many adventures, especially the ones involving boat rides. Thank you also to Samantha Zelade, Starla Simmons, Eva Hernandez, Thomas Fawcett, and Tyson Simons for being our community.

My family has patiently supported my work even when they did not fully understand what I was doing. I am grateful to my parents, Pura and Julio, and my siblings, Julio and Axel, for their unyielding love and for always telling the stories that led me to become a historian. My partner, Roger Reeves, has been my champion for the past sixteen years. I would not be the writer, thinker, or scholar that I am without his constant encouragement and critical mind. Our daughter, Naima, is the brightest and most joyous star in our constellation.

This book is dedicated to my brother, Germain Jiménez, whose death on October 2, 2010, fundamentally changed me, my thinking, and the questions I would ask about Puerto Rico. Though he is not here to see the culmination of the work I began just weeks before his death, this book is for him. This book is also dedicated to my cousin, Patricia Navarro Vélez. As this book was entering production, she became a victim of this country's indefensible failure to address gun violence. Patricia, who was an assistant professor like me, was killed at the University of Nevada, Las Vegas, while engaging in an activity all of us do regularly—work. That we have lost her brilliant mind and insight is lamentable, that her children and our family have lost the warmth of her love and touch is unconscionable, that we have let it happen again and again is simply shameful. *Patricia, querida, no te olvidamos.*

Abbreviations in the Text

AFL	American Federation of Labor
BIA	Bureau of Insular Affairs
ELA	Estado Libre Asociado (Free Associated State or Commonwealth of Puerto Rico)
FBI	Federal Bureau of Investigation
FLT	Federación Libre de Trabajadores (Free Federation of Labor)
FOMB	Financial Oversight and Management Board
MID	Military Intelligence Division (of the US Army)
NAFTA	North American Free Trade Agreement
NARA	National Archives and Record Administration
OAS	Organization of American States
PNPR	Partido Nacionalista de Puerto Rico (Puerto Rican Nationalist Party)
PPD	Partido Popular Democrático de Puerto Rico (Popular Democratic Party)
PREPA	Puerto Rico Electric Power Authority
PROMESA	Puerto Rico Oversight, Management, and Economic Stability Act
RG	Record Group
UN	United Nations
UTIER	Unión de Trabajadores de la Industria Eléctrica y Riego (Electrical Industry and Irrigation Workers Union)

Making Never-Never Land

Introduction

The stuffed bear my father gave me when he left Puerto Rico was pink. It wore flowered pajamas and an old-fashioned sleeping cap and had droopy plastic eyes. I clung to it as I watched his plane take off from Luis Muñoz Marín airport. "¡Mi papa! ¡Mi papa!" I cried inconsolably as my older brothers rolled their eyes at my drama. The memory is hazy, though I've heard this story often over the years. I remember the feeling of my father's departure and my sadness, though I cannot recall the sequence of events immediately before or after. But in my mind, I can still clearly see the bear's face and his sleepy pink eyes.

My family left Puerto Rico in the mid-1980s. Unlike previous waves of Puerto Ricans who had made their way to the East Coast of the United States or midwestern cities such as Chicago, we were part of a first wave of Puerto Ricans who moved to Houston, Texas, in pursuit of opportunities in the oil and gas industry. This group came mostly from southern, Caribbean cities and towns—Ponce, Guanica, Guayanilla, Yauco, Peñuelas—where previously they had been employed by the small petrochemical industry that had grown up and flourished there in the preceding thirty or so years. My father worked for Union Carbide in Puerto Rico for thirteen years before being laid off as the company wound down its operations in the archipelago.

Union Carbide, Phillips Puerto Rico, Caribbean Gulf, and several other petrochemical companies shut down their Puerto Rico subsidiaries as the incentives and financial benefits that had initially drawn them to the archipelago began to expire. For several decades, it had been profitable for the companies to settle in Puerto Rico, hire cheap Puerto Rican labor, and avail themselves of the multiple tax breaks available to them. However, by the mid-1980s, as those tax breaks expired, it became more profitable for these companies to move to other overseas locations rather than remain in Puerto Rico. So, they decamped for other parts of the Global South, leaving their storage tanks, chimneys, and other industrial rubble to rust and decay in the picturesque tropical landscape of Guayanilla Bay.

My father's departure was the first step in my family's tiered migration from Puerto Rico. When he arrived in Houston, he stayed with friends who had once been our across-the-street neighbors in the Jardines del Caribe neighborhood in Ponce. My father threw himself into finding work, purchasing a used car to drive to and from interviews. Though the Houston of the mid-1980s was experiencing a recession brought on by the collapse of global oil prices, my father was able to use his knowledge of the industry and his hustle to find work fairly quickly. In fact, in a full-circle moment, he eventually found his way to the Union Carbide plant in Texas City, an industrial town on the water just south of Houston.

After a few weeks, my father rented an apartment and furnished it with inexpensive secondhand furniture. A few months after his arrival in Houston, he was ready for the next phase of our move. My mother, my brother Germain, and I boarded a plane, leaving my two oldest brothers, Julio and Axel, both young teens, with an aunt. We left in the evening, arriving in Houston after dark. The city's lights and many highways loomed below us as Germain and I fought each other for access to the window. We left Puerto Rico in the spring, close to the Easter holiday. I know this because there were pastel-colored candies and treats waiting for Germain and me at the apartment when we arrived. My older brothers arrived a couple of months later after finishing the school year. By then, we had moved into a slightly bigger apartment where Germain and I shared one bedroom and Axel and Julio another. My parents purchased my older brothers a small stereo system and a handful of popular cassette tapes as a welcome gift. It is the image of Madonna's *Like a Virgin* cassette, with its black and white cover photo, that lingers in my memories of my brothers' arrival in Houston.

My aunt tells me that the move to Houston changed me. Whereas once I had been a gregarious and extroverted kid who loved to perform and sought attention wherever I could get it, after the move I became shy and reserved. I was afraid to speak to people or to ask questions or request help in stores. Though I learned English quickly, my voice in this new language was smaller, timid, and less sure than my previous voice—my first voice. Today, my partner tells me that when I speak in Spanish to friends and family, I am louder and more animated than I am in English, that I am a different person when I am home in Puerto Rico, a more excited and brighter version of myself.

My family's migration story is not exceptional. It is the story of thousands of Puerto Ricans who left before us and the thousands who followed. It is a story that has repeated itself for more than a century and continues to repeat itself daily. This story—the one where Puerto Ricans feel forced to depart from their homes and loved ones in order to seek employment and greater financial security, the one where they arrive in hostile cities and towns and experience racism and discrimination, the one where they become a part of what we now call our diaspora—is a product of a long history of colonialism. It is this story, or rather the repeating nature of this experience—indeed the repeating nature of Puerto Rico's colonial history—that drives my work.

THIS BOOK BEGAN from a seemingly simple question: What is Puerto Rico to the United States? I was a second-year law student asking myself a version of this question when I stumbled on a then-little-studied group of US Supreme Court decisions known collectively as the Insular Cases. These cases were decided in the first few years after the United States acquired the overseas territories ceded to it by Spain in 1898. The decisions, which covered a host of legal issues, ultimately sought to define the contours of the United States' relationship with its new overseas territories. The Court's opinions in these cases were so prosaically racist and eugenic in their logic that I was shocked (though I really shouldn't have been) when I learned that not only did they remain valid law, but in fact they continue to be the basis for the United States' relationship with Puerto Rico today.

Puerto Rico has been a colony of the United States for more than a century. Officially, it is an unincorporated territory under Congress's plenary power. This dynamic, which was set up in 1901 in the Insular Cases, has persisted through more than a century of large and small shifts in the global capitalist order. It has persisted despite the radical changes that Puerto Rican society has lived through and despite the reorientation of the world following two world wars and the Cold War. The mid-twentieth century saw the bulk of the colonized world move into other political statuses. This global turn from traditional extractive colonization to Western-led, neoliberal capitalist hegemony meant that for many in the Western world, formal colonies ceased to exist—but not for Puerto Ricans, who remained colonial subjects throughout all the upheavals of the twentieth century and into the twenty-first.

In the first few decades of the twentieth century, Puerto Rico produced sugar, tobacco, coffee, and tropical fruits for export to the United States. The plantations on which most agricultural laborers worked were owned by a small cadre of US-based corporations, and the profits from their labor flowed out of the archipelago and into the United States. By the mid-twentieth century, with the onset of global decolonization and the Cold War, Puerto Rico's economy underwent major shifts away from agricultural production and to industrialization and the production of goods and products destined for US markets. The territory also appeared to undergo major political shifts when it became the Estado Libre Asociado, or Commonwealth of Puerto Rico, in 1952. The establishment of local governance in Puerto Rico and the touting of those changes as moving the archipelago out from traditional colonialism facilitated the belief that Puerto Rico was something other than a colony of the United States. However, the economic shifts that had propelled Puerto Rico's economic growth began to stall as the century wound down, and Puerto Rico entered the twenty-first century with high levels of unemployment and an economy in decline. In order to fund the everyday functions of governance, Puerto Rico began to borrow heavily from US-based financial institutions. Thus, Puerto Rico was already burdened by severe debt when a series of catastrophes befell the territory beginning with the passage of Hurricanes Irma and Maria in September 2017.

Twenty-First-Century Colony

I'm often asked, what does Puerto Rico *do* for the United States? In other words, what is the benefit to the United States of having it as a colony today? To most people's thinking, colonies are sites of brutal, violent repression and of heavy extractive practices such as mining or plantation-based agriculture. Puerto Rico does not look like that anymore. There is no forced laboring in mines or plantations; there are no apparent riches or natural resources to be extracted; there is no apparent violent subjugation, as there has been historically in other colonies. To many people's thinking, there is a severe disconnect between what Puerto Rico looks like today and what a colony is supposed to look like.

Often when I receive this question, it is in the context of an interview or guest lecture with an audience that is just coming to know something about the condition of twenty-first-century Puerto Rico. Most people have the stereotypical Caribbean images in their minds—the ones put there by the Puerto Rico Tourism Company, which beckons people to "discover Puerto Rico" or to "live Boricua." Then, after learning about the archipelago's twentieth-century colonial history with the United States and its most recent economic and environmental crises, the question inevitably arises: What good is a bankrupt colony to the United States? Isn't Puerto Rico more of a governmental drain than a financial boon? Why does the United States keep it?

The answers to these questions are complicated and the subject of many books, including this one. But the simple, unvarnished answer that I give people is that what Puerto Rico currently "produces" is debt. Debt, that opaque concept, which many of us do not understand but which shapes our daily lives in ways both large and small. Debt, that dynamic that seems like a social ill, that points to the irresponsibility of the debtor, but that is in fact the basis for the world's financial system. Puerto Rico is a captive space for debt production. While the archipelago's financial crisis of the past decade has been reported as a debacle—and it certainly has been that for the residents of Puerto Rico, who have been paying off the archipelago's debt through harsh austerity measures—in fact, the financial crisis has been a boon for banks, hedge funds, contractors, and investors in Puerto Rico, who have made billions and stand to make billions more.

Puerto Rico—"the oldest colony in the world"—has experienced crises for more than a century.[1] Crisis is the status quo for many Puerto Ricans, and it is the background of life in the archipelago. At the start of 2016, Puerto Rico was in a debt spiral that led the governor to declare that the territory was insolvent and would not be able to pay its debts. After more than a decade of irresponsible borrowing and using debt to finance Puerto Rico's basic public functions, the government found itself hobbled by billions of dollars in unpayable debt. Large numbers of residents fled the archipelago daily, resulting in the largest out-migration Puerto Rico had seen since World War II. Those who remained were choked by austerity, rampant unemployment, the highest sales tax and utility costs in the United States, and the privatization and closure of the public sector.

In the midst of this dire situation, the passage of Hurricanes Irma and Maria in September 2017 exposed Puerto Rico's vulnerabilities for the entire world to see. Puerto Rico, which had been invisible to most people before Hurricane Maria, became hypervisible in its wake, and as a result so too did Puerto Rico's colonial condition.[2] The world watched as Puerto Rico went dark and remained so for months as a result of an unreliable and antiquated power grid that had not been properly updated due to mismanagement and corruption. Federal programs meant to help the territory in its recovery quickly became mired in bureaucracy, political infighting, and corruption. The Trump administration publicly insinuated that Puerto Rico was unworthy of federal aid, while in private the administration forced the territory's government to jump through hoops in order to access limited and conditional aid. All the while the archipelago's residents grew frustrated and exhausted with the lack of basic services and the slow pace of recovery.

The years since the hurricanes have seen thousands of Puerto Ricans take to the streets to protest the operations of an unelected and deeply unpopular Financial Oversight and Management Board imposed by the Obama administration in 2016 to address the territory's debt crisis. Puerto Ricans have protested cuts to state worker pensions proposed by the Board.

They have protested the privatization of the electric power sector, the education sector, and other services and utilities. They have protested the high costs of utilities even while those utilities continue to be unreliable and erratic. July 2019 saw Puerto Ricans' frustrations boil over into massive protests that shut down the streets of San Juan and other cities in the archipelago. The publication of private messages between then-governor Ricardo Rosselló and a cadre of his closest aides revealed not only corruption and collusion among the members but also a callous disregard for the thousands of lives lost in the aftermath of Hurricane Maria. The governor's messages and the attitude of disdain they revealed broke the dam of anger and frustration.

For fifteen days, Puerto Ricans took to the streets to demand the resignation of Rosselló and members of his cabinet. They protested the Rosselló administration's negligence, its arrogance, and corruption. They also protested the Board, the Trump administration, and Puerto Rico's colonial status. The protests of July 2019 acted as a moment of catharsis for residents of the territory who had lived through several years of trauma and upheaval. They made clear that Puerto Ricans understood that the disasters that had befallen them were not merely caused by nature but were exacerbated by the negligence of both the US and territory governments and directly attributable to Puerto Rico's colonial condition.

In the years since the hurricanes, a new round of tax incentives has brought large numbers of wealthy mainland US Americans to Puerto Rico, eager to reap the economic benefits available to them in the archipelago. According to a website run by Sotheby's International Realty, "few places on earth offer a return on investment the way Puerto Rico does."[3] This is because Puerto Rico's bankrupt government, wanting to attract capital to the archipelago, has created a tax haven for wealthy US Americans. "High net worth individuals" who move to Puerto Rico and live there at least 183 days out of the year effectively pay no taxes in Puerto Rico.[4] These tax breaks are available only to individuals who have not had a connection to Puerto Rico in the preceding six years, which means residents of the archipelago cannot access the benefits of these tax incentives even if they are "high net worth individuals." The incentives have created a deeply inequitable dynamic in which long-term residents of Puerto Rico are squeezed for every possible dollar to pay for the government's past unfettered borrowing while newly arrived US Americans are unburdened and free to live out their paradisiacal tropical fantasies.

Not surprisingly, the departure of Puerto Ricans in search of financial stability and greater opportunities has continued apace, and the empty homes and storefronts they have left, in combination with the government incentives, have opened up a new era of real estate development and hypergentrification. Furthermore, the closure of foreign destinations to US citizens during the COVID-19 pandemic spurred tourism to Puerto Rico, which could not close its borders to Americans the way other Caribbean nations did. As a result, in the past several years, rents have doubled in certain areas of the archipelago as more and more residential properties have been developed for short-term vacation rental through online platforms such as Airbnb and VRBO. Unable to pay the quickly escalating rents, longtime residents have been forced to move far from their communities and the homes they have known for decades. Puerto Ricans are being displaced at an alarming rate. Meanwhile, the government continues to court wealthy mainland Americans while often ignoring the needs of residents, leading many to believe that the government seeks to create a "Puerto Rico without Puerto Ricans."[5]

Puerto Rico is experiencing intense moments of political and societal reorientation that are forcing a reconsideration of territorial governance. However, undergirding all of this upheaval is the territory's long-standing colonial relationship with the United States, which, despite Puerto Ricans' demands, continues to limit the archipelago and its people's everyday possibilities and Puerto Rico's political future. This colonial status has left Puerto Rico susceptible to a repeating and overlapping history of crisis that has been made worse by debt, climate change fueled disasters, and most recently a global pandemic.

Race and Law

This book argues that despite Puerto Rico's unique position as a twenty-first-century colony, its path to that place was not exceptional. Race and law have acted as organizing principles in the United States–Puerto Rico relationship since its inception. In 1898, when the United States acquired the territory, race science was ascendant, and US residents overwhelmingly subscribed to ideas of social Darwinism and the unassailable conviction that the white race was better at democratic governance. Having been extolled by the likes of Rudyard Kipling to take up its rightful burden of educating and civilizing the poor, Asian, Black and mixed-race inhabitants in the overseas territories, the United States set about doing just that. However, almost immediately after acquiring the territories, questions arose as to what sort of relationship the islands would have with the United States. How would the islands be treated? What was permissible under US law? These questions arrived before the US Supreme Court soon after the United States began its imperial experiments. It is no surprise that just a few short years after enshrining segregation into law, the US Supreme Court would rely on racialized ideas of who the residents of the new territories were in order to decide how they could and should be treated.

These decisions, which might have seemed expedient at the time, have had deep and lasting impacts on the territories. The Insular Cases remain the legal underpinnings of the United States' relationship with its overseas territories. The structures they created more than a hundred years ago remain firmly in place. Though we have changed as a society and we reject blatant expressions of racism like those found in the Insular Cases, the decisions remain with us. As abhorrent as those decisions might seem to us today, at the time they sat comfortably within the Court's body of law regarding racial undesirables — groups that the US government sought to exclude because of race.

Therefore, in order to fully understand how Puerto Rico was constructed in law, we must look beyond the early twentieth-century moment of the Insular Cases, or rather we must look before, to a larger history of US settler colonialism and racial exclusion. Puerto Rico, and the federal policies and US Supreme Court law that created it, exists within a larger genealogy of law and policy impacting racially excluded others such as Native and African Americans. This body of law served to carve out states of exception for racial undesirables — lacunae of law and special legal designations that allowed the federal government plenary or complete power over these groups.

In these spaces of exclusion, Native tribes, Black Americans, and the inhabitants of the insular territories were left with little or limited rights and as a result they were exposed to the whims and repression of the state. While the histories of these groups are unique and complex, the ways they have been construed in law are quite similar. Thus, examining the legal apparatuses of their collective exclusion can fully illuminate the malleability of US law in its approach to racialized groups. The techniques and strategies adopted to control and exclude Native and Black Americans served as models for the Court in its decisions about Puerto Rico and the other insular territories.

Structure of the Book

This book is divided into two parts. The first, "Toward a Legal Genealogy of Racial Exclusion," focuses on the US Supreme Court decision of *Downes v.*

Bidwell, a foundational case that first established the limits of Puerto Rico's relationship to the United States, and places that decision within a longer historical context that moves backward to the years before the United States acquired the territory. Though scholars have often looked to the Insular Cases to understand the limits inherent in the relationship between the United States and Puerto Rico, this book seeks to place the Insular Cases within a longer legal history of racial exclusion. As a result, I look to early legal precedents addressing the status of Native and African Americans in order to understand how Puerto Rico is racially constructed through law and how this construction has worked to limit the territory's possibilities. By studying these cases together, as a genealogy, we can begin to see how the Court's logic in *Downes*, the most important of the Insular Cases—steeped in ideas of settler colonialism, anti-Black racism, and social Darwinism—created a state of exception, which continues to define the territory's relationship with the United States today.

This analysis is important not only because the Marshall Trilogy, which addressed Native exclusion, and *Dred Scott v. Sanford*, which addressed Black exclusion, serve as direct legal precedents to *Downes* but also because the Supreme Court in *Downes* engaged in a critical moment of racial formation. The Court relied on its previous precedents concerning racial undesirables to make Puerto Rico a racialized space and its inhabitants into a separate people intelligible within the racial and legal logics of the United States. It is not a coincidence that the most shameful cases in the United States' legal history of race should serve as direct precedents to a decision that continues to serve as the basis for Puerto Rico's exclusion more than one hundred years after it was handed down. This book interrogates how *Downes* and its antiquated ideas about race continue to undergird the United States' relationship with Puerto Rico and to circumscribe Puerto Ricans' lives. As Puerto Rico's crises continue to mount and residents continue to demand change with their voices and their bodies, the possibility of that change continues to butt up against the limits of *Downes* and the structures it created.

The second part of the book, "'American' State of Exception: Puerto Rico in the Twentieth and Twenty-First Centuries," traces the effects and logics of *Downes* into the present by focusing on several key moments in the history of Puerto Rico: the decades immediately following the *Downes* decision, the creation of the Commonwealth of Puerto Rico in 1952, and the events that have developed since June 2016. In the years immediately following the *Downes* decision, the United States set about reorienting the territory's economy and Puerto Ricans' daily lives, remaking Puerto Rico into part of the "American Sugar Kingdom" and residents into "Tropical Yankees." To that end, the US government quickly transformed the territory into a veritable experimental station. *Downes* opened the way for experiments in economic, agricultural, and environmental policy; health and sanitation; policing; and labor control and beyond. These experiments and the policies they ushered in were often perfected in Puerto Rico and exported to other parts of the US empire. Furthermore, Puerto Rico quickly became a plantation-based society with a majority of residents beholden to the whims of the US sugar market and the US-based corporations that dominated it. This situation persisted until the mid-twentieth century when global shifts in markets and an international move toward decolonization allowed for the possibility of change in Puerto Rico.

In 1952, the creation of the Estado Libre Asociado de Puerto Rico (ELA), or Commonwealth of Puerto Rico, seemed to usher in a new relationship between Puerto Rico and the United States. But did it actually do so? While it is clear today that the dynamic between the territory and the United States did not cease to be a colonial one after the creation of the ELA, in 1952 many believed that it had. The creation of the ELA obfuscated the colonial contours of the dynamic between Puerto Rico and the United States and seemed to provide residents with what they wanted at the time: a change in status for Puerto Rico and an end to traditional, extractive, plantation-based colonialism. It allowed Puerto Ricans to believe they had gained local autonomy and something like sovereignty. At the time, the ELA seemed to provide Puerto Rico with "the best of both worlds": its own local government, democratically elected by residents of Puerto Rico; a seemingly strong economy closely linked to the United States, with free trade between the two; and the ability to maintain Puerto Rico's own unique culture. What the ELA did not do was abrogate the structures set in place by *Downes*. Instead, the ELA operated within the racial and legal logics established in that case. As a result, the ELA did little to change the colonial nature of the United States–Puerto Rico relationship.

Debates about what the ELA was and what it did persisted from the time the ELA was put into place until the summer of 2016. In June of that year, Puerto Rico experienced three key political and legal moments that reinscribed its colonial status, reinvigorated Congress's plenary power, and ultimately undid what remained of the Estado Libre Asociado. In that single month, the Supreme Court handed down two important decisions about the territory: *Puerto Rico v. Sánchez Valle* and *Puerto Rico v. Franklin California Tax-Free Trust, et al.* These two cases collectively asked the court to define the limits of the territory's power to govern itself. The Court in these cases demonstrably grappled with what to do about Puerto Rico and how to resolve the disputes without fundamentally changing the nature of Puerto Rico's relationship to the United States. Ultimately, the court reaffirmed *Downes v. Bidwell*, 115 years after it was first passed.

June 2016 culminated with Congress's passage of the Puerto Rico Oversight, Management, and Economic Stability Act (PROMESA). PROMESA, which was meant to address Puerto Rico's billions of dollars of outstanding debt, established the much-reviled Financial Oversight and Management Board, or la junta, as it is known in Puerto Rico. Collectively, the actions of June 2016 signaled the death knell of the ELA and the reanimation of the kind of unrestrained plenary power that Puerto Ricans believed was done away with in 1952. This plenary power has its origins in those seemingly ancient and antiquated cases, discussed in part I of the book, which ultimately relied on racist notions of who was worthy of rights and who must be excluded. These events also set the stage for the political unrest and the constitutional crisis that took over Puerto Rico three years later in summer 2019, when thousands of Puerto Ricans took to the streets to demand the ouster of then-governor Ricardo Rosselló.

This book offers a *longue durée* view of Puerto Rican legal and political history in order to highlight the legacies of *Downes v. Bidwell* throughout Puerto Rico's twentieth and twenty-first centuries. It does so, not by telling a chronological and comprehensive story, but by focusing on key moments in Puerto Rico's history. In these moments, we see the logics of *Downes* at play again and again. We also see how the decision continues to constrain the archipelago. I do not believe that the Supreme Court could have imagined how its decision, which began as a banal dispute about the importation of oranges from Puerto Rico, would continue to resonate more than 120 years later.

THE STAKES ARE HIGH for Puerto Rico and for Puerto Ricans. As the environmental and human-made disasters continue to pile up, and vulture capitalists and gentrifiers set their sights on the natural beauty of the archipelago, Puerto Ricans are being forced to make difficult decisions under ever more impossible circumstances. More and more of the archipelago's residents are being forced to make the untenable calculus that my family made all those years ago: leave behind home, family, and community in pursuit of the possibility of greater economic security or stay and continue to resist the forces of displacement, corruption, and neglect. These are not easy choices, and the consequences reverberate across families and communities and across generations. Those who choose to stay are actively endeavoring to make new ways of living within the constraints of US colonialism; they are consistently pushing against the forces of displacement and of debt. Those who leave often do so with guilt or resentment. Many then live with an ever-present longing to return. They live, as Puerto Rican legend Bobby Capó crooned in the 1950s, "soñando con Puerto Rico." This book seeks to offer another narrative, a fuller one, that might help illuminate the path forward by highlighting from where we came.

PART I | Toward a Legal Genealogy
of Racial Exclusion

CHAPTER ONE

Downes v. Bidwell
Birth of an Exceptional Territory

The steamer *Ponce* entered the Port of New York carrying 576 boxes of oranges on November 20, 1900. Of those boxes, 543 had their origin in Mayagüez, Puerto Rico, while the remaining 33 came from San Juan, Puerto Rico. These oranges were the property of Samuel B. Downes, a merchant who was fast taking advantage of the commercial opportunities offered in Puerto Rico, the United States' newly acquired overseas territory. Upon arrival in New York, Downes's goods were intercepted and detained by George R. Bidwell, the collector of customs for the Port of New York. Bidwell designated the oranges "foreign goods" and levied $659.35 as import tax.[1] Downes sued in federal court, arguing that since Puerto Rico had been acquired by the United States in 1898, it had become a part of the United States, and thus taxation of goods from the archipelago was unconstitutional. After all, New York couldn't tax oranges arriving from Florida or California. This completely banal event—the arrival of tropical fruit from Puerto Rico at a port of the United States and the levying of import duties on that fruit—led to the most important legal precedent in the history of the archipelago and one that continues to define Puerto Rico's economic and political possibilities more than a century later.

The case of *Downes v. Bidwell,* among the first of the infamous Insular Cases that attempted to define the United States' legal relationship to its burgeoning overseas empire, was carefully followed by private business owners, legal scholars, politicians, the media, and the public at large. *Downes* and the other Insular Cases quickly became a referendum on the United States' imperial designs at the start of the twentieth century. The US Supreme Court, understanding the many interests at stake, attempted to toe a careful line in which it could allow the US government to hold onto the insular territories and reap the economic benefits available therein, while also not extending citizenship or too many rights to the territories or their inhabitants.

Though the Insular Cases were decided over the span of many years (1901–22), I focus extensively on *Downes v. Bidwell* (1901), because it was in that case that a plurality of the Supreme Court famously pronounced Puerto Rico to be "foreign in a domestic sense," a nonsensical declaration that continues to flummox and confuse today.[2] It was also in *Downes* that the court first declared Puerto Rico to be an "unincorporated territory" and set it on a course of legal exclusion that continues to define it today. The category of unincorporated territory, though novel at the time, had important precedents in the court's previous decisions dealing with Native and Black Americans; the *Downes* case reached back to those precedents and to their racialized and racist logics in order to find that Puerto Rico and its inhabitants were undesirable, unprepared, and not white enough to be Americans.

The United States' acquisition of its overseas territories in 1898 produced widespread debates about imperialism in the United States.[3] Many argued both the wisdom and the folly of the United States' course of action regarding expansion. There was grave concern that acquiring the territories meant integrating the inhabitants therein, making them US citizens, and allowing them to participate in the United States' political system. The rhetoric of the time in both the imperialist and anti-imperialist camps was undeniably white supremacist, anti-Black, and full of fear and disdain of the peoples occupying the island territories.[4] Secretary of the Interior Charles Schurz best summed up these concerns in a speech at the University of Chicago in 1899: "If they become states on equal footing with the other states . . . *they will take part in governing the whole republic,* by sending senators and representatives . . . *to help make our laws,* and by voting for president and vice-president. . . . The prospect of the consequences which would follow the admission of the Spanish creoles and the negroes of the West India [sic] islands and of the Malays and Tagals of the Philippines to *participation in the conduct of our government* is so alarming that you instinctively pause before taking the next step" (emphasis added).[5] Schurz's comments speak to the belief that the islands' inhabitants were too alien to be a part of the United States; too uncivilized to be clothed in the banner of democracy; utterly unfit to have a hand in making the laws of the United States; and, frankly, too Black and mixed-up to be US Americans. Later, in 1907, speaking specifically of Puerto Rico, Representative James Slayden of Texas summed up the problem simply: "We are of different races," he declared, "we are mainly Anglo-Saxon, while they are a composite structure, with liberal contributions to their blood from Europe, Asia and Africa. *They are largely mongrels now*" (emphasis added).[6] The moment of late nineteenth-century imperial expansion forced the United States to contend with the many "mongrels" who inhabited its new territories. In the midst of Jim Crow segregation, the US government understood the residents of the territories as decidedly not white and more Black than not. Thus, the United States turned to its history with its other nonwhite subjects for guidance on what to do with the "mongrels" inhabiting the overseas territories.[7]

It was in this milieu of fierce debate about the wisdom of allowing the peoples inhabiting the new territories to join the United States that the first of the Insular Cases were decided. In a series of decisions that spanned the first two decades of the twentieth century, the US Supreme Court made significant pronouncements about the place of Puerto Rico and the Philippines within the US body politic and made clear the limits of the US Constitution. Though much has been written about the Insular Cases and about *Downes*, my aim here is to make explicit how *Downes* fits into a larger geography of racialized legal exception that marked the United States during the early twentieth century.[8] While Puerto Rico and the Insular Cases are unique in many ways, the logics of *Downes* and the ways the Supreme Court racialized Puerto Ricans and the archipelago were not. In *Downes*, the court turned to those ignominious precedents discussed more fully in the next chapter—the Marshall Trilogy and *Dred Scott v. Sanford*—to map out the contours of the United States' relationship to Puerto Rico.[9]

While a full discussion of a legal genealogy of racial exclusion must necessarily include the court's treatment of Asians and Mexican Americans, among others, I focus on connecting *Downes* to the logics and legal reasoning of the Marshall Trilogy and *Dred Scott* not only because both are cited by the Court in that opinion but also because, as in those other cases, the Supreme Court in *Downes* engaged in a critical moment of racial formation.[10] The *Downes* court relied on its previous precedents concerning racial undesirables to make Puerto Rico a racialized space and its inhabitants intelligible within the racial and legal logics of the United States.[11] Within this legal genealogy, the Supreme Court carved out various states of exception—lacunae of law where the protections of the US Constitution do not apply or apply only in limited fashion, and where racial undesirables, such as Native Americans, Black Americans, and the inhabitants of the insular territories, were left exposed to the whims and violence of the state. The Court's decision in *Downes* created such a state of exception in Puerto Rico, where the US Constitution did not fully apply and the archipelago was left exposed to the vagaries of Congress's plenary, or complete, power.[12] Collectively, the Marshall Trilogy, *Dred Scott*, and *Downes* form but a part of a much larger legal genealogy of racial exclusion and help to illustrate how the court's reasoning, steeped in ideas of settler colonialism, anti-Blackness, and social Darwinism, underwent many contortions and legal gymnastics in order to create states of exception for racial others.

In this chapter, I focus on *Downes*, its legal reasoning, and the events surrounding the decision to offer a close reading of the case and to interrogate how its language created Puerto Rico's unique legal status. Additionally, I examine some of the immediate legal questions that remained after *Downes* and that were addressed in subsequent Insular Cases, chief among them the question of citizenship and what relationship Puerto Ricans had to the United States. Variations of these questions, as urgent as they were in the early twentieth century, have lingered and remain with us today.

Downes v. Bidwell, 1901

The United States acquired the archipelago of Puerto Rico with the signing of the Treaty of Paris that ended the War of 1898. This moment raised fundamental and contentious questions in US political, legal, and academic circles: Would the United States now become a colonial power like its former master? Would the inhabitants of Puerto Rico and the other island territories acquired by the United States after the war become US citizens? What were these new islands to the United States? Economically, it was clear the new island possessions could be a lucrative and profitable location for US corporate expansion; however, legally and politically, the islands were a bit of a quagmire for the United States. How exactly could the United States maintain these islands without making them a part of the nation? Did Congress have such power?

There were many who argued against the United States' retention of Puerto Rico and who saw it as inherently contrary to the United States' own political and legal ideology. Others argued for retention of the archipelago but wanted to see it maintained as separate from the United States.[13] As former president and Chief Justice of the Supreme Court William Howard Taft later wrote in reference to the debates surrounding the territory, "Few questions have been the subject of such discussion and dispute in our country as the status of our territory acquired from Spain in 1899. The division between the political parties in respect to it, the diversity of views of the members of this court in regard to its constitutional aspects, and the constant recurrence of the subject in the House of Congress, fixed the attention of all on the future relation of this acquired territory to the United States."[14]

In May 1901, the US Supreme Court decided the first of seven cases of the group that would be known as the Insular Cases and that defined the territorial relationship.[15] These cases arose almost immediately after the United States took power over the insular territories and dealt mostly with economic issues such as taxation and import restrictions. The second and most important of these cases was *Downes v. Bidwell*. In his suit against George Bidwell, the customs inspector at the port of New York, Samuel Downes argued that Article I, Section 8 of the US Constitution, which holds that "all duties, imposts, and excises shall be uniform throughout the United States," applied to the archipelago. Downes reasoned that since no duty on oranges existed for other parts of the United States, it was unconstitutional to impose such a duty on goods coming from the territory. In other words, Downes argued that the US Constitution applied to Puerto Rico, and it could not be discriminated against for taxation purposes.

The Birth of the Unincorporated Territory

The *Downes* case provided an opportunity for the many opinions about the constitutionality of retaining the overseas territories to be heard and explored in both the public square and in legal and political circles. In the run-up to the decision, senators, representatives, bureaucratic administrators, and President McKinley all played a part in shaping public opinion and ultimately the Court's as well. Yet, as legal historian Sam Erman has argued, aware that the justices would have the final say about the status of the new territories, "elected and administrative officials worked contemporaneously with legal academics to shape a new and congenial constitutional doctrine well before the Supreme Court was called to validate it."[16]

Legal scholars credit a series of five articles published in the *Harvard Law Review* between 1898 and 1899—which addressed the question whether, from a constitutional point of view, the phrase the "United States" included territories—with providing the bolstering the Court relied on in its *Downes* decision.[17] Two of the articles argued that indeed the territories were a part of the "United States," while two others argued that they were not. The fifth article, written by future Harvard University president Abbott Lawrence Lowell and titled "The Status of Our New Possessions—a Third View," is often credited with providing the Court with the novel approach that it ultimately adopted in the Insular Cases.[18] Lowell argued that some territories were a part of the "United States," while others were not. Lowell's idea became known as the doctrine of territorial incorporation, and it remains the basis for Puerto Rico's exclusion today.

However, when *Downes* was decided, the justices of the Court were divided as to the status of the new overseas territories. The Court was first tasked with determining whether Puerto Rico had become a part of the United States when it was acquired by the United States. Previous to the acquisitions of Puerto Rico and the other insular territories, the United States' doctrine of territorial expansion set out that territory acquired by the United States would be set on a course to statehood as soon as was legally feasible. Territories were incorporated into the United States and became a part of the United States until such time as they became states. As a result, the US Constitution and Bill of Rights "followed the flag" into those territories that the government acquired, and the protections of both documents applied therein. However, in the case of Puerto Rico, fear of incorporating the archipelago and its mixed-race population led the *Downes* court to break with long-held legal doctrine.

Before *Downes v. Bidwell*, the United States recognized four possible entities in relation to the United States (apart from the District of Columbia): (1) a state of the union on equal footing with others; (2) territories where the Constitution applied in full, and which were on the path to eventual statehood, such as Hawai'i in 1898; (3) sovereign foreign nations; and (4) Native American nations, which were so-called domestic dependent sovereigns.[19] In *Downes*, the Supreme Court created a new legal category, the unincorporated territory, to ensure that Puerto Rico would not join the union as a state until Congress deemed it ready, if ever that day arrived.

Prior to *Downes*, the Court did not distinguish between incorporated and unincorporated territories. Territory that was acquired by the United States might not be "ready" for statehood immediately on acquisition, usually due to the presence of indigenous groups, but once there was enough white settlement to displace the indigenous occupants, those territories would become states.[20] This is the logic that drove the United States' westward expansion and was in place when the United States acquired the islands of Hawai'i, annexed on June 15, 1898, mere days before the US invasion of Puerto Rico. At the time, the islands of Hawai'i still had a considerable indigenous presence; however, Hawai'i had been receiving white European and North American settlers for more than a century before the United States' acquisition.[21] With the overthrow of the Kingdom of Hawai'i and the establishment of the short-lived Republic of Hawai'i in 1894, the governing bodies of the Republic consisted of white, European, and US settlers who actively sought annexation by the United States.[22] Hawai'i became an incorporated territory and was given a system of self-government in 1901. It eventually became a state in 1959.[23]

Thus, the label "unincorporated territory," which Puerto Rico still bears, meant that Puerto Rico was not on a path to statehood and would not be placed on such a path for the foreseeable future. In 1901, as now, Puerto Ricans generally expressed feelings of ambivalence toward statehood. However, the more dire consequence of the label of unincorporated territory was that Puerto Rico and the other insular territories would be held under Congress's plenary, or complete, power with no foreseeable exit strategy. This power, granted to Congress by Article IV, Section 3 of the US Constitution, as enumerated by the Supreme Court in the Insular Cases, is startlingly broad and generally not subject to judicial review.

Ironically, the idea of the unincorporated territory was enumerated not in the Court's leading opinion, written by Justice Henry Billings Brown, who also infamously wrote the opinion in *Plessy v. Ferguson*, but in a concurring opinion written by Justice Edward Douglass White. While a majority of the justices agreed that the Constitution did not "follow the flag" into the overseas territories, they disagreed about why it did not. Though Brown's opinion contained many important pronouncements on the limits of the Constitution and Puerto Rico's new position in the US empire, it was White's ideas that became the dominant justification for Puerto Rico's ongoing exclusion.

The Critical Definition of "Appurtenance"

In one of the most famous assertions from the *Downes* case, Justice Brown determined that Puerto Rico as an overseas territory was "appurtenant to and belonging to the United States, but not a part of the United States within the . . . Constitution."[24] Almost as if Puerto Rico were a sidecar to the United States—along for the ride but not charting its own course. Thus, Brown declared that territory could belong to the United States but not be a part of it. This notion that an overseas territory could be "appurtenant to . . . but not a part of the United States" was first established forty years before the *Downes* decision in 1856, with the passage of the Guano Islands Act.

In the 1840s, farmers and agriculturists discovered that guano (dried bird and bat droppings) was extremely useful as a fertilizer. This spurred a worldwide race to discover and maintain control over guano deposits on uninhabited islands, keys, and other outcroppings.[25] In 1856, at the behest of North American adventurers who hoped to profit from discovering new guano deposits the world over, the US Congress passed the Guano Islands Act. The Act empowered US citizens to take possession of uninhabited, unclaimed islets containing deposits of guano for the purpose of extracting that commodity.[26] The Act stated that "whenever any citizen of the United States discovers a deposit of guano on any island, rock, or key, not within the lawful jurisdiction of any other government, and not occupied by the citizens of any other government, and takes peaceable possession thereof, and occupies the same, such island, rock, or key may, at the discretion of the President, be considered as appertaining to the United States."[27] In order to perfect proof of discovery, a citizen of the United States who discovered such an island, rock, or key had to provide a sworn affidavit to the State Department that the citizen was taking possession and that no others could lay claim to the territory.[28]

Finally, the Act conferred on the United States executive discretion to treat the islands in question as "appertaining to the United States," until such time as the guano had been exhausted, when the island would "revert and relapse out of the jurisdiction of the United States."[29] The Act specifically stated "nothing in this chapter contained shall be construed as obliging the United States to retain possession of the islands, rocks, or keys, after the guano shall have been removed from the same."[30] This clause was unique because it limited US sovereignty over these islands until such time as the guano deposits were depleted and then allowed for sovereignty to automatically revert out of US jurisdiction without any express legal maneuvering. There was no precedent for such a situation in the US legal framework at the time.

The question whether "appertaining to the United States" meant that these islands were a part of the United States came before the Supreme Court in 1889, thirty years after the establishment of the Guano Islands Act, with the case of *Jones v. United States*.[31] The dispute arose after a labor riot broke out on the Caribbean island of Navassa.[32] Working conditions on all guano islands were notoriously harsh, with men laboring long hours in the tropical sun while constantly breathing the ammoniac stench of the droppings they often mined by hand.[33] However, the Navassa Phosphate Company exacerbated the difficulty of such labor with its abusive practices, including forcing laborers to work for long hours under needlessly dangerous conditions, docking workers' pay on days they were injured, gouging them with highly inflated prices at the "company store," and punishing insubordination by placing men in "the stocks."[34] Men who complained about the abusive practices would forfeit all accrued pay.[35]

Under such barbarous and inequitable conditions, a labor riot broke out on Navassa on September 14, 1889. The riot began when a laborer, John Ross, emerged from a phosphate hole in which he had been working in order to explain to his supervisor, Charles Roby, that the phosphate was too hard to extract by hand and would need to be blasted out with dynamite. Roby responded by kicking Ross back into the hole, which prompted another worker to hit Roby over the head with a wooden tool, knocking Roby unconscious. As a group of workers brought Roby's unconscious body back to the main camp, other workers took their presence as a cue to lay down their tools, or conversely, to take up tools as weapons against other company officers. The rioting workers, who were all Black men, surrounded the homes of the supervisors, who were all white, and demanded an end to their inhumane treatment. The fighting lasted throughout the day with a series of skirmishes that left four white supervisors dead; a fifth would later die of his injuries.[36]

Notice was sent to the US mainland via a nearby British ship that a riot had broken out and the island needed to be evacuated. Eventually, workers were taken to Baltimore, Maryland, aboard several ships belonging to the Navassa Phosphate Company and the US Navy.[37] On their arrival, US Attorney Thomas Hayes investigated the case and identified eighteen men he believed to be the instigators. On November 6, a grand jury handed down five indictments against the men, charging five men with the murders of the supervisors and the rest as accessories to murder. In five separate trials, juries convicted three men of murder, fourteen men of manslaughter, and twenty-three men of rioting.[38] The three men convicted of murder, Henry Jones, George Key, and Edward Smith, were sentenced to death by hanging; they subsequently appealed those convictions to the US Supreme Court.[39]

The Brotherhood of Liberty and the Order of Galilean Fishermen, two African American benevolent societies, took up the men's representation and hired a legal team of three Black and three white lawyers to defend them.[40] The brief submitted to the Court on behalf of the three defendants in *Jones v. United States* did not contest the facts of the case but instead focused on legal arguments. The workers asserted that the impermanent nature of the United States' hold over the island of Navassa meant that the island was not considered a part of the United States, and thus the United States could not exert jurisdiction over disputes arising on the island.[41] They distinguished Navassa, which would revert out of US jurisdiction once its guano supply had been depleted, with territories in the Northwest, which had been permanently made a part of the United States. The brief inquired of the Court, "What is the significance of the desultory phrase, 'appertain to'?" Ultimately, the workers argued that in the context of the Guano Islands Act, "appurtenant to the United States" was devoid of meaning.[42]

The government's arguments did not directly address the workers' contentions regarding the meaning of appurtenance and instead focused on the United States' rights to acquire territory of any kind, permanent or temporary. Ultimately, the Court found for the government and held that Navassa must be considered "appurtenant to the United States" and thus within the jurisdiction of the federal government despite its impermanence. The Court reasoned that "the law of nations supported the Guano Islands Act, which used the word 'appertaining,'" that the government had taken the steps required by the act to establish "appurtenance," and that Navassa therefore "'appertained' to the United States" and was under the exclusive jurisdiction of the United States; however, the Court did little to clarify the precise legal status of Navassa and the other guano islands or the actual legal meaning of appurtenance.[43] What the Court's decision in *Jones* did do was set the stage for its legal reasoning in *Downes v. Bidwell*.

After the Supreme Court made its decision upholding the men's convictions, the lawyers for Jones, Key, and Smith petitioned President Benjamin Harrison for executive clemency. They argued that though the men had committed the acts for which they had been found guilty, the conditions under which they labored should be mitigating factors in the determination of their sentences. On May 18, 1891, Harrison granted the men executive clemency and commuted their sentences to life imprisonment rather than death by hanging. In his accompanying statements, Harrison was demonstrably appalled by the inhuman conditions on Navassa. He was particularly disturbed by the fact that the men were "American citizens, under contracts to perform labor . . . within American territory, removed from any opportunity to appeal to any court or public officer for redress or any injury or the enforcement of any civil right. Their employers were in fact their masters."[44] The fact that such a condition could exist—an American territory where American citizens were deprived of rights—was abhorrent to Harrison and played a large part in his decision.

However, despite Harrison's discomfort with such an inequitable dynamic, the *Jones* case, the Guano Islands Act, and the language of appurtenance were all part of a long US legal history of creating just such spaces of limited rights in which the state, or in the case of Navassa a private enterprise sanctioned by the state, could act with few limits. Similar dynamics existed on Native American reservations and plantations across the United States. The laborers on Navassa, the bulk of whom were Black men only twenty-four years removed from enslavement, were reduced to what philosopher Giorgio Agamben has called bare life—a condition in which the subjects' complete rightlessness leaves them exposed to the violence of the state.[45] In Navassa, the laborers, some of whom might have been previously enslaved themselves, were returned to a condition tantamount to slavery. What happened on Navassa was shocking and unjust, but the legal instruments that allowed for such a situation to exist had been forged over the preceding decades and they would be critical in making way for the Court in *Downes v. Bidwell*.

Puerto Rico: "Foreign in a Domestic Sense"

Given that Puerto Rico was merely appurtenant to but not a part of the United States, the Court next grappled with the question of whether the US Constitution extended to the archipelago at all. Did the US Constitution follow the US flag? In other words, must the protections of that document extend everywhere that US sovereignty did? Here the Court broke with its previous decision in *Dred Scott*, wherein Justice Taney pointed out what all assumed to be an obvious proposition: that the Constitution and the Bill of Rights applied in the territories. Instead, in *Downes*, Justice Brown wrote that in the overseas territories the Constitution was "operative," but this did not mean that every provision was "applicable."[46] For Brown, the fact that Puerto Rico belonged to the United States, but was not a part of the United States, determined the territory's fate. Because it belonged to this new class of unincorporated territories, the Constitution did not apply to it.

Brown's rhetoric in *Downes* paralleled that of the much-reviled *Dred Scott v. Sanford* in claiming that the US Constitution was not created for the people of the insular territories and did not conceive of them and thus did not apply to them. Brown wrote, "It is sufficient to observe in relation to these three fundamental instruments that it can nowhere be inferred that the territories were considered a part of the United States. The Constitution was created by the people of the United States, as a union of States, to be governed solely by representatives of the States. . . . *In short, the Constitution deals with States, their people, and their representatives*" (emphasis added).[47] Though ostensibly this distinction could be perceived as race-neutral and based solely on geography, it is clear that the overlying concern was about extending constitutional rights to groups deemed racially undesirable. Given that the inhabitants of Puerto Rico were not considered "people of the United States," in the same way that Blacks were not "people of the United States," at the time of the creation of the Constitution, Brown reasoned that the document did not apply to them. Because they were not considered "people of the United States" when the Constitution was drafted, they could claim no protections or rights under that document. As a result, Puerto Ricans were left exposed to the whims of the United States.

Indeed, the impetus for deciding that the overseas territories should be considered appurtenant to but not a part of the United States was a fear of the mixed-race inhabitants of the insular territories. To be sure, those new territories were held as separate from the United States because they were occupied by mixed-race peoples that the US government had no interest in bringing into the US body politic. This was borne out not only in the debates of the day, which highlighted the nation's eugenic and social Darwinian ideologies but also within the *Downes* decision itself. Brown wrote:

> A false step at this time might be fatal to the development of what Chief Justice Marshall called the "American Empire." Choice in some cases, the natural gravitation of small bodies towards large ones in others, the result of a successful war in still others, may bring about conditions, which would render the annexation of distant possessions desirable. *If those possessions are inhabited by alien races, differing from us in religion, customs, laws, methods of taxation and modes of thought, the administration of government and justice, according to Anglo-Saxon principles, may for a time be impossible*; and the question at once arises whether large concessions ought not to be made for a time, that, ultimately, our own theories may be carried out, and the blessings of a free government under the Constitution extended to them. We decline to hold that there is anything in the Constitution to forbid such action. (emphasis added)[48]

In these words, we get to the root of the Court's reasoning. These were alien races and alien cultures with which the United States had to contend, and special dispensations had to be granted so that the United States could deal with these new territories and their mixed-race people differently than it had previously done with other territories.[49] In Brown's view, there were some rights that might apply to Puerto Rico and its inhabitants, natural rights owed to all men. Though he did not enumerate what those natural rights might be, he was nonetheless certain that the Constitution itself did not follow the flag of the United States and thus its protections did not extend everywhere that the US government settled.[50]

Justice Brown proclaimed that even if the archipelago's inhabitants were regarded as alien races who were not a part of the United States, some rights did apply to them—mainly those laid out in the Bill of Rights: the right to life, liberty, and property. He stated explicitly, "We . . . disclaim any intention to hold that the inhabitants of these territories are subject to an *unrestrained power* on the part of Congress to deal with them upon the theory that *they have no rights which it is bound to respect*" (emphasis added).[51] This language, of course, directly echoes the language of Taney in *Dred Scott*, wherein he infamously wrote: "Blacks had no rights which the white man was bound to respect." In *Downes*, Brown was explicitly creating a limit on Congress's power lest he appear to take as extreme a position as Taney had in *Dred Scott*. However, beyond these three perceived fundamental rights—life, liberty, property–a whole host of others were not granted to the territory and were left at Congress's discretion.

The Court in *Downes* reasoned that Congress's benevolence would protect Puerto Rico's residents from any potential tyranny at the hands of the government. Justice Brown attempted to assuage the fears of those concerned that leaving the archipelago in Congress's plenary power, without the protections of the Constitution, could lead to Congress acting as a despot toward Puerto Rico's inhabitants. In direct response to those concerns, he wrote for the Court, "grave apprehensions of danger are felt by many eminent men—a fear lest an unrestrained possession of power on the part of Congress may lead to unjust and oppressive legislation in which the natural rights of territories, or their inhabitants, may be engulfed in a centralized despotism. These fears, however, find no justification. . . . There are certain *principles of natural justice inherent in the Anglo-Saxon character*, which need no expression in constitutions or statutes to give them effect or to secure dependencies against legislation manifestly hostile to their real interests" (emphasis added).[52]

Thus, as far as the justices of the Court were concerned, the territory's residents had nothing to fear. They could rely on the "natural justice inherent in the Anglo-Saxon character" to protect them from inequitable policies and laws at the hands of Congress. This inherent justice would protect them from the sort of inequality and oppression that the US government had perpetrated on Black and Native Americans for centuries. And while, undoubtedly, Puerto Rico's residents were spared from the sort of unrestrained and gleeful violence that those other groups were exposed to, nonetheless inequality, discrimination, hunger, and oppression were the fruits brought to bear on the territory by this legal policy. As the history of Puerto Rico and of nonwhites in the United States has demonstrated, despite Justice Brown's assurances to the contrary, the archipelago and its residents indeed had grave cause for worry.

The 1901 *Downes* opinion laid out not only the many reasons Puerto Rico and the other overseas territories could be considered something other than a part of the United States but also why they should be excluded. Again, while

Brown's opinion sought to offer the official word from the Supreme Court in 1901, it was the ideas established in Justice White's concurrence that were later adopted as the justification for Puerto Rico's legal and political exclusion. Though White agreed with Brown that Puerto Rico should be excluded from the United States and the Constitution, he based his opinion on the fact that Puerto Rico was not explicitly "incorporated" into the United States by the Treaty of Paris, in which Spain ceded the insular territories to the United States.

For White, the fact that the language of incorporation was not present in the Treaty of Paris, as it was in the treaty first contemplated to annex Hawai'i in 1854, was determinative.[53] He pointed to the provisions of that treaty to make the distinction that it was clear from the outset that the incorporation of Hawai'i was always intended. That intent was not explicitly made in the Treaty of Paris. Concomitantly, he used *Jones v. United States* and the Guano Islands Act to bolster his argument that the United States must have the power to acquire territory without incorporating it into the United States, but instead holding it as appertaining to the United States. White famously and nonsensically declared that "whilst in an international sense Porto Rico was not a foreign country, since it was subject to the sovereignty of and was owned by the United States, it was foreign to the United States in a domestic sense, because the archipelago had not been incorporated into the United States, but was merely appurtenant thereto as a possession."[54] As legal historian Christina Ponsa-Kraus has argued, White's reasoning meant that "appurtenant" could now be understood to mean "neither foreign nor part of the United States (though, in this context at least, emphatically subject to US sovereignty)."[55]

After *Downes*: Being Unincorporated

White's reasoning had also created an entirely new legal entity: the unincorporated territory—an exceptional space where the US Constitution did not fully apply and whose fate Congress had indefinite plenary power to decide. Here we see the Supreme Court again finding ways to exclude from the US polity those deemed undesirable. With *Downes*, Puerto Rico joined the pantheon of racially excluded others, Native and Black Americans, who had been deemed unprepared or undesirable for the United States. Here too we see the establishment of the indeterminate state that has circumscribed Puerto Rico ever since.

The *Downes* decision also left Puerto Rico in a state of limbo about what legal protections its inhabitants were due and what rights they were afforded by the US government. The question remained: What was Puerto Rico to the United States, and, more important, what were Puerto Ricans to the United States? Most notably, the question of citizenship was a contentious one. Many on the US mainland balked at the idea of granting US citizenship to the inhabitants of the archipelago.[56] The territory's mixed-race inhabitants were descended from Spaniards, enslaved Africans, and natives who had survived the Spanish conquest. They were overwhelmingly Catholic and predominantly spoke Spanish. The thought of bringing these mixed-raced "mongrels" into the US body politic offended US sensibilities.[57] But if Puerto Ricans weren't citizens of the United States, then what were they? In 1904, in the case of *Gonzalez v. Williams*, the Court declared that Puerto Ricans were not excludable aliens for immigration purposes. The Foraker Act of 1900 had explicitly established that Puerto Ricans were not citizens of the United States but instead were citizens of Puerto Rico.[58] However, since Puerto Rico owed allegiance to the United States, the territory's residents could not be excluded on arrival at ports of the United States. What exactly it meant to be a citizen of Puerto Rico was not clear. Nevertheless, Puerto Ricans could travel back and forth between the archipelago and the US mainland unhindered.[59] Puerto Ricans were decidedly not US citizens, but they also weren't aliens; rather, they remained in an undetermined and exceptional status.

The *Gonzalez* decision was later overturned by the 1917 passage of the Jones-Shafroth Act, which gave Puerto Ricans US citizenship on the eve of the United States' entry into World War I. However, citizenship granted through statute, rather than constitutionally, is inherently discretionary. Thus, the citizenship granted to Puerto Ricans in 1917 differed from that granted by the US Constitution in the Fourteenth Amendment in that it could be rescinded at the will of Congress without need for a constitutional convention, vote, or a subsequent amendment. Though subsequent laws have worked to nuance and further define the nature of Puerto Ricans' US citizenship, it ultimately continues to be a creature of statute.[60] Puerto Rico's US citizenship has often been described as a sort of "second-class citizenship," in that it is discretionary and does not bring with it the rights to representation in the US government that full citizenship brings.[61]

Furthermore, though the Jones-Shafroth Act appeared to some to have changed the legal status of Puerto Ricans, in reality the grant of citizenship and the Act's other provisions for greater home rule did nothing to restrain Congress's plenary power or to change the position of Puerto Ricans vis-à-vis the US government. The Jones-Shafroth Act's grant of citizenship also did little to change the lived experiences of Puerto Ricans. The archipelago's residents openly discussed what their new status as citizens actually meant.[62] Because of the 1904 *González* case, Puerto Ricans were free to travel to and from the United States, so the new citizenship did nothing to change that fact. Furthermore, after 1917, Puerto Ricans, though now citizens, nonetheless had no representation or participation in the federal government. Many believed that the citizenship provisions simply allowed the US government to conscript them into military service. Furthermore, Puerto Ricans who traveled to the United States as laborers or students continued to face the sort of inequitable treatment that other foreigners and people of color did, so in that respect the new status of US citizens did not, in effect, grant any new protections to the people of Puerto Rico. Puerto Ricans fell into a category of second-class citizenship similar to that of Native Americans and Black Americans in the United States. Nominally, this status gave them some rights; however, in practice, little changed for the archipelago and its residents.

Cementing the Unincorporated Territory

The final case of the initial group known as the Insular Cases came before a Supreme Court helmed by former president of the United States and former governor of the Philippines William Howard Taft in 1922. *Balzac v. Porto Rico* concerned the applicability in the territories of the Sixth Amendment's due process guarantees and asked the Court whether the Sixth Amendment's guarantee to trial by jury in criminal proceedings applied to prosecutions in Puerto Rico.[63]

Jesús Maria Balsac was a publisher from the city of Mayagüez on Puerto Rico's West coast.[64] A self-taught public intellectual, he was also heavily involved with the Puerto Rican Socialist Party and the Federación Libre de Trabajadores (FLT), Puerto Rico's worker union which was allied with the American Federation of Labor (AFL). Balsac was also the editor of the working-class newspaper *El Baluarte*, published in Arecibo, Puerto Rico, in which he wrote two scathing articles virulently criticizing the US-appointed governor, Arthur Yager.[65] As a result of these publications, Balsac was charged with two counts of libel, a misdemeanor offense—one count for each article. Balsac requested a trial by jury pursuant to the Sixth Amendment of the US Constitution, which he believed applied to the archipelago after the passage of the Jones-Shafroth Act.[66] However, at the time Puerto Rico had local provisions allowing for trial by jury in felony cases but not in misdemeanor trials, and as a result Balsac's request for a jury trial was denied.[67] Balsac was convicted on both counts and sentenced to four and five months imprisonment, respectively, as well as being ordered to pay fines.[68]

On Balsac's appeal, the Supreme Court was faced with two questions: (1) Was the Sixth Amendment applicable to Puerto Rico? (2) Did language found in the Jones-Shafroth Act effectively act to incorporate Puerto Rico into the Union? To answer these questions, the Court also had to address the issue of what effect the Jones-Shafroth Act and its grant of US citizenship had on the United States–Puerto Rico relationship.

The Court dealt first with the applicability of the Sixth Amendment to Puerto Rico. Taft reiterated that pursuant to the Court's decision in *Downes*, the Sixth Amendment applied to all territories of the United States except those that had not been incorporated into the Union. The Court cited its earlier decision in *Dorr v. United States*, which held that "the power to govern territory . . . does not require that [Congress] enact for ceded territory, not made part of the United States by congressional action, a system of laws which shall include the right to trial by jury."[69]

The Court then turned to the more novel issue before it: "[Had] Congress, since the Foraker Act of April 12, 1900, enacted legislation incorporating Porto Rico into the Union?"[70] Balsac's attorney pointed to the Jones-Shafroth Act as proof that Congress intended for the provisions of the Constitution to apply to Puerto Rico.[71] He argued that the legislation enacted several provisions that sought to bring Puerto Rico in line with US legal procedures such as (1) the creation of the Puerto Rico District Court, which had the same power as the district and circuit courts of the United States; (2) the fact that appeals from the Supreme Court of Puerto Rico went to the US Supreme Court; (3) the fact that US copyright statutes would be enforced in Puerto Rican courts; (4) the declaration that the laws of the United States not locally inapplicable had been applied in Puerto Rico; and finally (5) that the immigration laws of the United States applied to Puerto Rico.

Taft's response to these examples was to note that the Jones-Shafroth Act did not explicitly incorporate Puerto Rico into the Union. He pointed to the fact that the Bill of Rights contained in the Jones-Shafroth Act itself did not contain a provision guaranteeing the right to trial by jury in civil and criminal cases. Instead, he reasoned that if that provision of the Jones-Shafroth Act had intended to incorporate Puerto Rico into the Union of its own force, then it would have included the guarantee to trial by jury. He concluded that incorporation "is not to be assumed without express declaration, or an implication so strong as to exclude any other view."[72]

Furthermore, Taft argued that the grant of US citizenship contained in the Jones-Shafroth Act was "entirely consistent with non-incorporation" because when Puerto Ricans passed from under the government of Spain to that of the United States, they had the right to expect a status entitling them to the protection of their new sovereign.[73] This new status of US citizenship allowed Puerto Ricans to move back and forth between the United States and the archipelago and to become residents of any state and there "enjoy every right of any other citizen of the United States, civil, social and political."[74] Given that Puerto Ricans enjoyed that right before the Jones-Shafroth Act under the Court's *Gonzalez v. Williams* decision, it is unclear exactly what the Act's grant of citizenship provided. Ultimately, Taft concluded, "it is locality that is determinative of the application of the Constitution, in such matters as judicial procedure, and not status of the people who live in it."[75]

As a final matter, Taft entered into a discussion about the appropriateness of forcing a system of trial by jury on the Puerto Rican people. He mused that the jury system required citizens who were properly trained to exercise the responsibilities of jurors. He added that "Congress has thought that a people like the Filipinos, or the Porto Ricans, trained to a complete judicial system which knows no juries, living in compact and ancient communities . . . should be permitted themselves to determine how far they wish to adopt this institution of Anglo-Saxon origin, and when."[76] Furthermore, Taft argued that the United States had been liberal in granting the unincorporated territories most of the provisions of the Constitution but had been sedulous to avoid forcing a jury system on a Spanish and civil law locality until it desired that system. Taft's closing statements on this topic are especially noteworthy and thought-provoking: "We cannot find any intention to depart from this policy in making Porto Ricans American citizens, explained as this is by the *desire to put them as individuals on an exact equality with citizens from the American homeland*, to secure them more certain protection against the world, and to give them an opportunity, should they desire, to move into the United States proper and there without naturalization enjoy all political and other rights" (emphasis added).[77]

Twenty-one years after the *Downes* Court broke with long-held precedent and created the territorial incorporation doctrine, fear of Puerto Rico's mixed-race inhabitants remained the logic the *Balzac* Court relied on to keep Puerto Rico out of the US polity. Taft's language echoes Brown's in *Downes*.

He points to the fact that Puerto Rico's residents lived in "compact and ancient" communities that were not yet ready for the US legal system as a means of denying Puerto Rico the protections of the Sixth Amendment. Twenty-one years after *Downes* had produced such a split among the justices of the Court, *Balzac* failed to produce a single dissent or even separate concurrence. By 1922, the logic of White's territorial incorporation doctrine, with its inequitable results, was cemented into US legal precedent. Between 1901 and 1922, the Court used the doctrine to deny residents of the territories several legal guarantees that are believed to be fundamental to the US system of laws: the right to a jury trial, the protection of indictment by grand jury in cases of felony, the prohibition against self-incrimination, the right of the accused "to be informed of the nature and cause of the accusation" against him, the right of the accused "to be confronted with witnesses against him," and the right to "enjoy a speedy and public trial."[78]

I point to these US Supreme Court decisions to highlight the confusion that dominated this period and the United States' uncertainty as to the legal status of Puerto Rico. If the moment of the acquisition of Puerto Rico was an extra-juridical action with which the United States had to contend, retaining Puerto Rico presented far more problems. In its decisions regarding the territory, the US government and the Supreme Court broke with its own previous legal precedents in order to maintain the archipelago, and its population of racial others, outside of the US body politic. Before the acquisition of Puerto Rico and the other insular territories in 1898, territories had been placed on the path to statehood. This was the case with territories acquired through westward expansion and with Hawai'i. The logic held that these territories, mostly occupied by Native Americans, would wait for statehood until they had undergone a period of training in "American" ideas of democracy and law and until enough white settlers had established themselves in the territory and displaced or eradicated Native American communities.[79]

However, Puerto Rico could not be treated as previous territories had been. The archipelago was too densely populated with people who were of a mixed-race character and whose racial mixture included the abhorrent blood of the Spanish and African.[80] Fear and mistrust of Puerto Rico's inhabitants led Congress and the Supreme Court to create new and unique categories for Puerto Rico that would ultimately work to create a space outside of the established legal order. The archipelago's indistinct status as an unincorporated territory where the US Constitution did not apply and where residents were excluded from both full citizenship and the established legal order worked to leave Puerto Ricans in a state of exception that allowed for a myriad of experiments.

Conclusion

Downes v. Bidwell was the start of Puerto Rico's inequitable and nonsensical relationship with the United States. Born out of a desire to allow the US government to retain Puerto Rico but rooted in its racist ideas about the unfit nature of Puerto Ricans, their "mongrel" heritage, and their inability to comprehend and implement the superior form of US governance, *Downes*'s careful contortions has had lasting impacts that the Court in 1901 could not have imagined. The quagmire the justices created for the archipelago in that decision continues to flummox and frustrate more than a century later. And more than a century later, the racist notions that first fueled the *Downes* decision still firmly undergird the continued exclusion of Puerto Rico and its status of exception.

CHAPTER TWO

Legacies

Racial Exclusion and the "American" State of Exception

The *Downes* decision, with its convoluted legal reasoning, left Puerto Rico in the legal limbo in which it remains today. Puerto Rico continues to be a colony under Congress's plenary power more than a century later, and this status continues to shape nearly every aspect of life in the archipelago. However, the US Supreme Court did not create this status for Puerto Rico in a vacuum. The journey to determining Puerto Rico's unique legal relationship with the United States begins not with the War of 1898, but long before, when the young United States began its expansion west and south from the initial colonies. These forays out into what would become the greater United States brought settlers, and the nascent US government, face-to-face with Indigenous groups who had occupied the continent long before the arrival of the ancestors of those newly minted US citizens. Furthermore, from the earliest days of the United States, the tension between American ideals and the reality of enslavement pushed at the boundaries of US state formation.

The early nineteenth century was a period of radical transition in the United States. As the growing population moved south and west from the northeastern region of the United States, the populace became fractured. The question of sovereignty loomed over this era in US history, animating disagreements about the powers granted to the states and those of the federal government. Against the backdrop of these intense debates in the first few decades of the nineteenth century, the US Supreme Court was also carving out a role for itself. During this time of sectionalism, many in the southern states did not believe the Court had the power to review their state decisions, given that they were separate sovereigns. This power struggle was most visible in two areas of wide import and consequence: the abolition of slavery and the so-called "Indian problem."

To be sure, the ignominious history of the US government's treatment of these groups is well documented.[1] However, in this chapter I will revisit several key Supreme Court decisions concerning the rights of Native Americans and enslaved Africans and their descendants and the events that led to these decisions. These important precedents, which allowed for the dispossession of Native tribes, sanctioned the genocidal violence visited upon them, and subjugated enslaved and free Blacks, are essential to understanding the *Downes* decision and the Court's approach to Puerto Rico. Here, I offer a short genealogy of racial exclusion in law. I look to the precedents that led to *Downes v. Bidwell*, and I pull apart the legal logics on which they are built in order to better understand the fabric of the *Downes* decision. A full analysis of the Supreme Court's jurisprudence on racial exclusion could fill several volumes, so here I will focus on those precedents that are cited in and most directly lead to *Downes v. Bidwell* and the Court's analysis in that decision. As a result, I will focus on the group of cases known as the Marshall Trilogy (1823–32), *United States v. Rogers* (1846), and *Dred Scott v. Sanford* (1856). In these opinions, we see the birth and growth of plenary power and of the "American" state of exception. Native Americans and enslaved Africans were among the first nonwhite others with whom the US legal system had to contend, and the precedents established in these encounters have had lasting legacies that continue today.

As white settlers moved into territories previously occupied by Native Nations, the "Indian problem" remained ever present. Namely, what was to be done with Native peoples? The imperative to "civilize" and to put land into "productive use" was one shared across sectors of the US population, but the matter of what to do with the Native peoples who resided on those lands remained unresolved. There was great disagreement about whether Native Nations should be allowed to remain on their ancestral territories, whether they should be forced to sell them to the government, or whether the United States should employ the military to forcibly eject Native Americans from desirable areas. The majority of opinions about what should be done were couched in the racist and paternalistic assumptions of the day—that Native Americans were either fierce warriors who had to be restrained or simple children who needed to be educated and trained. It is against this backdrop of debate and contention over where power should reside in the young United States that the Marshall Trilogy was decided.

Native Americans, Discovery, and Plenary Power

Native American exclusion, like that of Puerto Rico, is premised on Congress's plenary power.[2] By the time the United States acquired Puerto Rico in 1898, the Court had affirmed Congress's power over Native Americans on multiple occasions. Importantly, the Court had also established that Congress's actions concerning Native Americans and their territory were not subject to judicial review, and as a result Congress's power over them was nearly absolute. Federal power over Native tribes was first established in a series of Supreme Court cases that began in 1823, which were known as the Marshall Trilogy because they were decided under the stewardship of Chief Justice John Marshall. This chapter begins with an analysis of the legal decisions that make up the Marshall Trilogy. These three cases are widely understood to be the genesis of the United States' Indian policies. The ideas and doctrines enumerated in the Marshall Trilogy form the bedrock of Indian law. The chapter then turns to a discussion of *United States v. Rogers*, referred to by legal historians as the *Dred Scott* of Indian law because it granted Congress plenary, or complete, power over Indians and left Indians with few enumerable rights in the face of that power.[3] In these decisions, the Court "rooted the power over Indian affairs and Indian lands firmly in the national government, providing fuel for westward expansion and its radical transformation" of the US landscape and geography and the lives of thousands of Native Americans.[4] In short, the Marshall Trilogy set the stage for the inequities Native Americans have experienced at the hands of the US government and the individual states since the cases were decided.

Johnson v. M'Intosh

Johnson v. M'Intosh, the first of the disputes to go before the court, was a test case that was orchestrated by land speculators interested in acquiring large tracts of land in the western territories.[5] It arose in a time of political tumult, when "settlers, Native American tribes and colonial forces competed for dominance over the new world."[6] From the earliest days of European colonization of North America, settlers had taken the position that purchases of land from Indian tribes were the prerogative of the government.[7] With few exceptions, most land acquired during that period was purchased by the colonies or the Crown, but rarely by individuals.[8] In 1790, the newly formed United States passed legislation to officialize this custom and thereby prohibited individuals and states from purchasing land from Native tribes.[9]

Prior to that date, in 1773 and 1775, leaders from the Piankeshaw Indian tribe sold several large tracts of land to the royal governor of Virginia and to a group of nineteen other people from several states, including speculators working on behalf of the Illinois and Wabash Land Companies.[10] The purchases were located in the present-day states of Illinois and Indiana within the boundaries of the Illinois Territory, west of the Allegheny Mountains. The tracts "were vast and ambiguously demarcated, constituting thousands of square miles of land."[11] The transactions were unlawful at the time they were made, because the Proclamation of 1763 prohibited private land purchases.[12] However, as historian Stuart Banner has explained, "land speculators remained active even after the proclamation . . . because they were gambling that the proclamation would be repealed or modified, and that their purchases would eventually be confirmed retroactively by the government."[13]

Thirty years later, on December 30, 1805, the Piankeshaw ceded much of the same parcel of land to the United States government via a treaty that was negotiated by William Henry Harrison, then the governor of the Indiana Territory. A portion of that parcel was later purchased by William M'Intosh, a speculator who held vast amounts of land in the midwestern territories and who was enlisted to participate in the lawsuit at the behest of the Illinois and Wabash Land Companies. Indeed, the case of *Johnson v. M'Intosh* was entirely orchestrated by the companies in an attempt to categorically legitimize their claims to the land in question.[14]

The companies' powerful and well-connected shareholders had tried numerous times to push through legislation that would have formalized their claims to the land. When those attempts failed, they turned to the judiciary and specifically to the newly formed federal district court in Illinois, whose appointed judge, Nathaniel Pope, was related by marriage to plaintiff Johnson's niece.[15] Thomas Johnson had himself been an original shareholder of the Wabash Land Company and the dispute was brought by his heirs who sought to legitimate their claims to his estate. Defendant M'Intosh was a vocal opponent of William Henry Harrison, who had become the governor of the state of Indiana. M'Intosh hoped that a win for the companies would lead to less government interference in his own large land holdings in Indiana and Illinois. With the companies' handpicked plaintiff and defendant in place and a sympathetic federal judge presiding over the dispute, and having also procured defendant's counsel, the companies set about manipulating the procedural elements of the case so that it could be appealed to the Supreme Court.[16] Through numerous legal maneuvers, the companies managed, in 1823, to get their case before the Court and argued by lawyers who were all working toward the same goal: a decision that gave the Wabash and Illinois Land Companies definitive title to the thousands of acres in Indiana and Illinois.

Unfortunately for the companies and for Johnson, the politics of the day did not work in their favor. Despite their careful machinations and collusion, they were unable to obtain a favorable decision. It was too obvious that the parties had conspired to obtain a decision the companies had sought since their original purchase of the lands fifty years earlier. Most glaring for legal observers was the fact that the parties had agreed on all the facts of the case. These facts had been in dispute since the original purchases, and some "could not be proved by evidence."[17] As a result of this stipulation of facts, the only question before the Court was "the power of Indians to give, and of private individuals to receive, a title which can be sustained in the Courts of this country."[18] In other words, could Native peoples legally convey their lands to private citizens of the United States? The Supreme Court found that Native tribes had no such power.

The Court relied on the doctrine of discovery to come to its conclusion that Indian tribes did not have the ability to convey their land to private individuals. Chief Justice Marshall's opinion began by first acknowledging that Indians had a sovereign right to possess their land "and to use it according to their own discretion."[19] However, Indian rights to complete sovereignty over their lands, as independent nations, had been diminished by European discovery. According to Marshall, the international law doctrine of discovery—that discovery gave exclusive title to those who made such a discovery—"gave the first European power to discover new lands an exclusive right, as against other European nations, to 'acquir[e] the soil from the natives, and establish settlements upon it.'"[20] Thus, discovery rendered the Indians' title imperfect by limiting their ability to alienate their lands only to the discovering power. Because the US government was the legal successor to the British Crown, in the United States Indians could sell their lands only to the federal government, and the United States had an "exclusive right to extinguish the Indian title of occupancy, either by purchase or by conquest."[21]

Johnson v. M'Intosh established that "US authority over Indian tribes, or at least the United States' exclusive right to acquire Indian property, originated from two sources: colonial prerogatives deriving from discovery, and the nature of Indians as savages and incomplete sovereigns."[22] Neither of these sources was based on the text of the Constitution. Instead, Chief Justice Marshall relied on his reading of international and common law to reach his decision. To be sure, though the Court relied on a seemingly well-established principle of international law in the *Johnson* decision, nevertheless the overlying logic was one of racism and the understanding of Native Americans as something other.

Indians were not fully human; they lacked civilization and Christianity.[23] In Marshall's words, Indians were "fierce savages, whose occupation was war, and whose subsistence was drawn chiefly from the forest. To leave them in possession of their country was to leave the country a wilderness."[24] He further explained that the "excuse, if not justification, for this doctrine lay in 'the character and habits' of the Indians."[25] They were of such a different character from the white Anglo-Saxon people that the Indians were incapable of being incorporated into the US polity. Although ordinarily conquest did not deprive existing inhabitants of their land rights, this rule did not pertain where the inhabitants were "a people with whom it was impossible to mix, and who could not be governed as a distinct society."[26] As a result, "Indians did not share the property rights enjoyed by 'civilized' whites."[27] This logic of Indian backwardness and savagery was, of course, par for the course at the time; as a result, it is also the ethos underpinning the Court's decision in *Johnson*.

Thus, despite their careful orchestration of *Johnson v. M'Intosh*, the Illinois and Wabash Land Companies could not prevail before the Supreme Court. However, the companies unwittingly opened the door for the Court to make a decision that would continue to reverberate in Native American communities for years to come. In *Johnson*, Marshall "began to assert and articulate a national power that extended beyond the Constitution."[28] As legal scholar Maggie Blackhawk has argued, Marshall "read the doctrine of discovery narrowly to serve as a restraint on only European sovereigns. . . . [Furthermore,] he created out of whole cloth 'Indian Title'—or the notion that Native Nations retained their inherent sovereignty and retained domain over their lands after discovery."[29] In doing so, Marshall also "laid the question of how the United States would treat the sovereignty of Native Nations squarely within the domain of domestic law."[30] The question of how the United States would treat the sovereignty of Native Nations came before the court a mere eight years later in the final two disputes of the Marshall Trilogy.

The Cherokee Nation Cases

Following the United States' acquisition of the Louisiana Territory, it became federal practice to "encourage" Native tribes in the east to exchange their lands for land in the western territories. The United States' purchase of vast territory in the west made it possible for the government to trade unoccupied land for desirable land in the densely populated eastern states. Generally, the government's approach was to encourage these trades rather than to forcibly compel them; however, often the sales were made under duress, through coercion, or through fraudulent agreements.[31]

In 1802, the State of Georgia entered into an agreement with the US government in which it ceded all its claims to land west of the Mississippi. In exchange, the federal government gave Georgia $1.25 million and a pledge to extinguish Indian title to lands within the boundaries of the state, "as early as the same can be peaceably obtained on reasonable terms."[32] However, by 1820, despite the migration of thousands of Native Americans to the western territories, tens of thousands still lived east of the Mississippi River, with large groups remaining in the southern states. Georgia, which had seen rapid growth in its population of white settlers in the first two decades of the nineteenth century, was one of these states.

In 1820, Thomas Cobb, a congressional representative from Georgia, complained that the federal government was not moving fast enough in acquiring land from the Creek and the Cherokee, who owned the most land in the state. He declared on the House floor, "The Indian title to fully one half, and *probably the most valuable half*, of the lands within the boundaries of the state is yet extinguished" (emphasis added).[33] By the end of the decade, Georgia had lost patience with the federal government's slow pace. The state moved to impose a series of new laws designed to make life for the Cherokee ever more difficult so that they would be forced to sell their land and move west.

Georgia took an aggressive step when it passed legislation that extended the state's jurisdiction and laws "over all the territory within her . . . limits" and declared that it had the right to "exercise, over any people, white or red, within those limits, the authority of her laws."[34] Georgia then barred Native Americans from testifying in court and from entering non-Indian areas of the state without first obtaining a permit. In 1830, when gold was discovered in the Cherokee territory, the state authorized the governor "to take possession of all gold, silver, and other mines on the Cherokee's land, on the grounds that all mines were 'of right the property of Georgia.'"[35] The culmination of Georgia's slow legal inundation of the Cherokee Nation occurred two weeks later, when the state authorized the seizure of all Cherokee lands and the distribution of that land to white settlers.

Against the backdrop of Georgia's onslaught against the Cherokee and the pressure it applied to force them to sell their lands, the passage of the Indian Removal Act in 1830 further signaled to the Cherokee that the federal government would not step in to protect the tribe from Georgia's encroachments. Nevertheless, after the passage of the Removal Act, the Cherokee wrote directly to Congress explicitly stating their desire to remain on their own lands within and surrounding Georgia.[36] However, when the federal government failed to uphold the tribe's treaty rights against the State of Georgia, the Cherokee turned to the Supreme Court. The resulting legal disputes, the Cherokee Nation Cases, were a last desperate attempt by the tribe to preclude Georgia from infringing on the tribe's long-established rights.

In *Cherokee Nation v. Georgia*, the tribe sought injunctive relief to prevent the state from executing or enforcing any of its laws within its territory, as recognized by treaty between the United States and the Cherokee.[37] The question before the Court was fairly straightforward: Could a Native American tribe sue a state in the federal courts? To answer this question, the Court had to determine whether the Cherokee were a state or a foreign nation. Lawyers for the Cherokee Nation argued that the Constitution "knows of but two descriptions of states—domestic and foreign."[38] Since the Cherokee Nation was not a domestic state, they argued, it must necessarily be a foreign nation. Article III of the US Constitution established that the Supreme Court has original jurisdiction to hear disputes arising between a foreign nation and a state of the United States. Furthermore, the tribe argued that it was an independent and sovereign nation because its people were viewed as noncitizen aliens by the federal government.[39] Thus, the Court had jurisdiction over the dispute.

Georgia made its position clear by failing to attend or participate in the proceedings. The choice not to appear before the Court was an argument in itself. Georgia maintained that because it was a sovereign state, the Supreme Court did not have jurisdiction over the state's internal affairs, and thus Georgia was not bound by any of the Court's decisions.[40] Participating in the proceedings would have suggested acquiescence to the Court's power; therefore, Georgia declined to take part.

The Court dismissed the case due to lack of jurisdiction.[41] The justices found that while the Cherokee had the *character* of "a state, as a distinct political society," the tribe was "not a foreign state" within the meaning of Article III of the Constitution and thus could not sue in US courts.[42] Instead, because the tribe resided "within the jurisdictional limits of the United States and its territory," it constituted a part of the United States.[43] As a result, the Cherokee were not a sovereign, independent nation but a "domestic dependent nation," occupying "a territory to which we assert a title independent of their will."[44] The Court likened the Indians' relation to the United States as "that of a ward to his guardian" and stated that the tribes were so "completely under the sovereignty and dominion of the United States, that any attempt to acquire their lands, or to form a political connection with them by a foreign state would be considered . . . an act of hostility against the United States."[45] In effect, the Court's decision precluded Indian tribes' ability to seek redress in the courts of the United States and placed Indians in the liminal status of being neither citizens of the United States nor aliens or citizens of a sovereign foreign state.[46]

A year later, the Court heard the second of the Cherokee Nation Cases. In *Worcester v. Georgia*, the plaintiffs, Samuel Worcester and Elizur Butler, were missionaries sent by the federal government to the lands of the Cherokee Nation to work as employees of the US Postmaster General. The State of Georgia prosecuted them for violating a state law that required whites residing in Cherokee territory to obtain a state license and swear allegiance to Georgia.[47] Worcester and Butler were part of a group of missionaries who not only failed to obtain licenses and refused to swear allegiance but also made public statements in support of the Cherokee, in clear defiance of Georgia law. The missionaries were tried and sentenced to four years of hard labor. They were later offered a pardon if they left the Cherokee territory or obtained a license from the state. Worcester and Butler declined the pardon and instead appealed to the US Supreme Court.

Once again, the State of Georgia declined to participate. The governor, Wilson Lumpkin, told the Georgia legislature that he would "disregard all unconstitutional requisitions, of whatever character or origin they may be."[48] Furthermore, the Georgia legislature itself declared, "the State of Georgia will not compromit [sic] her dignity as a sovereign state, or so far yield her rights as a member of the Confederacy as to appear in answer to, or in any way become a party to any proceedings before the Supreme Court having for their object a revival or interference with the decisions of the state courts in criminal matters."[49] Thus, as before, Georgia allowed its absence to be its argument.

Worcester and Butler were represented by the same attorneys who had argued *Cherokee Nation v. Georgia*. They maintained that the federal rights of the Cherokee Nation invalidated the Georgia statute because they were granted through treaty with the United States.[50] Ultimately, the case pitted the rights of the federal government over those of a state. There was no question that this dispute was squarely within the jurisdiction of the Court; therefore, the only question before the justices was the constitutionality of the Georgia statute. Worcester and Butler's attorneys asserted that "the statute of Georgia under which the plaintiffs in error were indicted and convicted was unconstitutional and void."[51]

Again writing for the Court, Marshall found that indeed Indian tribes had sovereignty. The Indian nations, he wrote, "have always been considered as distinct, independent political communities, retaining their original natural rights, as the undisputed possessors of the soil, from time immemorial."[52] The Court argued that both Great Britain and the United States had always treated the Indians as sovereigns and had never attempted to interfere with internal Indian affairs.[53] He emphasized that relations with Indians were the exclusive province of the national government and were conducted in the same manner as all other foreign relations.[54] In what has become the most cited language of the decisions, Marshall famously stated, "the Cherokee nation, then, is a distinct community, occupying its own territory, with boundaries accurately described, in which the laws of Georgia can have no force, and which the citizens of Georgia have no right to enter, but with the assent of the Cherokees themselves, or in conformity with treaties and with the acts of congress. The whole intercourse between the United States and this nation, is by our constitution and laws, vested in the government of the United States."[55] The Court was clear. The Georgia statute was unconstitutional. Worcester and Butler had to be released.

While *Worcester* was seen as a significant win for the Cherokee Nation, in fact, it did little to stop Georgia from infringing on the Nation's lands or its sovereignty. The Court's decision obligated Georgia to release the two missionaries from prison. However, the decision could not force the federal government to act on behalf of the Nation; nor could it invalidate acts of the Georgia government that did not directly relate to Worcester and Butler's convictions.[56] Following the decision, Georgia refused to acknowledge the Court's opinion, and Worcester and Butler remained in prison.

In the end, the missionaries sought guidance from the American Board of Commissioners for Foreign Missions. The board debated what course of action Worcester and Butler should take. It determined that the missionaries had been righteous in their refusal to abide by Georgia's statute and in pursuing the rights of the Cherokee before the Supreme Court. However, the board reasoned that the battle was clearly lost, and "the Cherokee must be advised that there was no longer any hope of resistance to removal."[57] Thus Worcester and Butler could honorably seek the pardon that Georgia had previously offered them. The missionaries were released on January 15, 1833.

The events that followed the Cherokee Nation Cases are well documented. For the next several years, the US government and the southern states worked to dispossess thousands of acres of Native sovereign land. The military was deployed to ensure that Native Americans would remove themselves to the Indian Territories west of the Mississippi River. The notorious Trail of Tears saw the culmination of Georgia's fight to divest the Cherokee of their ancestral territory. The US Army interned and forcefully relocated approximately

16,000 Cherokee in the fall and winter of 1838–39, under circumstances so extreme that thousands died along the journey.[58]

In these legal cases, a young Supreme Court and a young United States grappled with what exactly the Indian Nations were in relation to the nation. Did the Constitution apply to them? What sorts of rights, if any, were they due? Similar questions arose in the late nineteenth century after the United States acquired the insular territories. The Marshall Trilogy highlights the difficulty the Court had in toeing the line between maintaining federal control over Indian affairs and not seeming to trample the rights of states. Ultimately, the Court found justification for its conclusions that the federal government shared a unique relationship with the tribes and that it alone could regulate interaction with the tribes in the War, Treaty, and Commerce Clauses of the US Constitution, which "comprehend all that is required for the regulation of our intercourse with the Indians."[59]

The decisions in the Marshall Trilogy, because they are not firmly steeped in constitutional analysis but instead rely heavily on international and common law (prior precedents and judicial principles rather than legal codes or constitutions), have often been assumed by subsequent Supreme Court justices to be subject to change or not hard precedent.[60] In fact, subsequent decisions have limited the scope of the Marshall Trilogy.[61] However, despite possible interpretations and apparent contradictions, the Trilogy is seen to stand generally for the proposition that Congress has plenary power over Indian Nations.[62] With the *Johnson* decision, the Court essentially established the rule that the United States' power supersedes that of Indian Nations, despite their recognized sovereignty, while at the same time subjecting Native Americans to the laws of the United States. Thus, as Marshall wrote in *Cherokee Nation*, Indian tribes possessed sovereignty and had natural rights over property but were nevertheless reliant on the US government's "kindness and its power."[63] In this respect, Indian Nations are similarly positioned to the insular territories. As discussed in chapter 1, in *Downes* the Court also held that the inhabitants of the territories, though not granted the protections of the Constitution, nonetheless were owed those natural rights owed to all men. Additionally, they were also under Congress's plenary power and, though they could claim limited rights, nonetheless they too could rely on the benevolence of Congress to protect them.[64]

Likewise, by finding that Indians were aliens residing within a domestic dependent nation to which the United States held title, the Cherokee Nation Cases left Indians in a legal limbo in which they were neither foreigners nor citizens. This distinction, referred to as the alien-citizen paradox, meant that members of the Indian Nations were neither full citizens (with all the rights, privileges, and immunities associated with that status) nor completely foreign (because they enjoyed some form of formal relationship with the United States).[65] Again, this paradox would be echoed later in the *Downes* case with respect to the inhabitants of the insular territories. There as well, the residents of the territories were not citizens, but neither were they foreign because they too enjoyed a formal relationship with the United States. In the case of Puerto Rico, the *Downes* Court created the contradictory label of "foreign in a domestic sense" to grapple with the unique paradox it created.

United States v. Rogers

Twelve years after the Marshall Trilogy was decided, the Court made another important decision with respect to Native Americans that continues to reverberate today and whose legacy we see in *Downes*. The matter of *United States v. Rogers* arose in 1845 within the bounds of the Cherokee Nation located in the state of Arkansas. Like *Johnson v. M'Intosh* and *Worcester v. Georgia* before it, *Rogers* was a dispute in which no tribe was a party, and yet the outcome had immediate and lasting ramifications for all Native Nations.

William Rogers was a white man who moved to the Cherokee Nation sometime in 1836. There he married a Cherokee woman with whom he had several children. She passed away in 1843, but following her death Rogers remained in Cherokee country, where he raised his children. Having lived within the bounds of the Cherokee Nation and having incorporated himself into the everyday life of the tribe, Rogers was "treated, recognized, and had been adopted as a Cherokee by the proper authorities thereof, and exercised . . . all the rights and privileges of a Cherokee Indian."[66]

In September 1844, Rogers was involved in a fight with Jacob Nicholson, another white man residing in the Cherokee territory who had also married into the tribe. Nicholson, too, was a Cherokee citizen by the laws of the group. During the fight, Rogers stabbed Nicholson to death and fled. He was later arrested and indicted in the federal district court of Arkansas. Rogers, who represented himself, argued that the court lacked jurisdiction over the case because both he and Nicholson were Cherokee Indians. Under the 1834 Trade and Intercourse Act and established treaties between the United States and the Cherokee, the Nation had jurisdiction over criminal matters that arose in the Cherokee territory and that involved Indians. Samuel Hempstead, the US district attorney, disagreed and instead argued that "an American citizen could not expatriate himself, particularly to an Indian tribe, without some positive federal law authorizing him to do so."[67] Furthermore, Hempstead added that whites could not "join tribes by marriage, emigration, or adoption unless the federal law allowed it."[68]

Hempstead's claims were both inaccurate and misleading. They were misleading because any US citizen could choose at any time to renounce US citizenship and adopt that of a foreign nation without the say of the federal government.[69] And the claims were inaccurate because for years, white settlers had moved into Indian territories, had incorporated themselves into tribal communities, and had been held to tribal norms and rules upon doing so. Hempstead's primary concern in allowing Rogers and those like him to be considered Indians under the law was that to do so "would encourage worthless Americans to take refuge on the frontier."[70] The dispute posed novel and consequential questions of law, and the district court was divided. As a result, it sent the matter to the Supreme Court, posing several questions, such as whether a Native Tribe could naturalize a US citizen and whether a US citizen could renounce that status in order to claim citizenship in an Indigenous tribe.

Shortly after these events, Rogers and his cellmate overtook their captors and escaped imprisonment. Rogers for his part tried to return to Cherokee Country but drowned in a swollen river while trying to cross. Rogers's death, of course, should have been the end of the legal matter, since the defendant was no longer available. However, that information never reached the Court, and the dispute was heard several months later in January 1846. The Court's unanimous opinion was written by Chief Justice Roger Taney, who would also write the Court's opinion in the hateful case *Dred Scott v. Sanford*, discussed later.

The *Rogers* decision was short, and it pointedly did not address the questions that had been sent to the Court. Instead, according to American Indian law scholar David E. Wilkins, Taney "dramatically revised the actual history of the tribal-federal relationship, unilaterally redefined the legal and political standing of tribes — especially over questions related to tribal citizenship and membership — and mischaracterized the property rights of Indians."[71] The Chief Justice would employ a similar tactic in rewriting history to favor his desired outcome in *Dred Scott* a few years later. In *Rogers*, Taney declared that the area where the crime was committed was "a part of the territory of the United States."[72] He conceded that it was occupied by the Cherokee Nation, but he wrongly claimed it had "been assigned to them by the United States, as a place of domicile." Furthermore, Taney claimed that the Native tribes that had been present in the United States "at the time of its discovery have never been acknowledged or treated as independent nations by the European governments, nor regarded as the owners of the territories they respectively occupied. . . . The whole continent was divided and parceled out, and granted by the governments of Europe as if it had been vacant and unoccupied land, and the Indians . . . treated as, subject to their dominion and control."[73]

In making these statements about the history of Native Americans and their relationship to the federal government and their lands, Taney effectively rewrote the Court's decisions in the Marshall Trilogy and negated the long history of treaty making that had existed not only between the United States and Native tribes but also earlier, between the tribes and Great Britain. Most important, Taney's decision expanded the federal government's power over Native tribes and essentially established that "Congress held limitless power to regulate Indian Country and rooted this limitless power not in the Constitution but in the discovery doctrine," first enumerated in *Johnson v. M'Intosh*.[74] Furthermore, Taney stated that "were the right and propriety of exercising this power now open to question, yet it is a question for the lawmaking and political departments of the government, and not for the judicial."[75] Here, Taney not only affirmed Congress's plenary power over Indian affairs but also precluded the possibility of judicial review of those powers. After *Rogers*, the Court's "only legitimate concern is whether the political branches of government, federal or state, have exceeded constitutional limitations."[76] To determine whether the federal government acted "wisely or well is a political question, which is not for the courts to consider."[77]

In *Rogers*, the Court cemented Congress's unrestrained power over Native tribes while constraining the judiciary from reviewing that power. This precedent was dangerous indeed, as it effectively allowed Congress unchecked power over Native affairs. As Maggie Blackhawk has written, the decision opened the door for the United States to begin a violent campaign to solve the proverbial "Indian problem." *Rogers* allowed the United States to "establish military-run detention camps where the executive branch held limitless power. . . . In these camps, children were forcibly separated from their families and sent to federally run boarding schools that used violence to 'kill the Indian in him, and save the man.' . . . Native Americans were incarcerated for practicing their faith. Naming ceremonies were forbidden for children, whose hair was cut at the schools, where they were also forced to practice Christianity."[78] The list of abuses the United States committed against Native Americans is long and has been well documented by historians and scholars of Native American and Indigenous studies, as have the many ways that

Native communities have resisted, and continue to resist, the deracination of the United States.

However, what we see in these decisions is the Supreme Court and US government carving out legal lacunae in order to assert a nearly unrestrained power over Native tribes, while also limiting their rights and access to legal remedies. As Blackhawk described, these decisions quite literally allowed for the creation of reservations and camps where Native Americans were confined, neglected, and violated. Here we see the birth of the "American" state of exception—locations of Congress's unrestrained power, where residents are left with limited rights and few remedies. Plenary power "has been expanded beyond Indian Country to justify seemingly limitless power over all kinds of people at the margins of American empire."[79] This is the case in the United States' colonial rule over Puerto Rico and the other insular territories.

Dred Scott v. Sanford—Defining the "People" of the United States

Following the *Marshall Trilogy*, the Court continued to grapple with the status of racial others within the US body politic. These pronouncements, generally steeped in the racist language and ethos of the day, worked to create a legal map of exclusion for nonwhites in the United States. In 1856, in what has come to be known as the most disgraceful decision of the US Supreme Court, Chief Justice Roger Taney wrote that Blacks "had for more than a century before been regarded as beings of an inferior order, and altogether unfit to associate with the white race, either in social or political relations; and so far inferior, that *they had no rights which the white man was bound to respect*; and that the negro must justly and lawfully be reduced to slavery"[80] (emphasis added). The Court further explained that when the Constitution of the United States was created, it applied to all classes of persons who were recognized as citizens at the time of its creation, "but none other; it was formed by them, and for them and their posterity, but for no one else"[81] (emphasis added). Part of the Supreme Court's shameful decision in the case of *Dred Scott v. Sanford*, these pronouncements would be echoed in *Downes v. Bidwell* to justify Puerto Rico's exclusion from the protections of the US Constitution.

The legal ramifications of *Dred Scott* would later be overturned by several important pieces of legislation following the United States Civil War: the Thirteenth and Fourteenth Amendments to the Constitution and the Civil

Rights Act of 1866. However, Taney's pronouncements in *Dred Scott* remain important today, as they illustrate not only the racial animus and hatred that underpinned the workings of US government but also the continued development and deployment of the "American" state of exception.

How, the reader may ask, are Dred Scott and his plea for freedom from the shameful bonds of slavery relevant to a discussion of Puerto Rico's creation as a racialized space in need of legal exclusion? As we will see, the *Dred Scott* case and the United States' treatment of enslaved and free Blacks is integral to understanding how the United States and the Supreme Court furthered and perfected the legal lacunae of the American state of exception that would later be adopted in Puerto Rico—wherein Congress's power is plenary and residents are left with limited legal recourse.

The Court's declarations in *Dred Scott* with regard to the concept of territoriality and the limits of the US constitution were instructive to the *Downes* court in 1901. Furthermore, Taney's ideas with respect to the limits of citizenship and the role of race in deciding that citizenship also play a definitive role in the latter case. In *Dred Scott*, Taney created a category for Blacks outside of the legal order; he rationalized that this group could be maintained as something other than citizens without legal protections or rights. This same scenario, which had also played out in the Marshall Trilogy, would be echoed forty-four years later for the insular territories, and there too the logic would be steeped in racist ideas about the superiority of the white race and the inferiority of the mixed-race residents of the insular territories. Finally, and perhaps most important, Taney's declarations that Blacks had no rights that the white man was bound to respect marked them as rights-less individuals, whose bodies were available to state-sanctioned violence. If Black folks in the United States were not "people" under the Constitution, then they could claim no rights or privileges under that most revered document and were instead left to exist in the "American" state of exception.

Dred Scott was born into slavery in Virginia sometime around 1800.[82] In 1830, Scott's owner, Peter Blow, relocated to St. Louis, Missouri, taking Scott with him. In 1833, following Blow's death, Scott was sold to Dr. John Emerson, a surgeon in the US Army. From 1833 to 1836, Scott resided with Emerson at Fort Armstrong, in Illinois. While Scott was in Illinois, a free state, he could have sued for his freedom, but he did not do so, most likely because he was not aware that he could. In 1836, upon the Army's evacuation from Fort Armstrong, Emerson relocated with Scott to Fort Snelling in what is today Minnesota. At the time that area was within the newly created Wisconsin Territory, which had once been included in the Missouri

Compromise, where slavery was forever prohibited. Despite the fact that slavery was also banned in the new territory, Emerson was able to keep Scott enslaved because officials there did little to enforce the prohibition on slavery. Again, it is likely that Scott did not know that he had a legal claim to freedom while in the Wisconsin Territory.

While at Fort Snelling, Scott married Harriet Robinson, an enslaved woman belonging to Major Lawrence Taliaferro, who was stationed near the fort. Major Taliaferro, who was also a justice of the peace, performed the civil ceremony for the two in his official capacity. The fact of the Scotts' civil marriage before an officer of the peace was unheard of given that the enslaved were not legally allowed to marry. This was a unique situation because civil marriages were legal contracts and, as property, the enslaved were incapable of entering into contractual obligations. Furthermore, legal recognition of a marriage between enslaved individuals may have interfered with an owner's property rights to the enslaved if the couple were claimed by different individuals. Finally, if enslaved individuals were granted the legal right to marry, they might be able to claim other rights as well. The Scotts' legal marriage, performed by a justice of the peace in a territory of the United States where slavery was prohibited, pointed to the possibility that the Scotts had been freed. Scott's lawyers later made this very argument during his suit for freedom. However, it was also true that after the marriage, Taliaferro gave Harriet to Emerson, who continued to treat the two as enslaved property, thereby clouding the possibility of the Scotts' claim to freedom on account of their legal marriage.

In 1837, Emerson was once again reassigned and made his way to Fort Jessup in Louisiana, where he quickly met and married Irene Sanford. When the Scotts arrived in Louisiana, again they might have sued for their freedom, as Louisiana had for some time upheld the freedom of enslaved individuals who had lived in free jurisdictions. Yet, once again, the Scotts failed to make a claim for their freedom. Over the next nine years, the Scotts traveled with the Emersons back to Fort Snelling, to St. Louis, to Texas, and back to St. Louis, crisscrossing between slave states and free territories. In 1846, following Emerson's death, Dred Scott attempted to purchase his freedom from Emerson's widow, Irene. When she refused, Scott filed suit for his freedom and that of his wife and daughters.

The case of *Dred Scott v. Sanford* need not have been as historically significant and infamous at it became. At the outset, the suit Scott brought against John Sanford, Irene Emerson's brother, who had taken over her business affairs after she remarried and moved to Massachusetts, turned on the notion that Scott had become free via his many forays into free states and territories throughout his time enslaved to the Emersons. After many delays and legal technicalities, a trial court found for Scott and declared that he was free. This decision was fully in line with established Missouri precedents, which had repeatedly declared that enslaved individuals who resided in free territories or states were legally free. However, on its arrival before the Missouri Supreme Court, the case took a decidedly political turn when that court broke with thirty years of established precedent and overturned the lower court verdict. The Missouri justices held that under Missouri law, slave status *reattached* whenever an enslaved individual voluntarily reentered a slave state from a free state or territory.[83] Of course, one could argue that Scott's reentries into slave states were never voluntary since he was compelled to travel there.

This might have been the final verdict in Dred Scott's odyssey if not for the fact that in 1854, Scott acquired a new attorney who decided to begin a new case against Sanford in the federal courts. It is a basic tenet of US law that when a suit is between two parties who reside in different states, the federal courts hold jurisdiction to decide such a matter. Because Scott was a resident of Missouri and Sanford resided in New York, Scott's new lawyer decided to once again bring a case against Sanford, but this time before a federal court. Scott's new claim against Sanford was for battery and wrongful imprisonment and sought restitution in the amount of $9,000. Scott's lawyers hoped to win, not that full amount, but a token sum with which he could prove Scott's freedom.

At the outset of any legal dispute, a court must first determine whether it has jurisdiction to hear the particular controversy before it; this was true in the matter of *Dred Scott*, where the federal district judge had to first determine whether he had jurisdiction to hear the case. The question turned on whether the matter was a dispute between citizens of different states, which would grant the federal court diversity jurisdiction. Sanford's response to Scott's suit was a plea to dismiss the lawsuit for lack of jurisdiction. Sanford posited that the court should decline to hear the matter because, though he did reside in New York and Scott in Missouri, Scott was not a citizen of Missouri and thus did not have the right to sue in federal court. Because Scott's ancestors "were of pure African blood and were brought into this country and sold as negro slaves," Sanford argued that Scott was not a citizen of Missouri.[84] Sanford argued that no Black individual could be a citizen of Missouri and that, as a result, even if Scott was free, the court did not have jurisdiction to hear his case.[85]

The circuit judge rejected Sanford's plea and found that the court had proper jurisdiction. He surmised that free Blacks were entitled to minimal legal rights, including the right to sue in federal court.[86] The case then went before a jury with the instruction that Missouri law governed the dispute. Since the Missouri Supreme Court had already decided that Scott was not free and that court's decisions were the supreme law of the State of Missouri, the jury upheld the upper court's decision. Scott and his family remained enslaved.

When the federal court decided the matter, the case had already attracted much attention and had raised the interests of abolitionists and the proslavery camp alike. As a result, Scott's appeal to the Supreme Court of the United States, an undoubtedly prohibitively costly prospect otherwise, was bankrolled by several wealthy lawyers and abolitionists. Likewise, Sanford, too, received aid from the wealthy proslavery camp, which also had an interest in the Court's decision. After ten years of legal wrangling and delays, the case of *Dred Scott v. Sanford* finally reached the US Supreme Court in February 1856, and the stakes were higher than ever.

The primary issues briefed and argued before the Supreme Court were the questions whether Blacks could be US citizens, whether the US Congress had the power to prohibit slavery in the territories, and finally whether the Missouri Compromise was constitutional.[87] The exact holding of the Supreme Court is difficult to pinpoint, given that each of the nine justices wrote his own opinion.[88] The leading opinion, written by Chief Justice Taney, was but one of seven opinions written by the majority rejecting Scott's appeal.[89] Though a majority of the justices agreed with the overall outcome, they disagreed on the rationale. In the end, the Court did not need to decide the charged issues of citizenship, Congress's power to regulate the territories, and the constitutionality of the Missouri Compromise. The Court could have relied on its own precedent set in the case of *Strader v. Graham* a mere six years before.[90] That case held that "with the exception of runaway slaves, each state had complete authority to decide for themselves if a slave who had lived in the North had become free."[91] Relying on the *Strader* precedent would have dispensed with the *Scott* case in a fairly uncomplicated way. However, the justices had no intention of doing so.

By the time Scott's case made its way to the Court, the matter had become considerably politically charged. The justices could not avoid deciding on the politically contentious issues in large part because the proslavery faction among the justices, and especially the chief justice himself, wanted a decision that would deal with those prickly issues head-on. The southern justices wanted the issues in dispute to be resolved for the southern states. By making a clear pronouncement, the Court, and especially Taney, hoped to quiet the protests of abolitionists and to decide on the legality of slavery once and for all.[92]

From the outset, the Court had a tricky balancing act to maintain in deciding the case. Just as the federal court below it did, the Supreme Court first had to find that it held proper jurisdiction over the dispute. This posed a problem because, if the court found that Blacks were citizens of the United States, then Scott had a right to sue Sanford in federal court. However, if the justices found that Blacks were not citizens of the United States, then Scott had no right to sue, and the case was not properly before the Court. The southern majority wanted very much to find that Blacks were not citizens, could never be citizens, and thus could never sue in federal court. However, such a holding would have immediately ended the case, and the justices would not have been able to rule on the constitutionality of the Missouri Compromise, which was the political issue the southern justices most wanted to put to rest.[93]

Furthermore, because the circuit judge had ruled that Scott had a right to sue in federal court, Scott had not appealed that part of the decision. Because of this, some of the justices felt that the question of Scott's citizenship was not properly before the Court. That question had been answered, had not been appealed, and so was not in dispute. Likewise, because Sanford had won in the lower court, he also had not appealed the circuit judge's findings dismissing his plea in abatement. As a result, the Supreme Court did not need to answer the question of Scott's citizenship or his right to sue. Chief Justice Taney disagreed with all of this and instead argued that the question was properly before the Court because every court has the right to decide anew, and for itself, whether it has the jurisdiction to hear a dispute.[94]

Accordingly, Taney surmised that he and his fellow justices had every right to decide Scott's citizenship status. Taney argued that free Blacks may be citizens of individual states, but they could never be citizens of the United States and have standing to sue in federal court.[95] Here Taney's reasoning set up a framework for dual citizenship: one could be a citizen of a state of the union but not a citizen of the United States itself. Despite the existence of "a long popular and judicial tradition of considering the two [state and national citizenship] as inseparable dimensions of the same status," Taney found that nevertheless the two were separable.[96]

Taney's reasoning for this duality of citizenship was based entirely on race. He ignored the fact that free Blacks had played a role in the political processes of many states; since the ratification of the US Constitution, and indeed at the time of the *Dred Scott* decision, free Blacks exercised political rights in several states. Taney instead argued that at the founding of the nation, Blacks were either enslaved or, if free, were without any legal or political rights.[97] For Taney, the question boiled down simply "can a negro, whose ancestors were imported into this country, and sold as slaves, become a member of the political community formed and brought into existence by the Constitution of the United Sates, and as such become entitled to all the rights, and privileges, and immunities, guaranteed by that instrument to the citizen?"[98] Taney reasoned that the terms "people of the United States" and "citizens" were synonymous and thus the question was whether people of African ancestry formed part of "the people." He found that they did not because they were not intended to be included within the word "citizen," and they could not claim any of the rights or privileges granted by the Constitution.[99]

Additionally, Taney pointed to the fact that at the time of the creation of the Constitution, Blacks were considered as a "class of inferior and subordinate beings, who had been subjugated to the dominant race, and, whether emancipated or not, yet remained subject to their authority."[100] He went on to claim that it was not the province of the Court to decide on the justice or injustice of such a policy or of the laws—though, of course, the very purpose of Taney's decision was to do precisely that: to answer definitively the question of slavery and Black citizenship. As a result, Taney's opinion demonstrates the Supreme Court's insidious political activism in the most obvious and fraught way.

Having thus decided that Dred Scott was not a citizen of the United States and that he could not sue in federal court, the Court's decision should have ended. Given that Taney had just clearly stated that Scott had no right to properly be before the Court, the justices then did not have jurisdiction to decide on the remaining question. However, Taney was determined to find the Missouri Compromise unconstitutional and to give a victory to the southern states, which believed that the Compromise's prohibition on slavery in the territories was congressional overreach. Yet, because Scott had no right to be before the Court, Republicans and scholars at the time argued that Taney's pronouncements on the Missouri Compromise amounted to nothing more than dicta—musings of the Court that held no authority or binding effect.[101]

To find the Missouri Compromise unconstitutional, Taney relied on two very flawed legal arguments. The first claimed that the Territories Clause of the Constitution, from which Congress had traditionally claimed the right to acquire and administer territory, gave Congress rights only over territory held by the United States at the time of the ratification of the Constitution in 1787.[102] Taney cited no law or judicial opinions, nor did he provide any other evidence for his finding. In fact, his decision ignored the fact that at the time of the writing of the Constitution, the founders had their sights set on the acquisition of New Orleans from Spain.[103]

Taney further argued that the United States' power to expand its landholdings was granted, not by the Territories Clause, but by the Constitution's provision that "New States may be admitted by the Congress to the Union."[104] Thus, Taney declared,

> the power to expand the territory of the United States by the admission of new States is plainly given. . . . *It has been held to authorize the acquisition of territory, not fit for admission at the time, but to be admitted as soon as its population and situation would entitle it to admission. It is acquired to become a State, and not to be held as a colony and governed by Congress with absolute authority*, and as that propriety of admitting new states is committed to the sound discretion of Congress, the power to acquire territory for that purpose, to be held by the United States until it is in a suitable condition to become a state on equal footing with the other States, must rest upon the same discretion. (emphasis added)[105]

With this declaration, Taney enumerated the United States' doctrine of territorial expansion, which had been the custom in the United States to that date. The concept held that territory acquired by the United States had to be placed en route to becoming a state. In other words, the United States could not hold territories as colonies indefinitely. This portion of the decision, though often considered dictum, nonetheless was an important and long-held practice in US territorial expansion. However, as the reader knows, the acquisition of Puerto Rico would stretch and ultimately break this doctrine of law. Puerto Rico and the other insular territories would be transformed into "unincorporated territories," precisely so that Congress could hold on to them as colonies and govern them with absolute power.

Perhaps because he understood the weakness of his argument with respect to the Territories Clause, Taney next pointed to the Bill of Rights and the Fifth Amendment to buttress his holding that the Missouri Compromise was unconstitutional. He first argued that Congress could not violate the Bill of Rights in the territories. He explicitly stated that "no one, we presume, will contend that Congress can make any law in a Territory . . . abridging the freedom of speech or of the press, or the right of the people of the Territory to peaceably assemble."[106] Having established this proposition, which at the time seemed obvious to the justices and to legal scholars alike, he then turned to the Fifth Amendment's prohibition on unjust takings without compensation and due process.

The Fifth Amendment to the US Constitution holds that under federal law, no person "shall be deprived of life, liberty, or *property*, without due process of law; nor shall private property be taken for public use without just compensation" (emphasis added). Taney argued that prohibiting slavery in the territories was tantamount to a government taking of private property without due process or just compensation. He claimed that "an act of Congress which deprives a citizen of the United States of his liberty or property, merely because he came himself or brought his property into a particular territory of the United States, and who had committed no offence against the laws, could hardly be dignified with the name of due process of law."[107] For many at the time, Taney's arguments with respect to the Fifth Amendment went too far. It had been long established that individual states could ban pernicious and dangerous practices within their jurisdiction, such as the sale of alcohol and gambling, so why did Congress not have the same power over federal jurisdictions? However, Taney held the enslaved were a special sort of property that merited special protections of law because the right to hold slaves was explicitly granted in the US Constitution.[108]

Taney's goals in *Dred Scott* were clearly political. Had he wanted to, he could have easily dispensed with Scott's claims to freedom by relying on *Strader v. Graham*. While Taney hoped to quell political debate and dissent over the issue of slavery and the constitutionality of the Missouri Compromise, his decision had the opposite effect. Justices John McLean and Benjamin Robbins Curtis wrote lengthy and extensive dissenting opinions in which they contested Taney's historical arguments, showing that free Blacks had voted in a number of elections since the founding.[109] Curtis in particular argued that Blacks were constituent members of the nation and could not now be denied the right to claim citizenship.[110] These dissents became fodder for Republicans and abolitionists who argued that Taney's opinion was "wicked," "atrocious," "abominable," and "a collation of false statements and shallow sophistries."[111] As a result, rather than quelling dissent and political argument, Taney's opinion instead fueled further disagreement and ultimately helped precipitate the events surrounding the Civil War.

The *Dred Scott* decision, as controversial as it was, was not actually a surprise when it was made public. The various opinions had been leaked several months before the decision was officially announced.[112] And while the ruling did not free the Scott family, it did bring them into the national spotlight. The case, and the man himself, continued to garner national interest, and journalists continued to seek Scott out long after the decision was announced. The media attention in turn revealed that Irene Emerson's second husband, Calvin Chafee, who was a Republican representative from Massachusetts and purportedly an abolitionist, might have become Scott's owner on marrying Irene.[113] After the Court's decision was made public, Scott's attorney reached out to Chafee, notifying him that John Sanford had never been more than the executor of Emerson's will and Irene's affairs. As a result, the Scott family had never been under his control or ownership; that power had remained with Irene Emerson.[114] Thus, ownership of the Scott family had passed to Chafee when he married Irene. Chafee, apparently appalled and perhaps with an eye toward his reelection campaign, promptly conveyed the Scott family to Taylor Blow, the son of Dred Scott's first owner, Peter Blow. Blow, an abolitionist who had maintained a friendship with Scott and who had helped fund the initial case against Sanford, in turn manumitted Scott, his wife, and his daughters on May 26, 1857. Sadly, Scott, who had spent a decade fighting for his own and his family's freedom, was able to enjoy that freedom for only a little more than a year. Dred Scott died on September 17, 1858.

Conclusion

The important legal precedents discussed in this chapter form part of the genealogy of the "American" state of exception. By considering these precedents through this lens, we can better understand the reasoning behind these inequitable legal decisions and what sort of work they were really undertaking. To be sure, the government's intent was always to exclude and remove certain racial undesirables from the rights, privileges, and immunities enjoyed by the greater white population again and again. The US Supreme Court merely ratified this intent with these decisions.

This state of exception left racial undesirables outside of the established legal order and exposed to the vagaries of the state. For Native Americans, exclusion meant expulsion from their lands and an undermining of their traditional ways of life. It also meant violent warfare and brutal repression of any resistance to US subjugation. In the case of Black Americans, exclusion from citizenship and the protections of the Constitution meant that their bodies continued to be open to the unmitigated violence of enslavement without legal recourse to stop such violence. With the overturning of the citizenship provisions of *Dred Scott* and the creation of the Thirteenth and Fourteenth Amendments to the US Constitution, it seemed that Congress was working to incorporate African Americans into the US body politic. However, as we know, the brief window of full citizenship and true incorporation into the US political body that post–Civil War Reconstruction opened up was quickly closed. The era of Jim Crow segregation that followed, which lasted for more than seventy years, represented another carving out of a space of exclusion for Blacks Americans in which, despite their apparent inclusion in US citizenship, their rights nevertheless continued to be curtailed and their bodies continued to be open to violence with impunity.

In the case of Puerto Rico, the violence of the state of exception was not as overt or oppressive; nonetheless, the archipelago's exclusion from citizenship and the protections of the Constitution meant that Puerto Rico was exposed to the whims of Congress. This exposure to Congress's plenary power quickly took on the shape of a plantation economy fueled, not by slavery, but by peonage. The benefits of such an economic model flowed mostly into the hands of absentee US-based corporations and a small Puerto Rican elite. The vast majority of Puerto Ricans found themselves impoverished and trapped by these policies. Furthermore, Puerto Ricans' attempts to resist or reshape these policies were met with indifference and eventually with violence. The desires of the US government and of US investors overruled the political needs and desires of Puerto Rico's inhabitants. Puerto Rico was a new frontier that was open for business, and Puerto Ricans were a captive workforce available for exploitation.

Beyond the economic effects of the *Downes* decision, the archipelago became an experimental testing ground for US imperial policies, a situation that continues today. These experiments touched every facet of life in Puerto Rico, from English language policies, to the creation of so-called tropical medicine, to experiments in public health, agriculture, and policing. Resistance to these experimental policies was met with indifference, paternalism, and increasingly with violence.

CHAPTER THREE

Puerto Rico Remade

Days after the one-year anniversary of the arrival of the US military in the archipelago, on August 8, 1899, Puerto Rico withstood a crippling storm. Hurricane San Ciriaco swept through the Caribbean, flooding coastal areas and devastating the archipelago's central mountain region and, with it, Puerto Rico's coffee plantations. Dr. Bailey K. Ashford, in charge of the field hospital in Ponce, described the stream of "wax-like specters"—men, women and children—who spilled from the mountains the storm had swept bare and brown.[1] Ashford was stunned by the conditions of the poor, bedraggled creatures who streamed into his hospital and with whose care he was charged. So stunned, in fact, that he wrote extensively about his experience in his autobiography, *A Soldier in Science*. There, Ashford recounts how the sight of so many suffering and pathetic peasants led him to hypothesize that there must be a parasitic or pathogenic reason, beyond the purported rampant malnutrition, that so many of the territory's inhabitants were anemic and sick. Here, in this recounting of the aftermath of San Ciriaco, we are privy to the birth of tropical medicine in Puerto Rico and concomitantly the beginning of medical experimentation. Ashford's hypothesis and experiments eventually led him to discover the widespread problem of hookworm infection in Puerto Rico. He would go on to establish Puerto Rico's Institute for Tropical Medicine, which eventually, through a partnership with Columbia University, became the School for Tropical Medicine.[2] These experiments and treatments, which were perfected in Puerto Rico with the help of the Rockefeller Foundation, would then be exported all over the world, from Brazil to India, other parts of the Caribbean, and the mainland United States.[3]

These early experiments in tropical medicine are characteristic of Puerto Rico's experiences in its early decades of US rule. Puerto Rico quickly became a testing ground for experiments in medicine, hygiene, education, agriculture, economic development, and beyond. Indeed, in 1901 the US government established what was then known as the Federal Experimental Station in Mayagüez, Puerto Rico. Still in existence more than one hundred years later, the station is now called the Tropical Agriculture Research Station and continues to perform "research on problems of tropical agriculture."[4] This creation of Puerto Rico as an experimental station at large was possible because of the vast power that the Supreme Court granted to Congress over Puerto Rico and the limited power the court granted Puerto Ricans to push back in meaningful ways. The first few decades of the twentieth century saw US government agents' attempts to reorganize and reformulate life in Puerto Rico in service of US imperial designs; *Downes v. Bidwell* was the gateway to those policies.

Relying on a variety of sources, including newspapers and periodicals as well as correspondence and government labor records, this chapter focuses on some of the twentieth-century experiments and policy changes that remade Puerto Rico and the underlying racialized assumptions that fueled this remaking. While I focus on health, labor, and policing as three crucial parts of the US colonial project in Puerto Rico, these changes touched nearly every facet of Puerto Rican life. The perceived problems of overpopulation and of a sick and diseased populace loomed large for US government actors in Puerto Rico. Their concerns for the sickly and pathetic condition of the territory's inhabitants were expressed early on by military personnel and continued to be a source of consternation for US agents throughout the twentieth century.[5] These problems were addressed through a slew of policies that legalized divorce and birth control, encouraged migration to address overpopulation, and promoted medical experimentation in the case of health and sanitation issues.[6]

The impulse to experiment with the lives of Puerto Ricans, to remake them into proper colonial subjects who fit US ideas of respectability and who could be put to productive work in service of US capital, is the colonial impulse par excellence. This chapter offers an examination of some of the immediate shifts ushered in by the US acquisition of Puerto Rico and the Supreme Court's decision in *Downes v. Bidwell*. As the *Downes* court noted, the inhabitants of Puerto Rico were unprepared for the difficult work of governance. Puerto Ricans were "mongrels," in the parlance of the day; they were unsophisticated and suffered from indolence and laziness, conditions worsened by the tropical heat. Thus, the United States' overarching goal in the first decades of the twentieth century was to remake Puerto Rico and Puerto Ricans in service of US empire and of colonial capitalist structures. To accomplish this goal, Puerto Ricans had to be "Americanized" and educated in how to be proper US colonial subjects.

From the very start of the United States' colonial project in Puerto Rico, the government sought to reshape the archipelago's population across all sectors of life. This reshaping took many forms. Educational policies meant to indoctrinate the population in US politics, governance, history, and culture actively sought to undermine Puerto Rican identity, history, culture, and language in the service of "Americanization." Nutritional policies sought to increase the amount of dairy and meat Puerto Ricans ate. These policies served the dual purposes of providing "better" nutrition to malnourished peasants, while also creating a consumer market for US-produced staple foods. Family planning, marriage, and divorce laws sought to legitimate the informal unions common in Puerto Rico at that time and to address the rampant "problem" of illegitimate children. Public health and sanitation were also areas of supreme importance to the United States. Controlling diseases such as hookworm and malaria and ensuring the health of the populace were crucial to creating a robust labor force. While it is undeniable that Puerto Ricans garnered material benefits from some of these US-led experiments—the eradication of hookworm, for example, cannot be seen as anything but a societal good—nevertheless, the colonial logic that fueled these experiments and changes was concerned primarily with Puerto Ricans as a potential workforce and as productive subjects.

Relatedly, the colonial project also involved radical changes in economic and labor conditions that led to serious shifts in the lives of workers, from where they lived and worked to the type of labor they performed. The US government encouraged workers to resettle within the archipelago to bolster sugar production, as well as to resettle outside of Puerto Rico to ease the perceived problem of overpopulation. These shifts saw thousands of workers exit Puerto Rico in search of better economic opportunities and in service of US imperial projects. However, these individuals often found themselves at the mercy of US agents who took advantage of their labor and their bodies, exposing them to environmental extremes and harsh work conditions. In their search for economic stability, many workers paid the ultimate price of their lives.

Finally, an essential piece to the project of remaking Puerto Rico and reorienting Puerto Rican life involved the creation of a larger, better trained, and more equipped police force. Revamping the Puerto Rico Insular Police was necessary because the force would become the primary instrument by which the US government would ensure the smooth operation of the colonial capitalist project in Puerto Rico. To that end, the US government expanded the previously existing police force established under Spanish rule and provided it with military training. The Puerto Rico Insular Police quickly became the enforcement arm of US colonial capitalism. While it was essential to strengthen and remake the Puerto Rican physical body, it was also crucial to create an enforcement body that could ensure that Puerto Ricans set themselves to labor in service of US colonial projects.

Healing the Diseased Body: Bailey K. Ashford and the Birth of Tropical Medicine

From the early days of the arrival of the US military in Puerto Rico, the question of disease loomed large in the minds of US agents. As in Cuba and Panama, the US Army initially encountered problems with mosquito-borne diseases such as malaria and yellow fever.[7] Early accounts of the territory's inhabitants described Puerto Ricans as emaciated, sickly, and malnourished.[8] The population was further described as indolent and lazy, traits that were attributed to the tropical condition and heat of the archipelago.[9] Though some argued that this indolence would never allow Puerto Ricans to become proper enterprising US subjects, others saw these traits as in need of a remedy. Puerto Ricans only needed help from their US betters to leave behind a life of tropical lethargy and idleness.

The opportunity to address the problem of disease arrived early on, when Puerto Rico was struck by the worst hurricane in its history. The 1899 San Ciriaco storm left nearly 4,000 inhabitants dead and 250,000 homeless.[10] Shortly after the hurricane struck, survivors began pouring into cities from the mountain regions. Temporary encampments and infirmaries were set up in the twelve major districts. Ponce, along the southern Caribbean coast, was particularly badly hit. There, as the young doctor in charge of the Army field hospital, Ashford unwittingly stumbled upon the cause of Puerto Ricans' perceived indolence and lethargy. As the displaced residents began arriving at the makeshift hospital, Ashford noticed their pale and waxy complexions and flabby skin.[11] Recognizing the signs of anemia in the sickly and thin Puerto Ricans, he ordered that they be fed meat to supplement their iron intake. The soldiers in charge of feeding and caring for the patients began to report that rather than improving their health, the meat was making them sick and causing them diarrhea. The patients requested they be fed rice and beans and salted codfish, their staple diet, which they knew would not make them sick. Ashford acquiesced and ordered that the patients be granted their usual diets in the hope that their conditions would improve.[12] However, much to his dismay, the patients continued to look frail and sick, and many died under his care. "As soon as the sacred rice, beans and codfish arrived, everybody in camp began to purr," Ashford wrote in 1934, "but not the faintest tinge of red blood came into their faces. Moreover, they kept dying. It must be said that they died happily, and with their stomachs full. . . . I catechized my wife, but she only replied: 'That is the anemia of the country. They all die of it eventually. They say it is due to lack of food.' 'But I fed them by order! And the ungrateful things keep on dying!'"[13]

Ashford's frustration with the continued sickliness of his patients led him to sample and study their blood and eventually their feces. Through these studies, he discovered that the great lethargy and sickness afflicting so many of the territory's residents were in fact due, not to malnourishment, but instead to a parasite, hookworm, which entered the body through the feet. As many rural peasants lacked proper or, often, any footwear, the parasitic infection was widespread. Ashford began to experiment with procedures and remedies to rid his patients of the parasite, eventually stumbling upon a combination of purges and treatments that seemed to work. In April 1900, he published his findings in the *New York Medical Journal*, but it would be many more years before his findings were taken seriously.[14] Many doctors and patients held firm to the idea that the sickness of so many of Puerto Rico's residents was caused by malnourishment rather than widespread parasitic infestation.[15]

Ashford's early experiments led to several campaigns to eradicate hookworm and anemia in Puerto Rico. Eventually, Ashford's research and his efforts in the archipelago led the New York–based Rockefeller Foundation to offer its financial support to his work. A 1920 report in the Columbia, South Carolina, newspaper, *The State*, details the efforts of the Rockefeller Foundation and the great need present in Puerto Rico. Despite the fact that Ashford had been working to address the problem of hookworm and anemia since 1900, the article cited Dr. Victor Helser of the Rockefeller Foundation as stating that there was more hookworm in Puerto Rico in 1920 than any other place in the world.[16] "Hookworm is probably the most serious *economic* issue which Puerto Rico faces today. I have asked cane planters why they did not pay more wages and they said because the laborers *could not earn* it and probably, they are right" (emphasis added).[17] Anemia, the article goes on to explain, "which during the Spanish rule was believed to be due mostly to malnutrition, now is attributed to a great extent to infection. It is believed that the disease was brought in with the early slaves and thus spread uncontrolled throughout the length and breadth of the island."[18] In an attempt to address the problems of anemia and hookworm in Puerto Rico, the government and the Foundation would invest $357,000 to "bring relief to the unfortunate sufferers. A study undertaken by the Foundation has shown that nearly 90 percent of the population in rural areas harbor hookworm infection. Even light infection is said to cause mental retardation. Defective mentality thus produced renders the children incapable of assimilating instruction."[19]

The ability to assimilate instruction was, of course, paramount to the US government's colonial project in Puerto Rico. Tutelage in the American way of life was what the Supreme Court stated was most needed in Puerto Rico. "Americanization" and teaching Puerto Ricans how to be proper US subjects were essential steps in creating the tropical outpost the United States sought. Thus, it was essential to clear the populace of the scourge of hookworm, with its potential for diminished mental acuity, lethargy, and indolence. American ideals valued enterprising, hard-working people who lifted themselves up by their bootstraps. Puerto Rican laziness and idleness were counter to that great US American narrative. Thus, it was necessary to discover the cause of and cure the territory's inhabitants of their indolence. This of course, would in turn create better workers who would be able to cut greater amounts of cane and buoy Puerto Rico's economy. The fact that the greatest benefactors of such economic growth were US corporations and US investors was of course essential to the drive to eradicate disease.

While no doubt medical experiments in public health such as Ashford's were driven by a paternalistic desire to cure the poor Puerto Ricans of their disease and infirmity, an equally important motivation was to create a literal healthy body of workers. These peasants were necessary lives, and as such the state had an interest in ensuring they lived and were healthy enough to cut cane. Thus, the policies that funneled money into hookworm eradication and the creation of Ashford's Institute for Tropical Medicine were tied to the state's need to shape who lived and how. At the time, too many of the necessary workers were dying, with deep repercussions for the government's great moneymaker: the sugar industry.

Likewise, *The State* article also offers us a glimpse into the racialized ideas about the source of disease in Puerto Rico that were common in the day. The article points to no source for its belief that hookworm infestation arose with the importation of enslaved Africans to the territory, and yet that claim is asserted as fact. That the Spanish were incapable of managing their colonies and thus caring for their subjects was a "fact." That disease and infirmity were legacies brought by the enslaved to Puerto Rico was apparently also a "fact." In these "facts," we see the many beliefs undergirding the campaigns to eradicate disease in the territory. As important as it was to have healthy, productive workers, it was equally important to cleanse the United States' new charges, to sanitize them. Puerto Rican disease had its origins in enslaved

Africans, and that sickness had been perpetuated by Spanish cruelty and indifference; it was now up to the United States, Puerto Rico's white savior, to rid the inhabitants of their disease, to "Americanize" them and make them healthy and productive US subjects. The newspaper article's final sentence clearly illustrates the preoccupation with defects that US agents in the territory had. Puerto Rico had to be rid of disease lest that disease produce a class of mentally defective subjects who could not assimilate the lessons of "Americanization."

Defending the Colonial State: The "Porto Rico Experiment"

Concomitant with Ashford's experiments in tropical medicine were US government policies in the realm of social hygiene. The early decades of the twentieth century saw the US government, with the support of elite and middle-class Puerto Ricans, attempt to control and regulate the lives of poor and laboring women who were seen as disreputable and as bad mothers and who were often assumed to be sex workers. Policies meant to regulate and stem sex work had been in place since Spanish rule, but US agents' preoccupation with the sanitation of the poorer classes was fueled by Progressive Era policies and the activism of organizations such as the Women's Christian Temperance Union.[20] The onset of World War I led to the implementation of some of the most draconian and inequitable public health and hygiene policies, which relegated many poor and Black women to prisons and hospitals for experimentation in sexually transmitted infections.[21] These women, often powerless to refute accusations of their ill repute and diseased bodies, found themselves imprisoned in order to protect the far more valuable bodies of male US soldiers in the archipelago. While the United States sought to protect the bodies of the men who were tasked with defending the colonial state, poor and laboring women, deemed to be of lesser value, were open to the violence and control of incarceration and medical experimentation.

Such policies were enacted in the mainland United States with the creation of the so-called American Plan, and they were fervently exported and furthered in the archipelago.[22] The American Plan enumerated specific policies for protecting soldiers from sex workers and venereal disease. Key among these policies was the Department of War order banning sex workers from being within a five-mile radius of any military installation.[23]

According to military doctor Herman Goodman, the American Plan in Puerto Rico, or the "Porto Rican Experiment" as he aptly called it, was effective in corralling and containing the amoral state that prevailed in the archipelago.[24] Goodman, like the author of *The State* article, also attributed the rampancy of syphilis in Puerto Rico to the archipelago's racial origins. Puerto Rico, he wrote, consisted of an archipelago whose people "have been little changed by immigration, and the population has remained the off-spring of the Spanish settler, his black slave, and a mixture of two races in all degrees."[25] Goodman's description reveals the prevalent belief at the time that the descendants of enslaved Africans brought diseases to the Americas and that those diseases were made worse by Spanish neglect.

Goodman's article published in 1919 in *Social Hygiene* recounts several experiments performed on imprisoned sex workers and a sample of soldiers at Camp Las Casas in San Juan at the start of World War I operations. Goodman enumerated the various statistics for infection around the archipelago, including the fact that at the time 56 percent of men enlisted in the Puerto Rico Regiment were infected with syphilis.[26] He reiterated just how serious a risk to public health syphilis was and stated that "the problem faced in Porto Rico was an acute and pressing one if the twelve thousand men who made up the Porto Rico Army were to be protected from venereal disease."[27] Again, these soldiers, defenders of US empire, needed protection from the scourge of syphilis carried by the diseased women of Puerto Rico. Sex workers were seen as a threat to national security, and as such their bodies had to be surveilled, contained, and cleansed in order to protect the colonial state.

As a result, measures were implemented to limit soldiers' ability to travel within the archipelago. Certain barrios and towns known for their thriving red-light districts were completely off-limits to enlisted men. These travel restrictions eventually led to tensions among soldiers and their families who resided in banned barrios. When the affected families of the Puerta de Tierra barrio petitioned the military asking that their enlisted family members be granted permission to visit, the commanding general at Camp Las Casas responded, "The health of our soldiers is of such vital importance to our country that every reasonable and possible means must be employed to protect it."[28] The families' requests were denied, and Puerta de Tierra remained on the list of banned locations.

Goodman praised the intervention of the attorney general, Howard L. Kern, for ordering a change in the sex work policies that had previously existed. Before the onset of World War I and the perceived threat of venereal disease to national security, the archipelago had followed the old norms set out by the Spanish government wherein sex workers had been required to register with police and were inspected weekly at San Juan's Special Hospital for Women.[29] One week after the order of the commanding general of

Camp Las Casas banned travel for soldiers to certain parts of the archipelago, Kern issued new policies requiring that perceived sex workers be arrested and incarcerated for six months to a year.[30] Additionally, Kern extended the sex-work-free buffer zone around Camp Las Casas to ten miles and admonished judges and prosecutors that their past tactics had not been effective in containing the threat of venereal disease caused by sex workers.[31] He extolled the judicial branch to take a harder line on sex work and threatened that those who did not comply with these new, stricter policies would be dismissed and their places taken by others who were more efficient and more patriotic.[32]

Though the tactics of the US military and Attorney General Kern were well received among the conservative and elite sectors of Puerto Rico, who harbored similar racialized opinions of the poor and laboring classes of the archipelago, the majority of residents were affronted by these new policies. The newspapers *El Tiempo* and *La Correspondencia* became platforms where Puerto Ricans expressed their anger and resentment over the mistreatment of poor women who were perceived to be sex workers. Harsh criticism of Kern in particular appeared in the editorial sections of Puerto Rican papers, with writers claiming that Kern's actions in coercing the judiciary branch to adopt policies not mandated by legislation were illegal.[33] Journalist Luis Dalta accused Kern of coopting the judiciary's independence and of transforming the judges and prosecutors of the archipelago into puppets of the executive branch.[34] Prominent attorneys also joined their voices to the protest of US policies, insisting that the "repression against allegedly promiscuous women was a threat to the individual liberties of all Puerto Ricans."[35]

Furthermore, as historian Eileen Findlay has discussed, the opposition to these policies grew with the addition of socialists and labor union members.[36] The socialist press in Ponce took up the cause of the accused and imprisoned women and spent much ink protesting and decrying US anti-sex-work policies. Additionally, labor unions and working men and women came to the defense of the perceived sex workers, arguing that many were merely poor, working-class women who did not meet the standards of respectability set by the state and elite classes.[37] As Findlay explains, male allies of laboring women began to see the sex work crackdown as a "betrayal of the democratic promise that had cemented US colonial legitimacy for two decades among laboring Puerto Ricans of all races. The women came to represent hard-won civil liberties, cornerstones of that precious democracy."[38] As a result, workingmen saw the attacks against their fellow workingwomen as an assault on all laborers and ultimately against Puerto Rico as a whole.[39]

In the end, the anti-sex-work campaign in Puerto Rico was short-lived. The war came to an end about six months after the establishment of operations at Camp Las Casas, and so did the threat to national security posed by venereal disease and sex work. With the end of the war, the funding for the various prisons housing the women dried up, and the police's zealous arrests diminished. Those women who were already imprisoned at the end of the war remained there until their sentences were completed, but the flow of arrests slowed and eventually stopped. Over time, the police returned to their old ways of requiring registration and imposing fines for sex work.

The work of both Findlay and Laura Briggs offers us unique perspectives on the complexity of the US government's anti-sex-work campaign. Both highlight that women's bodies became blank canvases onto which the concerns of Puerto Ricans were projected. As Findlay argues, questions of democracy and citizenship became part and parcel of the treatment of women perceived to be sex workers. Accused and imprisoned women became stand-ins for the failures of US colonialism. Laura Briggs takes this a bit further, convincingly arguing that we can understand the moment of dissatisfaction and dissent concerning the "Porto Rican Experiment" as a stand-in for Puerto Ricans' growing resentment of, and dissent against, US policies in general and of the unsolicited grant of US citizenship in particular.[40] She argues that the sex worker's diseased body became a metonym for the Puerto Rican nation.[41] The trespass and injury that US agents perpetrated on poor Puerto Rican women who were accused, often wrongfully, of engaging in sex work became a stand-in for the injury and injustice perpetrated in the archipelago by the US government. As a result, Briggs and Findlay both agree, the treatment of sex workers during this time galvanized protest and created a point around which unhappy Puerto Ricans across sectors and classes could rally. This moment brought into stark view the limits of Puerto Ricans' newly acquired US citizenship and the murkiness of the limited rights granted to them by *Downes*.

Overpopulation and the Exportation of Puerto Rican Labor

Along with concerns for the health and social hygiene of the Puerto Rican populace was a preoccupation with Puerto Ricans' fecundity and the large families that were common in the territory at the time. Overpopulation in Puerto Rico was a central concern of the US administration from the early days of the military government and continued throughout the twentieth century. Government officials viewed large Puerto Rican families as examples of the ignorance and lax morals of the populace.[42] As the United States' rule over the archipelago pressed on and economic possibilities diminished for a greater portion of its residents, more and more discussion was devoted to the issue of overpopulation.

Notably, the archipelago's economic condition rarely featured in discussions of how to resolve the issues of hunger and malnutrition among Puerto Rico's poor and laboring classes. Instead, US agents joined the Puerto Rican elite to debate various ways to resolve the problem of overpopulation. Many among this latter group subscribed to Malthusian and eugenicist notions of the poor and working classes in Puerto Rico and sought to limit their reproduction while also seeking to curb the "racial degeneracy" of those groups.[43] The two schemes that came to dominate the debates were migration out of the territory, to other parts of the US empire, and birth control. During the mid-twentieth century, Puerto Rico, like poor and predominantly Black communities in other parts of the United States, would famously become a site for experimentation in contraceptive technologies and sterilization. However, in the first few decades of the twentieth century, migration seemed to be the more likely solution to the problem.

Labor migration as a form of population control began almost immediately after the United States' arrival. Puerto Rican workers were sought out to cultivate a slew of agricultural products from sugar, to fruit, to cotton and tobacco. Workers were recruited to the various insular territories of the US empire as well as to the US mainland itself.[44] These migrants toiled in various industries in Cuba, the Dominican Republic, the US Virgin Islands, the Philippines, and Hawai'i; they also worked alongside other Caribbean islanders on the construction of the Panama Canal.[45] In this way, Puerto Rican laborers resolved various labor shortages throughout the US empire and, in their removal from Puerto Rico, helped to alleviate perceived overpopulation.

As discussed earlier, World War I brought many of the tensions and problems of Puerto Rico's relationship with the United States to the fore. Policies related to labor, health, and sanitation took center stage in the years around the conflict. These discussions were couched in the exigencies of war and the need to further the US war effort; however, they were ultimately exertions of the United States' desire to contain the proliferation of Puerto Rican life and to wrangle the archipelago's inhabitants in ways that benefited the US government's imperial designs.

With the United States' entry into the war, the government experienced an acute need for laborers to aid in efforts at home. As soldiers were shipped abroad to fight, the War Department experienced labor shortages in the mainland United States. To address these shortages, the Department and the United States Employment Service worked together to recruit thousands of men from Puerto Rico. The importation of Puerto Ricans facilitated the business of war by providing male bodies to construct roads and to ready barracks and military outposts. For the US government, this labor operation held a twofold advantage: not only did it provide much needed labor in the mainland United States, but it also addressed the ongoing problems of unemployment and overpopulation in Puerto Rico. In May 1918, the Department of Labor published a post in the *United States Employment Service Bulletin* addressing the project: "As one of its means of augmenting the common-labor supply, the Department of Labor, through the United States Employment Service, will shortly begin bringing Porto Rican laborers to the continental United States. Within a month the first arrivals will be engaged in construction work on Government contracts, and the Employment Service already has arranged for the employment of more than 10,000 islanders on war work at Norfolk, Newport News, and Baltimore and vicinity. Approximately 75,000 Porto Rican laborers already are available for work in the mainland."[46]

After some discussion with Puerto Rican political leaders and the governor, the Departments of Labor and War settled on sending the men to construction projects located in the southern states because the climate would be most "suitable to their health."[47] An article in the *Official U.S. Bulletin* from early October 1918 described the arrival of the first group of men in New Orleans, Louisiana, in sunny tones stating that everything had been readied for their arrival and that the men would be paid wages equivalent to the going rate in the places they worked. The bulletin further described the enthusiasm of Puerto Rican laborers to join the war effort, stating that when the first call for workers was issued, the "entire police force of San Juan had to be requisitioned to keep traffic lines open, so great was the crowd of applicants."[48]

Though the initial impulse for the project may have seemed a mutually beneficial one, problems became apparent almost immediately upon the departure of the first group of men from the archipelago. Beginning in September 1918, about 3,000 Puerto Ricans left the archipelago for work projects in Fayetteville, North Carolina; Lexington, Kentucky; and New Orleans, Louisiana. On September 25, 1918, mere days after the second group of laborers departed, Arthur Yager, the US-appointed governor of Puerto Rico, wrote to Brigadier General Charles C. Wolcott Jr., chief of the Bureau of Insular Affairs, the agency then charged with matters relating to Puerto Rico. In his letter, Yager expressed concern for the families of the laborers who had left Puerto Rico for the US mainland and for the families of those who were scheduled to leave. Yager's overarching concern was that the Bureau and the Department of Labor had not made provisions for the families and dependents of the men who had been sent to the United States.

According to Yager, "practically all of the men who have been taken and who will be taken have dependents who are looking to them for support, and this class of people are so improvident that their dependents here will be almost in a starving condition within a week or ten days after the boats leave."[49] While Yager's letter makes obvious the low opinion he has of the undisciplined nature of Puerto Rico's poor and laboring class, his letter also highlights his frustration with the Bureau and the Department for not including in their plans provisions for those dependents who would be left behind and would surely be in dire straits without their men to provide for them. Furthermore, he explains that such a situation was completely foreseeable given the experiences of Puerto Rican soldiers and their dependent families in the past. Yager exhorts Walcott to communicate with those in charge of organizing the project to ensure that a workable solution would be reached quickly. He writes, "If the matter should be allowed to drift along for any length of time without some action, the conditions may rapidly reach a point where it would be necessary for me to take very prompt and radical action to prevent the starvation of thousands of women and children who would be left without any means of support."[50] Of course, despite Yager's insistence to the contrary, Puerto Rican women and mothers had long been skilled in surviving difficult situations, often on their own.

Furthermore, shortly after the start of the project, a steady stream of letters from the laborers themselves began arriving at the office of Félix Córdova Dávila, Puerto Rico's Resident Commissioner. These letters arrived from New Orleans, Little Rock, and Fayetteville, where conditions for workers were described as "pitiful," "atrocious," and "inhuman."[51] Some workers expressed concern that they were not receiving their promised wages: some received only part, others none at all. They worried that they would not be able to provide adequately for their families back home. These letters asked Córdova Dávila to send the workers home to Puerto Rico or to other parts of the United States where laborers had family that might assist them in getting home.[52]

At Camp Bragg in Fayetteville, North Carolina, the situation for the laborers was so bad that they selected a representative who wrote letters on their behalf and entered a sworn deposition to Puerto Rico's Resident Commissioner. In an initial letter dated October 7, Ramón Viña wrote that in the three weeks since the group of 1,700 men had left Puerto Rico for Fayetteville, three men had died, and "90 percent of the 1,700 are sick, some of them so very ill that they will also die."[53] Viña lamented that "a large number of the men who came in this expedition are anemic and of poor physical condition and should have never left Porto Rico under any circumstances at all. If one adds to this the fact that the majority of them wear just a pair of trousers and a shirt in the way of clothing, you will deduct that with thin equipment they cannot stand the climate and much less when the real winter weather sets in."[54] Somewhere in the planning for these labor camps, US officials had neglected to note the fact that despite the warmer temperatures in the US southern states, this climate was still far colder than that of tropical Puerto Rico. By and large, the men were not prepared for the colder weather, and large numbers of them became sick with pneumonia and influenza.

A subsequent letter dated October 12, and signed by 136 of the laborers at Camp Bragg, named Rafael F. Marchán as their representative and pleaded for the Resident Commissioner to send the men further south, where they had been promised that the climate would be similar to that of Puerto Rico. The letter stated that 12 men had died and 200 were seeking treatment for illness in the camp hospital.[55] On October 24, Marchán provided a deposition in which he describes the unsanitary conditions that the men found in the hospital at Camp Bragg and the ill care that they received at the hands of the doctors.[56] He recounts that the hospital staff often used the same instruments and supplies on numerous men without cleaning or sanitizing them, thereby helping the spread of the influenza from which so many suffered. He further relates tales of such "apparent neglect and criminal negligence as to permit a man to die from a wound on his foot which was infected and aggravated by the first aid bandage which was put on it and never removed for about a week until he passed away."[57]

Likewise, communications arrived at Córdova Dávila's office from workers stationed at other camps as well. A telegram from a laborer identified only as Reyes, who was working at a camp in Little Rock, Arkansas, sent shortly after his arrival requested the Resident Commissioner to come to the camp so that he might see for himself the conditions under which the men toiled. Reyes described the laborers being taken out of the camp under soldiers' guard and knocked about with butt ends of guns.[58] According to Reyes, some of these men had been paid only part of their salaries, and others had not been paid at all.[59] One hundred men were said to have perished in the labor camp in Little Rock, Arkansas, in the few months they were stationed there.[60]

By the end of November 1918, the war had come to an end, and the shipment of Puerto Rican laborers with it. A report in the *New York Times* from December 1 noted that 10,000 laborers had been shipped to various states through the program.[61] The paper described the program in laudatory tones and praised the work of the Puerto Ricans for having been a considerable asset during the war effort. The article also described the conditions that laborers experienced in fairly bright terms, claiming that laborers were paid full wages, that the program brought "unwonted prosperity" to many Puerto Rican families, and that it was "the best thing that ever happened in Puerto Rico."[62] These statements differ dramatically from the descriptions of conditions provided by laborers—the illnesses they experienced, the lack of pay, the poor treatment and harassment—as well as the concerns of Governor Yager, who saw the program as disastrous for Puerto Rican families.

In contrast to the praise and applause in the pages of the *New York Times*, in a letter dated just a few days later, on December 5, Gavin Payne, field director for the American Red Cross in Puerto Rico, describes the program and the laborers in much starker terms. Payne wrote to the chief of the Bureau of Insular Affairs to describe the scene at Camp Las Casas, San Juan, where he was providing emergency relief to the ships arriving from the United States with Puerto Rican laborers. He stated that despite the principles of the Red Cross to serve and not to criticize, "no American citizen, seeing these men, could resist the impulse to recite the story of this lamentable lapse in our vaunted humanity and efficiency. No fair description of conditions as I saw them can be made without indicating culpability somewhere along the line."[63] Payne's letter describes the pathetic condition of the laborers returning from the mainland on the "pestilential ship" the *City of Savannah*.[64] Most of the men were too sick to walk themselves off the vessel and needed assistance. Payne describes the deck of the ship as being "littered with the sick."[65] Furthermore, he claimed the "woeful emaciation in a number of cases brought vividly to mind pictures in the public prints some years ago of coolies in India when famines stalked abroad."[66]

Payne harshly criticizes US agents who dreamed up the scheme of sending the men to the United States. He laments that the "misguided theorist who advanced the idea of sending this type of men to our lusty mainland" had not been present at the harbor to see "what crimes are committed in the name of Human Uplift."[67] Payne describes the tattered and thin clothes the laborers wore on their return and the fact that most men were wearing the exact clothes they had been wearing when they left Puerto Rico. Furthermore, he angrily railed, "how the physical conditions of these men could have escaped the notice of any governmental agency at the time the transport sailed, and how the quality of their garments, with which they were to brave the inclement days of winter, passed inspection is beyond conjecture."[68]

Payne's letter buttresses the claims of Puerto Rican laborers themselves and their descriptions of the conditions under which they toiled. His outrage and his criticism of the program are important in understanding the real toll the men suffered during those short months. Of course, Payne's letter also demonstrates the paternalism endemic among US mainlanders who came to the territory during the early twentieth century. Payne affirmed and reified widely held notions that Puerto Ricans were ignorant, poor, helpless, and in need of white saviors such as himself. In this case, it was those very white saviors who had placed the men's lives in danger to begin with. US government needs for labor on the mainland in support of the war effort, combined with Puerto Rico's ever-present and growing problem of unemployment and the perceived problem of overpopulation, created the perfect storm that led to the woeful experiment in which the men were caught up. They left home to improve their situations and instead found themselves in a terrible nightmare.

This brief episode highlights several of the tensions and lasting questions that arose after the US occupation of Puerto Rico. In particular, the incident threw the territory's problem with unemployment into stark relief. This issue is one that had plagued Puerto Rico throughout its history and was terribly exacerbated by early twentieth-century US economic policies.[69] The debacle of the War Department and United States Employment Service's experiment with migrant labor not only illustrated the problems raised by the territory's economic dependence on large-scale sugar production but also highlighted the importance of the unanswered question of what Puerto Ricans were to the United States and what rights they were owed. As Justice Brown wrote in *Downes*, Puerto Ricans were owed some rights — natural rights owed to all men — but what did that mean in actuality? And where could laborers go to claim those rights? The question of worker rights would continue to arise throughout the early twentieth century as the US continued its colonial ambitions.

Controlling the Populace: The Puerto Rico Insular Police

In the early twentieth century, the Puerto Rico Insular Police were at the center of doling out violence in the service of US empire.[70] Since the beginnings of the Insular Police, intimidation was rampant, and from the force's earliest days, the Insular Police were used to curtail worker strikes and political protests. As early as 1905, the Insular Police were dispatched to handle a strike in the sugar districts of the territory.[71] Seventy-five officers were sent to handle the situation, which according to the police chief would have resulted in "the sacrifice of the sugar crop of the island" had police not intervened.[72] The Insular Police, often with the political and financial support of landowners, engaged in suppressing a number of major strikes throughout the early decades of US rule.[73] These displays of force were meant to discipline workers and ensure that they acted like good colonial subjects who remained quiet regarding the injustices of colonial rule and who broke their backs to generate profits for US capitalists and the Puerto Rican elites.[74]

With the imposition of US governance in Puerto Rico, in 1899 the police force was centralized and placed under the control of the US-appointed governor.[75] The police chief, usually a mainland American with former military training, was appointed by the governor and answered directly to him.[76] Though direct military rule lasted only two years, military control over the Insular Police lasted more than fifty years.[77] Until 1956, the force was directed by members of the US military who had reached the rank of colonel.[78] Police chiefs often arrived in Puerto Rico with little knowledge of local affairs and with their racial prejudices and misconceptions of residents firmly in place.[79] They also arrived with a firm belief in the United States' civilizing mission. Force would emerge as a key tool of Americanization efforts as the police played an outsize role in molding Puerto Rico's unfortunate inhabitants into proper subjects of empire.

In 1908, Governor Regis Post described the Insular Police as "semimilitary in both organization and appearance. The discipline, drill and regulations of the force are in many respects similar to those of the Army."[80] On the surface, the aim of the semimilitary training was to create a modern, professional, and nonpolitical force that would maintain the rule of law in the new colonial territory. In practice, the Insular Police were highly politicized and served to consolidate US rule and advance US political and capitalist interests in Puerto Rico. The force achieved these goals through violence, intimidation, and, perhaps most important, the expansion of politicized surveillance capabilities.[81]

Early on, the Insular Police was charged with surveilling and reporting on political activities around the territory.[82] Frequently, police higher-ups issued circular letters that included detailed information about the interests and policies of political leaders throughout the early period of US rule. One such circular letter, issued in 1904, contained orders to the district heads to ensure police surveillance and reporting on all political meetings and gatherings in the districts.[83] Such surveillance practices would only increase and expand over the course of the first several decades of US rule.

During World War I, US colonial officials again expanded the Insular Police and took steps to connect its officers with the US Army's Military Intelligence Division.[84] As we shall see, this marriage would prove extremely important during the 1930s with rising social and political unrest. The Military Intelligence Division (MID) began more heavily surveilling political and labor activities beginning in 1930 and continuing into the 1940s, with the heaviest surveillance activity taking place between 1935 and 1941.[85] The letters, memos, and reports of the MID total more than 2,000 single-spaced typed pages.[86] These reports were initially issued on a monthly basis but were later increased to weekly as political and social tensions began to boil over mid-decade.

During the 1930s, the Insular Police, the MID, and the nascent Federal Bureau of Investigation (FBI) all had a hand in implementing a widespread surveillance program that monitored so-called subversive activities.[87] With the ascent of the Partido Nacionalista de Puerto Rico (PNPR, or Puerto Rican Nationalist Party), "subversive" came to have a very broad definition for US officials in Puerto Rico, designating anyone participating actively in social and political life as a potential target for surveillance and scrutiny.[88] These subversive activities ranged from organized political events of the left-leaning and pro-independence parties, to student protests, to labor stoppages and strikes. The overtly politicized nature of policing and law enforcement in Puerto Rico during the early twentieth century provided countless benefits to powerful elites both in and outside the archipelago, at the same time that it bred mistrust and tension between many ordinary Puerto Ricans and the police. Nowhere was this mistrust more obvious than in the relationship between the police and laborers.

One of the most violent clashes between police and workers took place during a three-month period in 1915–16 in which 18,000 sugar workers brought work on twenty-four of the thirty-nine plantations in the territory to a halt.[89] Plantation owners, with the blessing of the government, hired armed men to break the strikes. The police, too, were ruthless in breaking up the strikes. Clashes in the districts of Vieques and Ponce resulted in the deaths of several workers, the injury of dozens of others, and the arrest of more than 300 laborers. The American Federation of Labor (AFL) condemned the government's actions in failing to negotiate or arbitrate with workers and instead resorting to violence and police intimidation to deal with worker demands. Prominent labor organizer and Puerto Rican politician Santiago Iglesias Pantín stated that workers' legal right to strike was effectively denied the moment the armed forces were placed in the service of the sugar corporations.[90]

This practice and police clashes with workers continued throughout the early decades of the twentieth century and finally came to a head during the 1930s as frustration over poor labor practices and unemployment boiled over. As unrest grew in nearly every employment sector of the territory, the US government cracked down on dissent and protest, and the Insular Police force was its chief instrument in these crackdowns.[91] Strikes broke out in the major commodity industries of sugar, coffee, and tobacco, as well as in public works; baking; needlework; button, hat, and shirt manufacturing; highway construction; transportation; and printing.[92]

Tellingly, the US government files relating to the various strikes of the 1930s were labeled with the words "Puerto Rico Pacification." The term "pacification" is defined by the Oxford English Dictionary as either "the act or process of pacifying, the state of being pacified" or "the act of forcibly suppressing or eliminating a population considered to be hostile."[93] As Tyler Wall, Parastou Saberi, and Will Jackson note, the history of pacification is embedded within the development, expansion, and survival of modern capitalism and colonialism.[94] Pacification, they urge us to recognize, is not merely "a synonym for repression"; rather, pacification "involves the (re)production of a new social order, as well as the destruction of any opposition." During the 1930s, we see pacification forming a key aspect of police work in order to ensure the smooth functioning of colonial capitalism. The working class and poor became key targets for police intervention, not because of actual involvement in criminal activities, but because their resistance to labor discipline threatened the colonial capitalist social order being constantly produced and reproduced during those early years of US rule. The police acted as strikebreakers and sought to eliminate any resistance by violating the rights of Puerto Rican workers. Despite the protected nature of labor strikes as political speech, the government sought to forcibly suppress and eventually eliminate all signs of opposition.

The general air of discontent in Puerto Rico at the time touched every part of life. During the first four decades of US rule, the territory's economy underwent major restructuring. These changes were in response to the Great Depression and shifts in the global economic market and in the United States specifically. As a result, the territory's agricultural sector, its primary economic engine, saw a prolonged decline throughout those decades. Such economic contraction and agricultural decline led to widespread unemployment and, with it, the shrinking of laborers' buying capacity. The overwhelming result of these changes was that malnutrition, hunger, and deterioration of health conditions became more prevalent during the 1930s.[95]

The tempest of desperation and frustration came to a head in 1933–34, when workers from several sectors went on strike across the archipelago. In the six months between July and December 1933, there were eighty-five strikes or actions by workers in tobacco, sugar, needlework, baking, transportation, and dock works, and by the public car drivers.[96] Needlework, in particular, was a harsh industry employing hundreds of women and paying them poverty-level wages. Women regularly worked late into the night with poor lighting and little to eat.[97] In August of that year, 2,000 needle workers went on strike in the city of Mayagüez.[98] The women demanded a 25 percent pay increase and modifications to a proposed industrial code. Reports of the strike from San Juan's *Porto Rico Progress* described the women stoning the factory of Maria Luisa Arecley. A riot subsequently ensued when sympathizers and the unemployed joined the workers and the group swelled to about 6,000 people.[99] Police fired on the crowd, killing Maria Feliciano, one of the striking women; injuring a child who was present; and wounding another man in the abdomen. The report further detailed the injuries of a man who was clubbed by police, as well as those of a police officer who was seriously hurt.[100] All told more than thirty strikers and thirteen police were injured in the tumult. The confrontation, along with other strikes in Yauco and Caguas in the weeks preceding it, led needleworkers to receive a 15–20 percent raise.

A MID report chronicling the subversive activities of December 1933 painted a broad picture of the strike events in the archipelago that month. The report began by declaring that "a serious situation in reference to strikes confronted the Insular Government."[101] The report then described the various strikes occurring in Puerto Rico, including the possibility of a general strike if the individual sectors were not dealt with. The report focused in particular on two strikes taking place simultaneously: a dockworkers strike at the important Port of San Juan and a Puerto Rico–wide chauffeurs' union strike to protest high gasoline prices. Both strikes elicited a slew of communications between Puerto Rico–based government officials and the US secretary of war, as well as residents, merchants, and business groups. Both strikes were able to hobble Puerto Rico's commerce and thus posed serious threats to the government, US capital interests, and local elites. In both instances, the threat of police violence loomed, and Acting Governor Benjamin Horton availed himself of police and military help in quelling the labor actions. Ultimately, both groups of striking workers were able to win concessions because their work and their sectors were essential to the continued movement of goods and capital to and from the United States and Puerto Rico. A MID report for January 1934 confirmed that once the strikers and gas companies reached a temporary agreement for the reduction of gasoline prices, the chauffeurs' strikes virtually disappeared.[102] However, the same MID report described another strike brewing in the sugar sector.

A few months before the January MID report, in September 1933, sugar workers on the eastern coast attempted to bring production to a halt in protest of low wages and corporate policies that paid workers in vouchers to company stores rather than cash.[103] These initial attempts at protest led to fierce confrontations with police and at least one riot, with one dead and three wounded.[104] Another attempt at a Puerto Rico–wide strike took place in December 1933, with the strike moving to several large sugar plantations throughout the archipelago.

On January 5, 1934, the Federación Libre de Trabajadores (Free Federation of Labor or FLT) entered into a collective bargaining agreement with sugar employers.[105] In existence since 1899, the FLT was a workers' union whose ideals were similar to the AFL and whose political arm was the Partido Socialista (Socialist Party). This marked the first time that the FLT signed a contract for all sugar workers in the territory with the Sugar Producers' Association.[106] Unfortunately, the agreement mostly benefited the employers and left many of the workers' demands unaddressed. Most sugar workers repudiated the agreement for several reasons: the minimum wages proposed were lower than the ones they already earned, the workday continued to be twelve hours, workers did not share in the industry's vast profits, employers continued to enjoy large tax exemptions, and employers continued to pay workers with vouchers instead of cash.[107] As a result, on January 10, five days after the initial agreement was signed, 14,267 sugar workers were on strike.[108] Sugar workers protested not only against employer practices and low wages but also against the FLT leaders and government policies.

Shortly after the start of the strike, on January 11, sugar workers from the city of Guayama in the south-central part of Puerto Rico called on nationalist leader Pedro Albizu Campos to head up the strike.[109] Workers sought Albizu Campos's support in the strike because they believed that Socialist Party leaders were allied with the FLT in support of the agreement.[110] This was an unprecedented move in Puerto Rican labor history. Previous strikes had relied on the political support of the Socialist and Communist Parties and had focused on wages and labor policies but had not taken an anticolonial tone.[111] The introduction of Albizu Campos to the 1934 dispute meant that workers were ready to publicly and politically relate their labor disputes with US imperialism. In joining with the nationalist leader, workers acknowledged the colonial dynamics that kept their wages low and exploited their labor. They were vocally rejecting colonial capital's abuse of their bodies and demanding an end to those abuses. In appealing to Albizu Campos, workers were also declaring that the previously established rules of strike and protest no longer applied.

The January 1934 MID report expresses concern for the political dimensions of the strike and the explicitly anti-US turn that it took. The report claimed that Albizu Campos, recognizing the strike's political possibilities, headed to Guayama, where 1,500 workers were on strike, and "attempted to take over the leadership of the strike. Since that date he has visited a number of Centrals making highly inflammatory speeches of an independence [sic] nature. Finally, Socialist leaders seeing the progress made by Campos made strenuous efforts to retain their hold on the labor groups."[112] The MID report expresses deep concern for the potential for violence as a result of Albizu Campos's involvement in the strike. The violence that Albizu Campos's presence fomented, however, was not that of the PNPR's armed insurgents. Instead, it was the violence of the state, as government officials deployed police forces and colluded with both capital and organized labor to reimpose order in the sugar districts.

On January 12, Albizu Campos travelled from Ponce to Guayama and held a rally for 6,000 striking workers.[113] This was in stark contrast to the 500 workers who had arrived for a rally held by prominent FLT organizer Francisco Colón Gordiany a few days before. Once workers understood that Colón Gordiany was interested, not in listening to their demands, but in urging them to accept the agreement and return to work, the majority began to protest loudly and criticize the labor organizer and the agreement. Police arrived at the scene of the protest and removed 400 laborers from the assembly hall, preventing them from voicing their demands or concerns to Colón Gordiany and other labor representatives.[114]

On January 19, Albizu Campos published his thoughts on the sugar strike and the role of the Insular Police in the newspaper *El Mundo*. There he decried the agreement struck between the FLT and the sugar corporations and wrote, "The government and the sugar corporations constitute one entity. The government [and sugar] have created an agreement among themselves and want to impose on workers those conditions that would best suit the sugar industry. It has mobilized the Police in order to intimidate striking workers. In Guayama there are more than 200 police officers. The sugar carts and trains leave protected by the police, because they so fear the strikers."[115] He stated that "the government wants to impose these slave conditions on workers who represent about 90 percent of the population. This is sugar slavery imposed by force. It is up to us to abolish it."[116] Albizu Campos's appeal to workers, especially those in the southern region where he was from, was apparent in the numbers that showed up to hear him speak. In Albizu Campos, workers found an ally willing to forcefully speak on their behalf and denounce both the state and sugar capital, as well as the Socialist Party and the FLT, which had betrayed workers.

The FLT, the Socialist Party, plantation owners, and US agents all pointed to Albizu Campos's role as a politician and not a labor organizer as a way to delegitimize his involvement with the strike.[117] Government and labor organizers had frequently blamed "outside agitators" for inciting strikes as a way of delegitimizing worker demands.[118] From this point of view, workers were simply pawns of outside agitators who had their own interests in mind, rather than capable individuals with legitimate and real demands and concerns about their labor and bodies.[119]

In response to Albizu Campos's involvement in the strike, the FLT held meetings at the various striking plantations. In meetings held on the northern side of Puerto Rico, the FLT was able to persuade some of the striking workers to accept the agreement and return to work. These meetings were often marked by heavy police presence meant to intimidate workers and to prohibit any "outside agitators" from speaking to them. In one such meeting held on January 15 in Fajardo on the northeastern coast, FLT representatives explained the agreement to the striking laborers. Also present at that meeting, however, were forty-five police officers from a special force trained in the maintenance of public order during protests and strikes.[120] During the meeting, FLT organizer José Salvá informed the workers that police were there to maintain public order, but workers understood that police were there, not to protect them, but rather to keep out members of the Nationalist Party and other pro-independence or pro-labor activists.[121]

The topsy-turvy nature of this strike is particularly evident in the events that took place in Yabucoa along the southeastern coast. On January 19, the newspaper *El Día* published a report written by politician Cayetano Coll y Cuchí, an opponent of Albizu Campos: "the agitation in that town [Yabucoa] is tremendous [and] is headed by Sr. Pedro Albizu Campos, who the police are afraid to arrest, despite the many entreaties to the police chief and Governor Horton to do so."[122] In response to Albizu Campos's presence and worker interest in his rhetoric and leadership, the FLT warned workers that if they did not sign on to the labor agreement and return to work, the FLT was prepared to hire others to replace striking workers.[123] This was an unprecedented threat, given that the FLT was the representative body of the workers. Never before had the workers' own union threatened to hire scabs and call on the police to remove striking workers if they refused to return to work. The FLT had traditionally lobbied on behalf of workers and advocated in their interest. In fact, the organization had often clashed with the Insular Police in its work in support of workers' rights. Here, instead, the FLT joined up with the Insular Police and colonial capital to suppress worker demands and threaten workers' bodies and livelihoods. These threats only further angered workers.

The situation was so charged that the usual dynamic among organizers, workers, and politicians was turned completely upside down. This was in part due to the presence and leadership of Albizu Campos. When workers sought him out, they broke with the established dynamics of past strikes. They threw their lot in with the PNPR rather than the Socialist Party, and this sent the FLT and Socialist Party leaders scrambling for ways to maintain control over laborers at the expense of workers' interests. Unprecedented poverty and hunger led desperate workers to break with the established roles they were expected to inhabit during these strikes. Workers were enraged that the FLT was not advocating for their best interests, and they sought out other ways to voice their discontent and make themselves heard. Albizu Campos was happy to oblige workers who called for support and leadership. His presence and the workers' turn toward direct confrontation with capital and anticolonial rhetoric proved dangerous to organized labor, the insular government, and opposition parties such as the Socialist Party. In response, organized labor colluded with state officials to discipline workers through police power.

As the strike continued throughout that January, worker exhaustion and hunger led many to accede to the FLT's agreement and return to work. Laborers received pressure from the FLT, politicians, the government, and the police to break the strike. Acting Governor Horton himself called on police and local judges to "investigate and immediately take before the courts of justice any person who evidence tended to show committed defamation against labor organizers."[124] Horton's call for the criminalization of such statements was a direct response to Albizu Campos's fiery declarations against labor organizers and the government. Horton hoped that by cracking down on so-called defamation, he could silence Albizu Campos and workers who took harsh positions against the FLT and the US government. The governor's call for greater arrests for defamation had an immediate chilling effect on worker protests.[125]

By January 24, only 1,025 workers remained on strike.[126] As the month wore on, laborers from the various plantations accepted the agreement and returned to work. Smaller-scale, localized strikes, however, continued to arise throughout the sugar sector as workers claimed their employers were not meeting the terms of the agreement. Laborers in Guánica and Humacao held work stoppages due to disputes concerning work start times and longshoremen wages.[127] Despite efforts to continue the strike and have their demands for greater wages and better conditions met, by the early days of February 1934, exhaustion, lack of income, and state pressure led the last of the sugar laborers to return to work.

In the end, the sugar strike of 1933–34 did not result in improved economic conditions for sugar workers. Predictably, resentment and frustration with labor policies continued to bubble up throughout the decade. Between 1934 and 1935, 50,000–60,000 laborers went on strike, and between 1936 and 1937, 13,119 workers went on strike.[128] The continued decline in the agricultural sector resulted in the growth of strikes in other employment sectors such as dockyards, telephone, ground transportation, and needlework. In January and February 1938, Puerto Rico saw its second major strike of the decade: dockworkers paralyzed commerce when they held a monthlong strike demanding wage increases and control over the unloading of cargo shipments.[129] The presence of the police continued to haunt these moments of labor unrest. Not surprisingly, police presence also continued to have a chilling effect on protests and attempted to intimidate workers into accepting poverty wages by using violence to break strikes.

The 1930s saw the effects of years of inequitable and untenable economic and social policies come to a crashing climax in Puerto Rico. In response to growing inequality, falling wages, and hunger, workers took to the streets to demand change. The police took to the streets with them. In these disputes, it was clear that both government and police were willing to work with employers to ensure the continuation of the political-economic status quo. However, more and more this status quo could not provide for the masses of frustrated, angry, and hungry residents who demanded change by all means available to them. The state was also willing to employ all means available to quell the growing discontent. Nowhere is this more evident than in its dealing with labor and nationalism. The documents of the MID, produced by US government agents, demonstrate the extent to which the Insular Police were used to intimidate Puerto Rican laborers and to force them back to work. These actions are but a part of a long history of state use of police as a labor-controlling entity.

Conclusion

The United States' efforts to reshape Puerto Rican society in the first decades of the twentieth century were marked by their experimentation with the lives and bodies of residents and their use of police violence to buttress those changes most beneficial to US capital interests. Attempts to reshape agricultural, economic, and labor policies often exposed Puerto Ricans to brutal conditions in which their lives were of little value. The machine of US corporate interests cared very little about the bodily integrity of the territory's residents. Consequently, Puerto Rican laborers and those perceived to be diseased or a threat to the United States' colonial project often found themselves at the mercy of the US government and the Insular Police, their bodies open for experimentation, surveillance, imprisonment, and violence, with little recourse to resist.

As a result of these continued social and economic experiments, dissatisfaction with US policies grew throughout the early decades of US colonial rule in Puerto Rico. More and more of these tensions were manifested in protest that often turned violent. Labor strikes in the ports, sugar plantations, and the tobacco and needlework sectors grew more frequent and more violent throughout the decade of the 1920s and into the 1930s. And police violence grew right along with the strikes. Likewise, Puerto Ricans were also ready to protest those policies that were perceived as invasive to their bodies and detrimental to their health and livelihoods.

The first few decades of US rule saw Puerto Rican society undergo radical changes as the archipelago became a place for experimentation in service of US colonial capitalism. The Insular Police were critical instruments in maintaining the colonial order that US capital and the Puerto Rican elite demanded. The reconfiguration that took place in the early twentieth century was made possible by the broad powers granted to Congress in *Downes v. Bidwell* and the limited rights that Puerto Ricans had to contest that power. Puerto Ricans, nonetheless, expressed their anger and frustrations with the colonial order with their words, their bodies, and all means available to them.

CHAPTER FOUR

No Longer a Non-Self-Governing Area
Creating the Estado Libre Asociado de Puerto Rico

Antonio del Valle, my grandfather, was born on September 5, 1911. Toño, as he was known, was born a citizen of "Porto Rico," the anglicized name given to the archipelago in 1899, which it bore until a resolution of Congress officially returned the name to its Spanish spelling in 1932. At the age of six, Toño became a citizen of the United States when the 1917 passage of the Jones-Shafroth Act changed Puerto Ricans' citizenship status overnight. In the short span of his first six years of life, Puerto Rico and Antonio had undergone dramatic legal shifts that likely went unnoticed by him and the majority of impoverished Puerto Ricans like him.

At the time of these momentous shifts, Toño's parents, Felix del Valle and Monserrate del Toro, lived in the rural mountain barrio of Quebrada in the northeastern municipality of Camuy. Felix worked as an agricultural laborer, while Monserrate tended their home and family. When Antonio was born, the couple already had four children. They would go on to have six more, for a total of eleven, though not all would survive into adulthood. Felix's work as a rural laborer was seasonal, and the family balanced on the edge of poverty. Theirs was a struggle of occasional work in the coffee plantations or cane fields, followed by scrambling to make ends meet during the dead months, *el tiempo muerto*. The family got by through subsistence farming, with Monserrate and the children growing the food they needed to survive, in addition to whatever Felix was able to bring in through his work.

The youngest children might have attended school for a few years, but as soon as they were old enough to contribute to the household, they were put to work. Toño had the equivalent of a first- or second-grade education when, at the age of nine or ten, he left home and set off on his own. Though he loved his mother fiercely, there were simply too many children to feed and clothe, and Toño, being one of the older boys in the family, did not want to be a burden. So shoeless and with little more than the clothes he wore, he left Barrio Quebrada on foot and made his way alone. The year would have been about 1920; economic conditions in Puerto Rico were fairly dire and headed toward calamity with the approaching Great Depression.

Antonio worked his way south, doing whatever jobs he could for whoever was willing to hire him. He eventually settled in the southern port city of Ponce, along Puerto Rico's jewel-blue Caribbean coast, where he cobbled together a life for himself. For a time, he labored in the sugarcane fields around Ponce, engaging in any sort of work available, from cutting and collecting to transporting cane by horse-drawn cart. Eventually, he found work as a deliveryman for local small grocers. He also had the gift of gab and was a consummate salesman, selling everything from tropical fruit and vegetables to shoes. Family stories have it that he was such an effective salesman, he sold the same pair of shoes to two different buyers.

Toño was never still. Being a child of poverty is a great motivator, and he was not a man to rest when there was work to be done or a dollar to be made. In my memories of him as a much older man in his eighties, he was always moving, slowly, but nevertheless always in motion, tinkering in the yard or tending to his unmanicured and lush garden. His hard work and drive to survive, combined with the economic and political changes that were afoot in Puerto Rico in the mid-twentieth century, allowed him, and many laboring Puerto Ricans like him, a level of upward mobility that the previous generations had not had.

The period after World War II and into the early 1970s saw a boom in industrialization and modernization in Puerto Rico. The creation of the Estado Libre Asociado (the ELA, or the Commonwealth of Puerto Rico), and the economic policies known as Operación Manos a la Obra (or Operation Bootstrap) transformed the archipelago's economy from a largely agricultural one to an industrialized one. With these changes came the creation of a middle class composed of former rural laborers, like my grandfather Toño, who moved to cities and suburbs to work in newly built factories and refineries. Furthermore, federal and Puerto Rican government policies effectively made Puerto Rico into a tax haven for US corporations, attracting many companies to the archipelago. In mid-twentieth century Puerto Rico, industry boomed, and an economic miracle took place.

Antonio, never one to squander an opportunity, managed to save enough money to buy himself a small, heavy truck with which he could haul and deliver products such as cement and gravel to construction sites all over Puerto Rico. In this way, he became a small business owner. With little more than a first-grade education, Antonio pulled himself up by the proverbial American bootstraps and managed to move into Puerto Rico's blooming middle class. By all accounts, my grandfather was a Puerto Rican success story, an exemplar of the purported miracle that befell the archipelago following the creation of the ELA and in the era of Operation Bootstrap. In very concrete ways, his success and prosperity were made possible by the shifts that took place in Puerto Rico in the mid-twentieth century.

My grandfather's story is the story of so many of our poor and rural elders in Puerto Rico. The policies enacted in the years leading up to the adoption of the ELA, under Puerto Rico's version of the New Deal, created the infrastructure that ultimately allowed for industrialization and the powerful, though short-lived, economic boom that came with it. Antonio's successes, and those of other Puerto Ricans like him, became intricately tied with the creation of the ELA. For many of his generation, the ELA, the Popular Democratic Party that ushered it into existence, and the governor who negotiated its creation were directly responsible for their prosperity, their jobs, their new hurricane-proof homes, their cars, and the stability that those material gains had brought.

In the mid-twentieth century, Puerto Rico underwent many radical shifts that dramatically transformed life in the archipelago. In this chapter, I will focus on the people and events that created the midcentury miracle that allowed so many Puerto Ricans to move out of poverty. The lead-up to the creation of the ELA was a turbulent time, with Puerto Ricans clamoring for change and the world undergoing a global reorientation. Puerto Rico's election of its first governor, the creation of the ELA, and the economic policies that were ushered in as part of Operation Bootstrap all did much to convince Puerto Ricans that the archipelago had become something other than a colony of the United States. This moment seemed to assuage people's desires for change, and the material gains of those decades convinced many that Puerto Rico's unique association with the United States was an overall good.

As radical as those mid-twentieth century shifts were at the time and as much as things appeared to be improving in Puerto Rico (and things did improve for thousands of people), the ELA and Operation Bootstrap would show themselves to be utter failures.[1] The gains of those halcyon decades would erode over the latter half of the century, and Puerto Rico and Puerto Ricans would enter the new millennium in bondage to debt. The failure of the ELA and of Puerto Rico's economic miracle were due in large part to the fact that they were built on a mirage, or as journalist Ed Morales put it, a fantasy.[2]

Puerto Rico's relationship with the United States did not change in 1952. Instead, Congress delegated to Puerto Rico the ability to self-govern, but that delegation was subject to Congress's whims and desires and could be chipped away or undone. Indeed, many of Puerto Rico's "powers" have been eroded and undermined in the decades following the creation of the ELA. Perhaps most important, the ELA did not overturn *Downes v. Bidwell* or its racist logic. Despite the pomp and celebration surrounding the ELA, Puerto Rico remained an unincorporated territory under Congress's plenary power. The ELA was colonialism with a shiny new veneer, meant to fool Puerto Ricans and the world into believing that Puerto Rico was something other than what it had always been—a colonial possession. Likewise, the prosperity created by Operation Bootstrap was also illusory and fell victim to congressional whims; the financial incentives that brought industry to Puerto Rico and created a miracle were eventually undone by Congress, and Puerto Rico's economy cratered horribly as a result.

Luis Muñoz Marín: The Consummate Politician

As we have seen, the first few decades of US rule in Puerto Rico brought radical transformation to every sector of life in the archipelago, from education, to diet, to labor and employment. In the first three decades of the twentieth century, Puerto Ricans' per capita income grew as a result of the rapid growth of sugar production and exports.[3] However, despite these transformations, the standard of living for the majority of Puerto Ricans did not improve. Puerto Rico's turn toward greater reliance on goods imported by the United States meant that the cost of living outpaced salaries. While, undoubtedly, some of the changes implemented during these early decades improved life for Puerto Ricans, by the 1930s it was clear that the promises of prosperity under US colonial rule had not been borne out. The convergence of the outsize growth of capital colonialism, economic depression, and several wars led many working class and rural Puerto Ricans to lose economic footing and to slip deeper into poverty.

This dissatisfaction came to a head in the decade of the 1940s, when events in Puerto Rico converged with global shifts that allowed for a reorientation of life on the archipelago. Following World War II, with the Soviet Union in ascendance and the rearrangement of the global order, the United States found itself claiming the mantle of the world's exemplar of liberal democracy, a paragon of newly enshrined human rights, the shining city on the hill. The desire to occupy that exceptional space and to be seen as the leader of the "free world" presented some domestic challenges for the United States. It would not do for the protector of the world to hold colonies in a quickly decolonizing world. It would also not do to have racial segregation and overt racism. These things could all be used to discredit the United States before the world. This moment of global reorientation created an opening for activists and community groups to demand an end to segregation and racism enshrined in law. It also allowed Puerto Ricans to demand a change to the United States–Puerto Rico relationship. One particularly savvy Puerto Rican politician stepped in to steer those demands and the changes they brought.

Luis Muñoz Marín, the first governor elected by the people of Puerto Rico, was the founder of the Partido Popular Democrático de Puerto Rico and the architect of the ELA.[4] He was instrumental in brokering the concessions that allowed for the creation of the ELA and was instrumental also in negotiating the terms of the ELA itself. Born into a prominent family at the turn of the twentieth century, Muñoz Marín was the son of Luis Muñoz Rivera, who was himself a notable politician. A founder and leader of the Autonomist Party, he had fought for self-rule for Puerto Rico under Spanish rule.[5] When Spain finally granted Puerto Rico's Autonomous Charter, allowing the archipelago to determine its local affairs and establish a local government, Muñoz Rivera became the head of the new government.[6] He held that position only briefly, as shortly thereafter the US occupation ended Puerto Rico's autonomy and its relationship with Spain. Later, Muñoz Rivera would serve as Puerto Rico's Resident Commissioner, a nonvoting member of Congress who lobbies on behalf of Puerto Rico.

Much has been written about Luis Muñoz Marín, his youthful literary ambitions, the bohemian years he spent in New York's Greenwich Village, his turn to journalism and later politics, his role in negotiating and enacting the ELA, his time as governor, and the changes to Puerto Rico that he oversaw. For some he was the consummate politician, able to move easily between political circles both in the US mainland and in Puerto Rico; for others, he was a brilliant strategist able to negotiate some of the biggest deals in the history of the archipelago; and for others still, he was a shape-shifter who betrayed his political beliefs on multiple occasions.[7]

In his youth, Muñoz Marín was an avowed and unyielding socialist. In a letter written to a mentor in 1922, at the age of twenty-four, he apologizes for his militant socialist attitude and for his dismissive and abominable behavior toward mutual acquaintances.[8] Like many other youths who are introduced to a radical political or religious ideology, Muñoz Marín went all in on socialism, to the point of offending and rejecting those of his own class in his sympathy for workers and the rural poor. Though Muñoz Marín grew out of his militancy, his socialist beliefs influenced his politics for the rest of his life. In fact, it was his past as a socialist that was often raised by suspicious US politicians who sought to dismiss and discredit him.

Eleven years later, in 1931, Muñoz Marín, in a public letter addressed to US-appointed governor Theodore Roosevelt Jr., described himself as "a radical nationalist, for moral . . . and for economic reasons."[9] He clarified that he was in support of Puerto Rican socialism insofar as it did not seek to curtail Puerto Rican sovereignty or to hinder any future self-determination. But he was adamant that he did not belong to any political party. During these years, he was also said to profess an admiration for Nationalist Party leader Pedro Albizu Campos, who in some ways was a perfect foil for Muñoz Marín.[10] If Muñoz Marín's political ideology was malleable and shifted over time, Albizu Campos's was the complete opposite; he was unyielding in his vision of Puerto Rican independence and an end to US colonial occupation. The two men's political paths were entangled through much of the 1940s and 1950s, when Muñoz Marín turned away from independence and embraced autonomy.

In a 1936 letter to journalist and close friend Ruby A. Black, Muñoz Marín expressed his dismay at the proposal for independence put forth by Maryland senator Millard Tydings. Tydings famously proposed his bill for Puerto Rico's independence in response to the assassination of his friend and the chief of the Insular Police, E. Francis Riggs.[11] If Puerto Ricans wanted independence, let them have it, the Tydings bill set forth, but without any of the economic safeguards or the gradual phasing-in that had previously been proposed and adopted for the independence of the Philippines. For many Puerto Ricans, Muñoz Marin among them, the unfavorable terms of the bill were retribution for Riggs's death at the hands of a group of nationalists. For Muñoz Marín, the bill was a nonstarter, as it would have eliminated free trade between the United States and Puerto Rico with few transitional measures and would have been economically devastating for the archipelago.

"I am working towards Puerto Rico's independence," he wrote. "Independence, for which we have to fight, perhaps under all circumstances, is preferable for the future of our children and grandchildren." Independence, he explained, must be obtained through nonviolent and orderly means. "The [US] Government's approach of proposing an independence project that is fundamentally unjust . . . places upon the shoulders of the US government the blame for any collective tragedies that might take place in Puerto Rico. . . . In any situation that might develop, *no Puerto Rican official should shoot at a student or any other Puerto Rican. I say this with certainty because Puerto*

Ricans are not at fault, rather the situation that exists in Puerto Rico is the fault of the US government, and it is [the government] that constantly stimulates these collective tragedies" (emphasis added).[12] The collective tragedies to which Muñoz Marín refers consisted of the upheaval caused by the Insular Police's arrest and presumed execution of two young nationalists in retaliation for Riggs's death. While Riggs's death was shocking, the police response and the deaths of the two nationalists galvanized Puerto Rican sentiment against the police and the US government. Many saw the excesses of the police as emblematic of the US government's power over the archipelago and Puerto Ricans. Here Muñoz Marín places the blame for that upheaval squarely on the shoulders of the US government.

This letter, written at the height of the turbulent 1930s and as his political star was rising, shows us the fiery Muñoz Marín who cleaved to his convictions and remained unapologetically pro-independence. His belief that Puerto Ricans were not at fault and should not be held responsible for resistance to US rule is significant. Later, as governor of Puerto Rico and in an attempt to smooth the way for the passage of the ELA, Muñoz Marín would himself deploy the police to quell dissent and enforce the infamous gag law, *ley de la mordaza*, that punished those who supported nationalism and independence. But in the 1930s, he had yet to turn away from independence, and his anger at US policies in Puerto Rico was obvious.

The fervent political activity of that decade and Muñoz Marín's growing political ambitions led him and a group of others formerly aligned with the pro-independence Liberal Party to break with that party and found the Partido Popular Democrático de Puerto Rico (PPD, or Populares) in 1938. The PPD's slogan, "Pan, Tierra, y Libertad," spoke to the priorities of the party; though independence for Puerto Rico was part of the new party's platform, its focus was directed more toward social and economic reforms. Born, in part, out of Muñoz Marín's activism during the New Deal era, the Populares' foremost goal was to improve the standard of living for Puerto Rico's workers and rural poor. *Pan y tierra*, bread and land, were the first priorities for the party. Puerto Rico's poor were in desperate need of land and of sustenance. The question of status could wait.[13]

The PPD's first few years in existence were focused on educating poor and rural workers about the importance of voting. For decades, labor bosses would bribe or coerce their workers into voting for the bosses' preferred candidates, and it was common practice for poor laborers to sell their votes for a few dollars.[14] Furthermore, corrupt election officials often informed labor bosses whom workers had voted for, resulting in the potential blackballing of workers who did not follow orders.[15] One of the PPD's most effective strategies in those early years was in convincing poor workers that their votes mattered and they should vote in their own interests, not their employers'. The party urged rural voters to reject the plantation-based economic status quo and instead support the PPD's project of land reform. The Populares crisscrossed the archipelago, meeting with rural peasants and speaking directly to their needs. This campaign was effective in cementing the working poor's support for the PPD for years to come.

The success of the PPD's reformist agenda and its growth in popularity were made possible by the convergence of several events in the early 1940s. In 1940, Luis Muñoz Marín became president of the Puerto Rico Senate, at that time the position of highest political leadership in the archipelago.[16] This political victory marked the start of the PPD's ascent in Puerto Rican politics and its nearly thirty years of political dominance in Puerto Rican elections. The victory also made way for the beginning of the Populares' reformist policies. Key among them was the 1947 passage of the Industrial Incentives Act, which exempted private corporations from income and property tax contributions for an initial ten-year period with the possibility of extensions. This was the beginning of Operation Bootstrap and the start of the "economic miracle" that was the engine for Puerto Rico's industrialization program.

A second pivotal change that made the PPD's reforms possible was the US Supreme Court's decision in the case of *Puerto Rico v. Rubert Hermanos, Inc.* in 1940.[17] That decision upheld a Puerto Rican statute that sought to enforce a federal law, first established in 1900, that limited the amount of land a single owner could own to 500 acres. The federal law, which had been in existence for four decades, had been largely ignored by corporate landholders and unenforced by the government. The PPD's plan for agrarian reform was premised on the notion that corporate ownership should be limited to the 500 acres mandated by statute and that land in excess of that amount should be redistributed to the landless peons who worked it.

Equally essential to the success of the PPD's agenda was the appointment of Rexford G. Tugwell as governor in 1941. Tugwell and Muñoz Marín had known each other for some time prior to Tugwell's appointment, and, crucially, Tugwell's support of land reform aligned with the ambitions of Muñoz Marín and the PPD.[18] In the first few years of the 1940s, an agrarian reform program began, its success aided by infrastructure projects that created new water, sewerage, and electric utilities.[19] Additionally, several government agencies were created to facilitate industrialization and development and to make way for the modernization of the archipelago.[20]

During this period of economic reform, Luis Muñoz Marín also began to turn away from the idea of independence for Puerto Rico. While statehood had always been a nonstarter for Muñoz Marín, he had cleaved to the notion that Puerto Rico deserved decolonization and full sovereignty; however, over time he began to embrace the concept of autonomy for Puerto Rico.[21] As we saw earlier, he had consistently been a fierce critic of US economic policies in Puerto Rico and of US domination over the archipelago. However, as the decade of the 1940s wore on, he became convinced that independence would not be possible given the Puerto Rican economy's heavy reliance on US markets. Muñoz Marín's change in stance regarding Puerto Rico's status has been heavily debated for decades. For many, his turn toward autonomy in connection with the United States was a betrayal.[22] For Muñoz Marín and the PPD, it was a matter of pragmatism. The way to move Puerto Ricans out of poverty, to create a middle class, to modernize, was in coordination with the United States and in close connection with the US economy. Muñoz Marín believed that free trade with the United States was essential for Puerto Rico to industrialize and for Puerto Ricans to build wealth. So it was that the one-time radical nationalist and militant socialist positioned himself to become the father of the ELA.

Negotiating a Change: Public Law 600 and the Creation of the Estado Libre Asociado

Mid-twentieth-century Puerto Rican history is rife with important milestones. Perhaps one of the most notable was the 1947 passage of Public Law 382, the Elective Governor Act, which for the first time allowed Puerto Ricans to elect their own governor, the highest executive position in Puerto Rico.[23] That election made Luis Muñoz Marín the first governor elected by the people of Puerto Rico, a position he would hold for sixteen years. The election also made it possible for him and the Populares to more forcefully continue their reformist agenda.

When Muñoz Marín took office in January 1949, Operation Bootstrap was well underway and already bearing fruit. In its first two years in operation, the new tax exemptions had attracted more than 80 new manufacturing plants to the archipelago.[24] By 1955, that number would grow to over 300. These new plants not only employed Puerto Rican laborers and paid them better wages than agricultural jobs but also created many ancillary jobs in construction, utilities, education, health, and so on. Thus, the impacts of these first few years of Operation Bootstrap created a ripple effect across Puerto Rican society.

With the overwhelming success of the new economic strategies and the positive changes they were producing in Puerto Rican society, Muñoz Marin argued that "a new kind of state" was being created in Puerto Rico, one in association with the United States.[25] He argued that Puerto Ricans had exercised their democratic rights by electing their own governor and that the archipelago was undergoing a democratic revolution that could become a model in Latin America. Puerto Rico, he argued, could showcase to all the world that economic development, prosperity, and democracy could be forged in close association with the United States. Puerto Rico's economic miracle could help to counter anti-American sentiments in the region during the fear-filled early years of the Cold War.

The Truman administration happily took Muñoz Marín up on his suggestion, and Puerto Rico became the United States' showpiece in the Caribbean, a capitalist success story in the face of creeping socialism. Muñoz Marín and a cadre of close PPD collaborators—including the up-and-coming young lawyer José Trías Monge, who would later go on to become chief justice of the Puerto Rico Supreme Court, and Puerto Rico's Resident Commissioner Dr. Antonio Fernós Isern, a former cardiologist who had been a close ally to Muñoz Marín since the founding of the PPD—seized on the Truman administration's goodwill and the US government's global ambitions to press for a change to Puerto Rico's status. The stage was thus set for another historic milestone.

The Truman administration and Congress gave Muñoz Marín and Fernós Isern the go-ahead to begin a process wherein Puerto Ricans would draft their own constitution and create what would become the ELA. The negotiations and drafting of Public Law 600, which would eventually be adopted as the Puerto Rico Federal Relations Act and be made part of the Puerto Rico Constitution, took place over the two-year period from the summer of 1949 to the summer of 1950. However, the initial groundwork for the law was laid a few years earlier, with the Tydings-Piñero bill of 1946. Jesus T. Piñero, then Puerto Rico's Resident Commissioner, proposed the bill with Senator Millard Tydings, who ten years earlier had proposed the bill for Puerto Rico's independence that had incensed Muñoz Marín.

Unlike the previous Tydings bill, the Tydings-Piñero bill called for a referendum on independence, statehood, and what was then called Associated State or Dominion status, modeled after the political status of former British colonies such as Canada and Australia. As initially proposed, the main elements of that status included provisions that would set up a constitution and local government for Puerto Rico; once those were in place, the United States would have given up full sovereignty over Puerto Rico. The United States would have retained property rights over military bases in the archipelago and other federal installations; however, Puerto Rico would have held sovereignty over its own political and foreign affairs. The proposed legislation also provided for reciprocal but not common citizenship. In other words, Puerto Ricans and US citizens would have had the ability to travel back and forth freely, but Puerto Ricans would have retained their own citizenship and would have enacted their own immigration laws. The common market and free trade between the United States and Puerto Rico would have continued to exist, and federal assistance laws would have continued to apply. Additionally, Puerto Rico would have been able to enter into treaties with other sovereign nations, except for treaties of a military nature. In military affairs, US laws and declarations would have continued to bind Puerto Rico.[26]

The initial proposal contained in the Tydings-Piñero bill was no doubt naively aspirational, and not surprisingly, it failed to move out of committee for consideration. However, the proposal demonstrated Piñero's and the Populares' desires for a robust form of self-determination for the archipelago. As Trías Monge later explained, the provisions of that failed bill had three key components that the drafters believed were important and that later informed the negotiations for Public Law 600: "It represented an attempt to advance self-government through the recognition of the right of the people of Puerto Rico to adopt a constitution of their own; it explicitly placed the relations between the United States and Puerto Rico on a mutual consent basis; and it proposed substantial changes" to those relations.[27]

With the Tydings-Piñero bill, as with Public Law 600 a few years later, Puerto Rican political leaders were seeking a greater measure of self-determination and of sovereignty—one that would have allowed Puerto Rico not only to decide issues of a local character but also to play a role on the international stage. It is noteworthy, also, that the Tydings-Piñero bill would have reverted residents back to Puerto Rican citizenship, rather than the US citizenship granted by the Jones-Shafroth Act. This suggests that even after thirty years of US citizenship, these political leaders believed that residents saw themselves as not quite Americans, or at least as more Puerto Rican and not completely a part of the United States. This dynamic, which the Supreme Court had first established in law in *Downes v. Bidwell*, was prevalent in the mid-twentieth century and persists still; it often reappears in important moments such as the major hurricanes of 2017 or discussions of the Puerto Rican debt crisis. That many Puerto Ricans did not feel themselves a part of the United States body politic in 1950 is clear not only by their desire to hold sovereignty over themselves and move out from under the thumb of the United States' plenary power but also by the fact that they desired their own citizenship.

The failure of the 1946 bill, with its sweeping ambitions, led PPD leaders to adopt a narrower focus when it came time to draft Public Law 600.[28] According to Trías Monge, he and the other drafters initially hoped to draft Public Law 600 in a way that would unambiguously move the archipelago out from under Congress's plenary power. However, the drafters also understood what a careful balancing act they had to engage in order to not upend the hard-won goodwill that Congress and the president felt toward the Muñoz Marín administration. Over the course of the negotiations, Public Law 600 underwent many changes and would ultimately emerge as a much different statute from the one initially proposed in 1946—one that would be less offensive to Congress and the US president.

In contrast to the ambitious provisions of the 1946 bill, Public Law 600 focused instead on the first aim of the 1946 legislation—to advance Puerto Rican self-government. The law completely dropped the last prong of the Tydings-Piñero bill and did not seek any radical political changes to the relationship between the United States and Puerto Rico. As for the other aim of the 1946 bill, the law made a murky attempt to establish a relationship of mutual consent between the United States and Puerto Rico. This murkiness, which the PPD leaders hoped would open the door for Puerto Rico to move out from under Congress's plenary power, became the source of much debate in the years following the passage of Public Law 600 and the creation of the ELA.

The drafting of Public Law 600 is attributed to a handful of prominent men: Luis Muñoz Marín, Antonio Fernós Isern, José Trías Monge, and Abe Fortas, a mainland lawyer and close friend of Luis Muñoz Marín who later became a US Supreme Court justice. Trías Monge warned Muñoz Marín and the others early on that in order for the legislation to truly create "a new kind of state," it had to repeal the Foraker and Jones-Shafroth Acts, which formed the basis for the United States–Puerto Rico relationship. Simply drafting and adopting a constitution would not be enough to end Puerto Rico's colonial condition.[29] For the law to truly change the colonial nature of the relationship, it would need to be drafted as a "a bilateral, mutually binding 'compact.' Congress would then explicitly acknowledge that the island was no longer a 'possession' under the constitutional 'territorial clause.' Only after this happened . . . would it be correct to declare that 'Puerto Rico is not a colony.'"[30]

Despite Trías Monge's warnings, Muñoz Marín and Fernós Isern took a different approach. They opted to keep the legislation as simple as possible. They aimed to obtain as large a grant of powers as possible for Puerto Rico without appearing to undermine Congress's control over the archipelago.[31] Muñoz Marín and Fernós Isern believed that adopting a simplified version of Public Law 600 would not foreclose the later adoption of more permanent and just changes to the Puerto Rico–United States relationship.[32]

For some time, Fernós Isern had been a vocal advocate for the need to establish that the legislation would take the form of a bilateral compact between the United States and Puerto Rico. Such a provision would be modeled after language included in the Northwest Ordinance of 1787, which created a government for the Northwest Territory, provided a method for admitting new states from the territory to the union, and established a bill of rights guaranteed in the territory. The "bilateral compact" language would address the problem of the unjust applicability of federal law in the archipelago without Puerto Rican consent and representation in the federal government.

Despite this belief, Fernós Isern gradually backed off the inclusion of the compact language, as it became clear that Congress would not approve it. He did not want to endanger the rest of the provisions in the draft—the creation of a constitution and local government for the archipelago. Instead, he took the position that the existence of a compact could be assumed based on the mere existence of the process they were enacting.[33] During the congressional hearings about Public Law 600, Fernós Isern stated that "should Puerto Rico adopt its own constitution, it would certainly constitute a compact between the United States and the people of Puerto Rico."[34] For him, the mere act of Puerto Rico creating its own local government was enough evidence of an agreement with Congress, a demonstration of Puerto Ricans' democratically chosen desires.

Abe Fortas suggested that the drafters of the law meet somewhere in the middle. The idea of a compact was too important to abandon. Instead, he suggested they include language to the effect that the agreement would be "in the nature of a compact." The final version of Public Law 600 thus included the following language: "Fully recognizing the principle of government by consent, *this Act is now adopted in the nature of a compact* so that the people of Puerto Rico may organize a government pursuant to a constitution of their own adoption" (emphasis added).[35] Though ambiguous, the language, the drafters hoped, might provide an avenue to legally argue, and for the courts to eventually determine, that Puerto Rico was no longer a territory of the United States.[36]

In the congressional hearings about Public Law 600, both Muñoz Marín and Fernós Isern were pressed on the meaning of the "compact" language and whether anything in the proposed statute would change federal power over Puerto Rico or whether the territory would become incorporated upon passage of the statute. Though both men artfully engaged in a game of semantic wordplay and sidestepping, Fernós Isern assured Congress that the law "would not change the status of the island . . . relative to the United States. . . . It would not alter the powers of sovereignty acquired by the United States under the terms of the Treaty of Paris."[37] In attempting to assure House leaders that Public Law 600 did not go too far in granting rights to Puerto Ricans, Muñoz Marín claimed, "if the people of Puerto Rico should go crazy, Congress can always get around and legislate again." Here acknowledging that Congress's plenary power remained firmly in place, Muñoz Marín nevertheless was certain that Congress would not need to step in to rein in Puerto Rico: "I am confident that the Puerto Ricans will not do that [go crazy], and invite congressional legislation that would *take back something that was given to the people of Puerto Rico as good American citizens*" (emphasis added).[38]

As he did throughout the hearings, Muñoz Marín appealed to Congress by calling forth the notion that Puerto Ricans were good US citizens who had earned this concession from Congress with their half century of obedience and by having proved themselves capable of exercising a proper democracy. At one point in the hearings, he stated that "Puerto Rico is one of the best working democracies of the world. . . . The United States has not always received the credit it rightly deserves, especially in the Latin America area, for its basic democratic and equalitarian attitude toward civilized people of a different culture."[39] Thus, not only was Puerto Rico's exercise in democracy attributable to the United States, and presumably its years of tutelage, but enacting Public Law 600 would also allow the world to see for itself what the United States had done for Puerto Rico. Muñoz Marín was now a long way from the young politician who had blamed the United States for Puerto Rico's tragedies; instead, here he was appealing to the United States' desire to be seen as just and equitable in the growing Cold War.

With Muñoz Marín's and Fernós Isern's assurances that nothing in Public Law 600 would change the existing prerogatives of the US government in Puerto Rico, the statute sailed through Congress and was signed by President Truman in July 1950. Now that it had been enacted, Puerto Rican leaders could draft a constitution, and the people of Puerto Rico would vote on whether to ratify it. Once Puerto Rican voters ratified the constitution, it would go back to Congress, which would assure that the constitution complied with the requirements set out in Public Law 600. After Congress certified the constitution, it would go into effect, and the Puerto Rican government would be reorganized in compliance with the new constitution. In this way the ELA would be brought into existence.

The language of "in the nature of a compact" and its ambiguity quickly became the source of endless debate. For many, especially those who supported independence and statehood, the idea that Public Law 600 created a compact between the United States and Puerto Rico was merely empty rhetoric. The fact that Muñoz Marín and Fernós Isern had both agreed that nothing would fundamentally change about the archipelago's relationship with the federal government was definitive proof that the so-called compact was a lie. If the relationship remained a colonial one, then Public Law 600 was a farce. If Puerto Rico remained unincorporated, then it was still a colony under the thumb of Congress's plenary power.[40]

For Muñoz Marín and the PPD, however, the statements made in the hearings and the ambiguity of the "compact" language were just semantics. What mattered, he argued, was that Puerto Rico's legal status had changed, even if the terms had not. Even if Puerto Rico remained unincorporated, it was no longer a non-self-governing territory; its political status had changed. Furthermore, the "compact" meant that the application of federal law in Puerto Rico was no longer due to Congress's plenary power but due to the compact itself, the agreement between Puerto Rico and the United States, with the consent of the Puerto Rican people. This compact, Muñoz Marín argued, could not be amended without the consent of the people.[41]

The referendum on Public Law 600 took place on June 4, 1951. Despite opposition from the Independence, Nationalist, and Statehood Parties and ambivalence on the part of many, Public Law 600 was approved by 76.5 percent of voters.[42] A constitutional convention was elected in August 1951, and the delegates met from September 1951 to February 1952 to collectively draft a constitution for Puerto Rico. The proposed constitution followed the basic outlines of many state constitutions, but it contained some key differences. The provisions in its bill of rights were modeled after the newly created Universal Declaration of Human Rights approved by the United Nations and the American Declaration of the Rights and Duties of Man, approved by the

Organization of American States (OAS). Both of these documents contained broad provisions for civil and political rights.

When the constitution was sent to Congress for approval (a sore spot for Muñoz Marín and the PPD, who saw the need for approval as undermining the principles established in Public Law 600), many in Congress balked at the socialist-leaning provisions that mirrored the UN and OAS declarations.[43] They demanded the removal of sections that enshrined the right to social protections in the event of unemployment, sickness, old age, or disability; the right to work; the right to an adequate standard of living; and the rights of mothers and children to special care and assistance.[44] Other provisions about compulsory public education also ruffled Congress and so had to be removed. In the end, the constitution was approved pending the removal of those "unfavorable" provisions that sought to guarantee Puerto Ricans fuller rights.

After the constitution was drafted, it was sent to President Truman for his approval with a letter from Muñoz Marín attached. That letter stated that "the relationship between the United States and Puerto Rico, although increasingly liberal, was established by unilateral action. . . . The present process is based on bilateral action through free agreement. . . . The principle that the relationship is from now on one of *consent through free agreement*, wipes out all trace of colonialism" (emphasis added).[45] Though we know that the constitution of Puerto Rico did not wipe out all traces of colonialism in the United States–Puerto Rico relationship, it is striking how often the language of consent was repeated, not only by Muñoz Marín and the PPD but also by US officials. Truman's own letter of transmission of the constitution to Congress repeats the language of consent.[46] With this constitution, Puerto Ricans were consenting to be governed, and concomitantly, the United States could not take unilateral action with respect to Puerto Rico without its consent. The Constitution of Puerto Rico came into force on July 25, 1952, and with it, the Commonwealth of Puerto Rico was born.

The United States, Puerto Rico, and the United Nations

Despite the back-and-forth between the PPD leaders and Congress and despite the explicit assurances that the ELA would do nothing to displace congressional power in Puerto Rico, the United States and Puerto Rico quickly moved to have the archipelago recognized as a self-governing territory before the United Nations (UN). The United States hoped that recognition of Puerto Rico's self-governance would burnish US human rights bona fides in the international community. Meanwhile, Muñoz Marín and the Populares hoped that quick recognition at the UN would force the United States to acknowledge Puerto Rico's new sovereignty as well as definitively settle the question of Puerto Rico's colonial status for those in the archipelago who were skeptical of the new legal entity.[47]

Formed at the end of World War II and in the wake of the Holocaust, in 1952, the UN was still a fairly young international organization. In the years after its formation, with the ascendency of human rights organizations and legal instruments, the promise of the UN seemed great, and powerful nations jockeyed for position while smaller countries sought recognition and a voice in the global order. As the Cold War years wore on, the UN became the stage for countless disputes between the United States and the West, on one side, and the Soviet Union and other communist or socialist governments, on the other.

In 1947, UN members who administered non-self-governing territories were asked to identify their respective territories. The United States identified and agreed to transmit information to the UN secretary-general on Alaska, American Samoa, Hawai'i, the Panama Canal Zone, Puerto Rico, and the US Virgin Islands.[48] Furthermore, the UN General Assembly also took the position "that as the aim of dependent territories was full self-government, it was indispensable for the United Nations to receive information on political and constitutional development [in the territories]."[49] The adoption of these provisions and the creation of committees to administer them became somewhat contentious, with the United States and other reporting nations quibbling over the requirements.

Against this backdrop, it is not surprising that on January 19, 1953, six months after the creation of the ELA, the United States notified the UN about Puerto Rico's new status and that the United States would no longer transmit reports on the status of the archipelago. Furthermore, the United States requested that Puerto Rico be removed from the UN's list of non-self-governing territories. Fernós Isern appeared before the Committee on Information from Non-Self-Governing Territories in August 1953 to proclaim that Puerto Rico had attained full internal self-government in political, economic, social, and cultural affairs in 1952, with the adoption of the Constitution of the Commonwealth of Puerto Rico.[50] Furthermore, he stressed that the compact and the constitution had both been initiated by the people of Puerto Rico and were based on free decisions by the electorate.

The debate concerning Puerto Rico's status began in October 1953 and led to lively discussions among the delegates regarding reporting requirements and what constituted self-governance under UN regulations. The question up for debate was, as stated by the delegate from Guatemala, whether "the new status warranted the territory's being regarded as a territory which had achieved a full measure of self-government in one of the accepted forms, that is, *association with a metropolitan country on an equal footing*" (emphasis added).[51] This equal footing provision was the sticking point for several delegates. The Indian delegate stressed that Puerto Rico remained economically dependent on the United States, while Mexico and Honduras pointed out that the ELA "suffered from certain defects" that warranted the continuation of reporting.[52] Guatemala voiced the strongest opposition, stating that while "Puerto Rico had made an important step towards self-government, it did not yet correspond to the full measure of self-government required by the UN Charter, and did not therefore justify the cessation of the transmission of information by the US."[53] Not surprisingly, the Soviet Union, the Ukrainian Soviet Socialist Republic, Czechoslovakia, Poland, and Yugoslavia all opposed Puerto Rico's removal from the list and the cessation of transmission of information on the archipelago. The Ukrainian delegate simply stated that the terms of the ELA "could not disguise the fact that [Puerto Rico] continued to be a United States colony."[54]

The US delegate rejected the many arguments made by the opposing delegates and declared, "The previous status of Puerto Rico was that of a territory subject to the *full authority of the Congress of the United States in all governmental matters*. . . . The present status of Puerto Rico is that of a people with a constitution of their own adoption, stemming from their *own authority, which only they can amend*. The relationships previously established . . . have now become provisions of a *compact of a bilateral nature whose terms may only be changed by common consent*" (emphasis added).[55] These arguments rang particularly disingenuous given that Congress retained its full authority over Puerto Rico and had insisted that it retain that authority throughout the process of the creation of the ELA. The matter of the compact of a bilateral nature was again raised, even while it was already clear to many in Puerto Rico and the United States that the rhetoric meant very little without legal teeth to back it up. Nevertheless, the magic words assuaged the concerns of hesitant delegates. In the end, the politics of the day, as well as the power the United States held in the region and in the UN, played a large part in moving the delegates to vote in favor of the United States' proposal. After much back-and-forth and spirited debates, on November 27, 1953, the General Assembly of the United Nations removed Puerto Rico from its list of non-self-governing territories and passed a resolution stating that it thought it appropriate that information on Puerto Rico cease to be transmitted.[56]

In light of these events and the US delegate's arguments before the UN, Muñoz Marín and other PPD leaders argued for years that Puerto Rico had ceased to be under Congress's plenary power and was no longer a colony of the United States. According to these leaders, with the creation of the ELA, the federal government's power arose from the compact itself, which they understood to mean that Congress could not unilaterally amend the Constitution of Puerto Rico. This type of arrangement was "a new and novel form of government. It did not, like earlier home rule arrangements for territories, presuppose eventual Puerto Rican statehood; it was seen as responding to Puerto Rico's desire to remain part of the United States while retaining a distinct culture and language."[57]

Conclusion

While it is clear today that the dynamic between the archipelago and the United States did not cease to be a colonial one after the creation of the ELA, in 1952 many believed it had. For my grandfather, Antonio del Valle, the ELA, Operation Bootstrap, and the industrialization they ushered in offered a lifeline. Gone were the days of reliance on seasonal, agricultural work to survive, of hustling to make enough to eat, of poverty and precarity. The mid-twentieth century in Puerto Rico was full of possibilities for those willing to take advantage of them, and for many of my grandfather's generation, those possibilities were opened up by Luis Muñoz Marín, the PPD, and the ELA.

The ELA allowed the people of Puerto Rico to believe that the colonial relationship had been, if not dissolved, then at least radically reconfigured. In conjunction with the material gains that Operation Bootstrap had afforded broad swaths of the Puerto Rican population, for a time the ELA obfuscated the colonial contours of the dynamic between the archipelago and the United States. The ELA seemed to provide Puerto Ricans with what they wanted at the time: a change in status for the archipelago and the end to traditional, extractive, plantation-based colonialism. The ELA allowed Puerto Ricans to believe they had gained local autonomy and something like sovereignty. After all, the changes ushered in during the mid-twentieth century had radically improved the lives of thousands. The fact that those changes had been negotiated by Muñoz Marín and the PPD also pointed to the effectiveness of both Operation Bootstrap and the ELA.

Beyond the material changes in Puerto Rico, the ELA also established a new common sense of local autonomy in close association with the United States. Over the next sixty-five years, Puerto Rican identity became deeply enmeshed with the notion of the ELA. In the mid-twentieth century, the political project of the ELA was part of a two-pronged governmental approach. On the one hand, the Puerto Rican government set out to modernize the archipelago through economic and land reform, to industrialize and to "bootstrap" the Puerto Rican economy to that of the United States. On the other hand, the government also sought to instill a sense of pride in Puerto Rican history and identity through a project of cultural nationalism known as Operación Serenidad (Operation Serenity). This project emphasized the unique history, language, and culture of the archipelago while also stressing that Puerto Rico could maintain these unique attributes while being closely associated with the United States. The project of cultural nationalism sought to integrate into the ELA those who had fought for a political nation for Puerto Rico and those who viewed Puerto Rican identity and culture as distinct from and irreconcilable with US American culture.[58]

Perhaps one of the most lasting effects of the ELA's creation was the organization of Puerto Rican politics along two main ideas and two parties: one in favor of the ELA and one against it and in favor of statehood and mainland integration. For the past seventy years, political conversations in the archipelago, and indeed ideas about Puerto Rico's future possibilities, have been framed either in opposition to or in alignment with the ELA. The many referendums on Puerto Rico's status that have been held over that time period have all been framed to some extent around this dichotomy. On both sides, political leaders, academics, journalists, and others have understood the archipelago's possible future either as a state of the United States or as a continued commonwealth. The possibilities of independence and political nationhood have long been nonstarters for a majority of Puerto Ricans.

In the end what, if anything, did the events of 1952 do to upend the logics put in place by *Downes v. Bidwell*? The simple answer is very little. *Downes* made it through the creation of the ELA unscathed and in place. Subsequently, in the 1956 case, *Reid v. Covert*, a plurality of the US Supreme Court stated that "neither the [Insular] cases nor their reasoning should be given any further expansion."[59] However, that ruling did nothing to walk back or undo the colonial dynamics put into place in *Downes* and the other Insular Cases. So, despite the decades of arguing over whether Puerto Rico and the United States entered into a compact or not and what the terms of that compact might have been, *Downes* remained the underlying structure of the United States–Puerto Rico relationship. Congress and Trías Monge certainly understood that whatever compacts the United States entered into with Puerto Rico and whatever new legal labels were created, without an abrogation of *Downes*, little would change in the relationship between the United States and the archipelago.

In the first few decades of the twentieth century, Puerto Ricans were clamoring for decolonization. For some, that took the shape of statehood; for others, it took the shape of independence; and for still others, it took the shape of a sort of dominion status. The ELA was the compromise solution that was marketed as offering decolonization. It didn't. And political leaders across the spectrum understood this well. Puerto Rican Nationalist Party leader Pedro Albizu Campos stated as much in his rejection of Public Law 600. "In Puerto Rico only the US has jurisdiction," he stated. "That law can be annulled by the US Congress [at any time.]"[60] Former ally of Muñoz Marín and PPD leader Vicente Geigel Polanco also understood this to be true, and his insistent rejection of Public Law 600 caused his break with Muñoz Marín and the party.

Downes v. Bidwell remains binding law, and Puerto Rico remains an unincorporated territory. Over the course of the decades since the ELA's creation, Congress has exercised ever-greater power in Puerto Rico. The Supreme Court has affirmed *Downes*'s supremacy, proclaiming that any powers Puerto Rico has to govern itself were delegations of congressional power and not sui generis. The fact remains that Congress continues to hold plenary power in Puerto Rico, and the reasons articulated in *Downes*—that Puerto Ricans are racially inferior and are incapable of exercising a proper democracy—continue to undergird that plenary power.

CHAPTER FIVE

Puerto Rico in Never-Never Land

On July 25, 2016, a death notice appeared in the print edition of the newspaper *Primera Hora*.[1] It announced the demise of the "Estado Libre Asociado (ELA, 1952–2016)" and thanked the people of Puerto Rico for having withstood sixty-four years of political limbo. The notice also called on "the spirit of self-determination to illuminate every heart and grant them courage to face that which appears impossible." The announcement coincided with the sixty-fourth celebration of Puerto Rico's Constitution Day—a holiday in the territory—which commemorates the signing of Puerto Rico's constitution and the creation of the ELA, or Commonwealth of Puerto Rico. That same day, a group of opponents of the ELA and pro-statehood activists led a procession through the streets of the Puerta de Tierra sector of San Juan from the Capitol building to Luis Muñoz Rivera Park, where a symbolic liberty bell hangs. The procession was led by a group of *lloronas*, veiled female mourners dressed in traditional funereal black. Mourners carried a coffin in which the symbolic ELA was laid to rest, which they deposited outside the headquarters of the Partido Popular Democrático de Puerto Rico, the pro-Commonwealth party founded by Luis Muñoz Marín.

Though this dramatic performance was orchestrated by proponents of statehood for Puerto Rico, nevertheless it was emblematic of many Puerto Ricans' understanding of the archipelago's place as a US colony. When the death notice, which was actually the creation of Puerto Rican artist Karlo Andrei Ibarra, entreated Puerto Ricans to have the "courage to face that which appeared impossible," to proponents of statehood that undoubtedly meant making Puerto Rico the fifty-first state. However, Ibarra's tongue-in-cheek invocation aptly spoke across the political spectrum. The events of that summer called Puerto Ricans to imagine what a future without the Commonwealth might look like. For many, that meant the time for statehood had arrived. For others, the events of the summer of 2016 and the proverbial death of the ELA meant that the possibility of a different political future might be near.

This chapter focuses on Puerto Rico's recent past, beginning in June 2015, when Puerto Rico's then-governor, Alejandro Garcia Padilla, declared the territory's debts to be unpayable. Since then, the United States' actions toward

Puerto Rico have reverted to a form of blatant and obvious colonialism that, for many, hadn't been visible since before the creation of the ELA. June 2016 saw the US government and Supreme Court reinstitute the types of colonial policies that many Puerto Ricans believed to have died with the creation of the ELA. For others, the United States' actions in June 2016 were entirely expected and unsurprising; Puerto Ricans were living in a colony, after all. No matter how much the ELA had tried to obfuscate or dress up Puerto Rico's relationship with the United States, its colonial underpinnings were still present. And significantly, the legal logics that had first established the colonial relationship were still present. Despite more than one hundred years and countless changes in policy, the 1901 *Downes* decision was still good law and, I argue, still the guiding logic with which the United States related to Puerto Rico.

June 2016 began with the US Supreme Court's decisions in two important cases about Puerto Rico: *Puerto Rico v. Sánchez Valle* and *Puerto Rico v. Franklin California Tax-Free Trust, et al*. Collectively, these cases asked the Court to define the limits of Puerto Rico's power to govern itself. June culminated with Congress's passage of the Puerto Rico Oversight, Management, and Economic Stability Act (more commonly referred to by its acronym, PROMESA), which was meant to address the archipelago's billions of dollars of outstanding debt. For many Puerto Ricans, it was obvious that, collectively, these actions of June 2016 spelled the demise of the ELA. Unfortunately, June 2016 also saw the reentrenchment of the sort of unapologetic and unabashed colonialism that had existed in the archipelago prior to the creation of the ELA.

The events of June 2016 ushered in a new era of United States–Puerto Rico relations. The ELA's veneer of efficacy and the notion of local autonomy that it had offered were stripped away. PROMESA's implementation of an unelected financial control board to oversee Puerto Rico's economy made apparent to everyone that Puerto Rico was set to live a new moment of colonial domination in service of US capital. As I watched the events of that month unfold, I could not help but think of *Downes v. Bidwell*. Though the Court took great care to not directly invoke that decision, its legacy loomed large. Here, after more than one hundred years, was *Downes* rearing its head and affirming once again that federal power was firmly in place in Puerto Rico and that despite the changes that a century had brought to the world and to the archipelago, little had changed in the structures between the two. The Court's 2016 decisions acted as legal bookends to *Downes*; we had come back full circle to the case and to its affirmations of colonial power and the racialized logics that initially produced it. In 2016, the Court took great pains to uphold *Downes* without ever naming the decision or invoking its racialized logic.

Four years later, in June 2020, the Court once again affirmed *Downes* in *Financial Oversight and Management Board for Puerto Rico v. Aurelius Investment, LLC, et al.*, but this time the Court explicitly stated as much. *Aurelius* gave the Court another opportunity to correct a century-old injustice. Indeed, the Court received amicus curiae (friend of the court) briefs from many Puerto Rican lawyers and politicians urging it to do just that. However, the Court, while acknowledging *Downes's* ignominious history, opted to leave it firmly in place, even as the Court repudiated the racism that had spawned the decision.

However, the *Downes* decision cannot be separated from its racist logics and underpinnings. The impulse to exclude Puerto Rico and its residents from the US body politic and civil and constitutional protections, and to uphold federal power to do just that, was born in the racist thinking of the late nineteenth and early twentieth centuries. We cannot divorce *Downes's* outcome from its racist intent, just as we cannot divorce the Supreme Court's decision in *Plessy v. Ferguson*, that separate could indeed be equal when it came to race and accommodation, from its racist intent. *Downes* and *Plessy* are fruit of the same racist tree. As a society we revile *Plessy*, and it was effectively overturned by the Court's *Brown v. Board of Education of Topeka* decision in 1952 and the subsequent passage of the Civil Rights Act of 1964. Yet *Downes* lives on and continues to perpetuate the exclusion and inequality of Puerto Rico. As legal historian Maggie Blackhawk has argued, "constitutional law comprised by colonialism, like that comprised by slavery [and segregation,] should be identified as constitutional failure."[2] Those failures of constitutional law must then be rejected as poisoned fruit, as both *Dred Scott* and *Plessy* were rejected. Yet, decisions like those of the Marshall Trilogy and *Downes* live on and continue to have effect. This chapter considers how *Downes's* racist legacy is lived in Puerto Rico, and how *Downes's* logics continue to constrain the archipelago's political possibilities, its future trajectory, and its residents' everyday existences.

Death of the Estado Libre Asociado de Puerto Rico: A Performance in Five Acts

Act I — *Setting the Stage: How Did We Get Here?*

The past twenty years have been a period of massive upheaval and deterioration in Puerto Rico. The material gains many residents saw in the mid-twentieth century—access to property and credit, stable incomes, accessible health care, healthy pensions, and the creation of a middle class in Puerto Rico—have all but disappeared. Today, nearly half of Puerto Rico's populace is living below the federal poverty line and accessing some form of government assistance.[3] These conditions have only been exacerbated by the events of the past several years—economic policies driven by debt and austerity, the contraction of the public sector, and several environmental disasters. Over that time, we have seen the Puerto Rico government declare itself unable to pay its assumed debts. We have also seen a flurry of lobbying on behalf of banks, hedge funds, and other financial entities to ensure that no matter the outcome, Puerto Rico must pay. And perhaps the most obvious outcome of the events of the past several years has been the renewed visibility of United States–Puerto Rico colonial dynamics.

The spring of 2016 saw Puerto Rico take center stage in US mainland political debates and media. Puerto Rico, which usually only got the attention of mainland media after a devastating storm or when a presidential primary created the brief obligatory discussion about where Puerto Rico is and why it is allowed delegates in primaries, was suddenly everywhere. What was happening in spring 2016 that led Puerto Rico, the otherwise invisible, often forgotten colony of the United States, to be at the center of mainland political discussions?

The road to that memorable spring was paved during the decade preceding it, when the government of Puerto Rico, mired in a deep recession, accrued billions of dollars in debt. The colony's economy had been contracting since the height of the purported Puerto Rican economic miracle in the mid-twentieth century.[4] This so-called miracle was created and sustained by industrialization that was fueled by a series of federal and local tax incentives that made the colony attractive. Puerto Rico became a hub for manufactured goods that were exported directly back to the United States. The subsidies were extremely attractive to many US industries, and throughout the second half of the twentieth century hundreds of US corporations set up shop in the territory. The incentives were established for a term of years; when the term expired, industries would often close down their operations and move to other destinations, such as the Dominican Republic, where labor was cheaper. These subsidies saw the development and eventual departure of several major industries in the latter half of the twentieth century. For example, a bustling petrochemical corridor developed along the Caribbean coast in the Guayama municipality in the mid-twentieth century, attracting major chemical refiners such as Union Carbide and the Phillips Petroleum

Company.[5] This industry eventually wound down in the early 1980s, leaving an industrial graveyard that now sits rusting along the picturesque coastal highway.

In the early 1990s, the federal tax subsidies that created the miracle in Puerto Rico were ended as part of the negotiations to enact the North American Free Trade Agreement (NAFTA). The incentives would have a ten-year phaseout period to allow industries to plan for the end of subsidies and, presumably, to allow Puerto Rico to attract other industries and diversify its economy.[6] By 2006, with the end of the last of the tax subsidies, an exodus of industry out of Puerto Rico was well underway and, concurrently, so were the loss of jobs for residents and the loss of an income base for the government. As a result of these changes, Puerto Rico was already in a substantial recession when the global Great Recession began. In the face of this loss of industry and economic decline, Puerto Rico's government began borrowing to sustain itself. It also began implementing a regime of austerity that saw the implementation of a value-added tax (VAT) in Puerto Rico for the first time. That tax currently stands at 11.5 percent, among the highest in the United States. Furthermore, government austerity measures radically reduced the government work force; the territory's government, once the largest employer in Puerto Rico, began to shed jobs at an alarming rate. Concomitantly, the government also began a regime of privatization of government services and infrastructure, such as education and roads. Schools began to close at a dizzying pace, with students shuffled to new locations, while the number of jobs for teachers shrunk greatly. Finally, and perhaps most detrimentally to government workers, the Puerto Rico government began reducing pension contributions and cutting benefits.

These measures meant that the colony's government limped along during the late 2000s and into the early 2010s. During this time, Puerto Rico began to see a slow drain of its population as more and more Puerto Ricans decamped for the mainland United States. Many of these migrants were college-educated and looking for professional opportunities that were unavailable in Puerto Rico. Life for Puerto Ricans in the archipelago became ever more difficult as the decade wore on. Meanwhile, the territory government continued its borrowing, often committing itself to ever more untenable adhesion contracts created by the banks and hedge funds that lent to Puerto Rico. The contracts contained outrageous terms, high interest rates, and unpayable balloon payments.[7]

For observers in the United States, the first that they heard of Puerto Rico's financial troubles came in June 2015 when then-governor Alejandro

García Padilla publicly stated for the first time that Puerto Rico's debt had become unpayable.[8] Much like the millions of individuals who find themselves overwhelmed by credit card debt, Puerto Rico was "caught in a vicious circle where it borrowed to balance the budget, raised the debt, and had an even bigger budget deficit the next year."[9] Puerto Rico's declaration came on the heels of the very public municipal bankruptcies in Detroit, Michigan, and Stockton, California. However, Puerto Rico's municipal bond obligations were worth over eight times more than Detroit's. Furthermore, unlike municipalities in the US mainland, the Constitution of Puerto Rico contained a provision, meant to attract investors to the territory, that required general obligation debts—those debts taken on with the backing of the government—to be paid before other obligations, including payments to worker pensions and government services.[10] And crucially, US federal bankruptcy laws barred Puerto Rico from seeking relief and restructuring its debts through bankruptcy, as the mainland municipalities had. The situation was unprecedented. Thus, García Padilla's public declaration that the colony would not be able to make future debt payments raised a slew of questions about what was to be done with Puerto Rico. Short of restructuring its obligations with its individual lenders and seeking more favorable terms—a proposition that seemed unlikely—Puerto Rico was looking at a potential default the likes of which had not been seen in US history.

Puerto Rico quickly became dubbed the "Greece of the Caribbean" in a comparison to the Greek debt crisis that had hobbled that country and sent the Eurozone into a tizzy following the worldwide Great Recession of 2007-8.[11] Pundits, politicians, and academics began weighing in with ideas and suggestions about what should be done with Puerto Rico. Meanwhile, García Padilla's government lobbied Congress to allow it to restructure its debt as Detroit had done in 2013. Wanting to be paid in full, and unwilling to negotiate more favorable terms for Puerto Rico, the colony's creditors struck back. Millions of dollars poured into lobbying Congress against a bailout that would have seen the archipelago's debts restructured to the detriment of the banks. More was spent on political advertisements meant to scare the US public about a potential bailout for Puerto Rico. The ads played on people's ignorance about Puerto Rico and employed racist fear tactics. In one ad, a voice can be heard saying, "After years of wild overspending, Puerto Rico is out of money. Who will bail out Puerto Rico? Washington says you will."[12] While these ominous words are spoken, images of visibly angry older people frowning are displayed. The ad then claims that the cost of a bailout would be borne by "savers and seniors" in the mainland United

States. In another ad, an older woman, Teresa, explains that she bought Puerto Rico bonds thinking they were safe because they were government-backed. As we see Teresa impassively looking at the camera, we hear the words "Congress wants to bail out Puerto Rico with Teresa's retirement savings."[13] The ads raised the specter of the hard-working retirees and seniors of the US mainland paying to help the Spanish-speaking Black and brown islanders of Puerto Rico, who had been too irresponsible to prevent the debt crisis. These tactics worked to turn the US public, most of whom could not find Puerto Rico on a map, against allowing Puerto Rico to restructure its debts through a federally permitted bankruptcy process.

On the other side of the debate were the countless Puerto Ricans, both in the archipelago and in the diaspora, who called on Congress to find an equitable solution, one that would not require the people of Puerto Rico to pay for the billions in debt through further austerity. In the years leading up to 2016, the people of Puerto Rico had been saddled with ever more austerity, from new forms of taxes, to higher utility rates, to bigger fees for basic services. Countless opinion pieces appeared in major newspapers offering ideas and arguing both sides of the issue.[14] The *New York Times* editorial board even chimed in with essays, titled "Don't Abandon Puerto Rico" and "Congress Needs to Throw Puerto Rico a Lifeline," that urged Congress to facilitate a debt restructuring.[15]

On May 1, 2016, Puerto Rico's largest debt payment to that date, $422 million, was due. As the May deadline approached and it became clear that Puerto Rico would default on its obligations, the frenzied interest in Puerto Rico grew. As so many times both before and after this moment, Puerto Rico was most visible to those in the continental United States in the midst of crisis. Perhaps the most lasting image many have of this time is of playwright and actor Lin-Manuel Miranda, then at the height of his *Hamilton* fame, lobbying Congress to do something, anything, to address Puerto Rico's debt crisis. In March, during a visit to Congress, he famously offered up *Hamilton* tickets, which were nearly impossible to get, as an incentive to urge members to act. One month later, he visited *Last Week Tonight with John Oliver* and performed an original rap:

We have to help our island, just 100 miles across.
To recap, 3.5 million American civilians are on the hook for billions.
Vulture funds are circling and lobbying for payout.
There's nothing left to tax or cut,
We're stuck, we need a way out.

Allow them to restructure.
There's no structure for what happens if you let this crisis play out,
When May is only a day out.
It's non-partisan.
The hard part is in convincing Congress Puerto Rico matters,
So their heart is in the fight for relief,
Not a bailout, just relief.
A belief that you can pass legislation to ease our grief.
   (emphasis in the original)[16]

Miranda's heartfelt performance tried to undo some of the disinformation about Puerto Rico's debt crisis that had been sown in the attack ads, while also trying to persuade Congress to act to address the plight of Puerto Rico. In doing so, he also slipped into well-worn tropes used in the past to urge Congress to act on behalf of Puerto Rico. He invoked the fact that Puerto Ricans are US citizens, and so Congress and the US people owe them care and protection. In the three-minute performance, he emphasized the small size of Puerto Rico several times, again attempting to move the viewer. The performance was meant to elicit sympathy for Puerto Rico and to supplicate Congress to act on its behalf. But in doing so, the performance invoked long-standing stereotypes of Puerto Ricans as helpless and in need of salvation from Congress. These same narratives were used in the early twentieth century to justify the initial invasion and colonization of Puerto Rico, as well as policies meant to Americanize Puerto Ricans and train them to be proper US subjects. Indeed, these narratives were invoked by the Supreme Court in *Downes*, when the justices declared that the territories, being as they were inhabited by racial "mongrels" who were untrained in the ways of Anglo-Saxon governance, would need the aid of the United States to become full-grown democratic citizens.

The performance also highlighted the fact that Puerto Rico's lack of representation left it in the position of supplicant to Congress. Over the century of Puerto Rico's colonization under US rule, the colony has had to rely on spokespeople in the diaspora to bring its issues before Congress and the US people. Miranda, as a successful, highly visible, and well-regarded Diasporican, was just the latest to step into that role in order to make Puerto Rico's situation visible to the US public. Surrogates for Puerto Rico often rely heavily on the logic that Puerto Ricans are US citizens and, as such, Congress owes them protection. These surrogates traffic in the same stereotypes that US Americans make about Puerto Rico being helpless without Congress, as well as shaming Congress and the United States for the poor treatment of Puerto Ricans and poor conditions in Puerto Rico.

As was expected, Puerto Rico missed the May deadline and failed to pay the $422 million owed on that date. This default led to much speculation about what would happen next. The territory had another payment due two months later, in July, and that one was even larger, at $2 billion. That payment included about $800 million in general obligation bonds, which the Constitution of Puerto Rico required to be paid. While the month churned on, the territory continued to negotiate with bondholders and continued to lobby Congress to allow it to file for federal Chapter 9 bankruptcy, which is available to certain municipalities and governmental entities. Speaking on the eve of the May 1 default, García Padilla said, "If Congress fails to authorize a mechanism to restructure our debt, the 3.5 million American citizens who live in Puerto Rico will continue to suffer."[17] Puerto Ricans in the territory and in the continental United States waited to see how Congress would respond.

Meanwhile, two major legal cases that could resolve some of the overarching questions of Puerto Rico's crisis were pending before the US Supreme Court. These cases, *Puerto Rico v. Sánchez Valle* and *Puerto Rico v. Franklin California Tax-Free Trust, et al.*, had been argued before the Court the previous October, and many awaited the Court's opinions, some with hope that the Court would resolve some of the uncertainties about Puerto Rico's status vis-à-vis the United States and others with trepidation that the Court would double down on the territory's colonial status. The two opinions were released within days of each other in June 2016. The Court, anticipating congressional action on the debt crisis and not wanting to take any definitive stance that could be understood as a declaration about the status of Puerto Rico, took its usual approach to the territory and put the issue back to Congress. In failing to take a strong stance, the Court effectively doubled down on its *Downes* decision by affirming Congress's plenary power and leaving the ultimate fate of Puerto Rico entirely to Congress.

A few weeks after the Court issued its opinions, Congress did indeed act, though perhaps not in the way Lin-Manuel Miranda and other Puerto Ricans who had lobbied Congress might have wanted. On June 30, Congress passed the much-reviled Puerto Rico Oversight, Management, and Economic Stability Act, or PROMESA, as it is commonly known. With its passage, Congress reaffirmed its plenary power over Puerto Rico and effectively stripped the territory of its ability to self-govern. PROMESA tore off the veneer of self-governance that had lingered over Puerto Rico since the creation of the ELA in 1952 and reinstituted the sort of colonial structures that had existed in the first half of the twentieth century. June 2016 saw the Supreme Court and Congress collectively take Puerto Rico and its residents back more than a century, to *Downes* and to a colonial dynamic many thought they'd left behind.

Act II — June 9, 2016: Puerto Rico v. Sánchez Valle

On June 9, 2016, the Supreme Court handed down its decision in the case of *Puerto Rico v. Sánchez Valle*.[18] This was the first of a series of sledgehammer-like blows to Puerto Rico's last semblances of local autonomy and purported local sovereignty. After sixty-five years of the ELA and much squabbling about the meaning and parameters of that status, the Court finally offered some definitive answers.

Luis Sánchez Valle was indicted for selling a gun to an undercover police officer on September 28, 2008. He was charged with the illegal sale of a firearm and ammunition without a license and the illegal carrying of a firearm, violations under the Puerto Rico Arms Trafficking Act. Shortly after, a federal grand jury also indicted him on similar charges under federal arms trafficking laws, which carry more lenient penalties than the Puerto Rico charges. Sánchez Valle pleaded guilty to the federal charges and was sentenced to a five-month prison sentence followed by five months' house arrest and three years' supervised release. After accepting guilt for the federal charges, Sánchez Valle moved to have the Puerto Rico charges dropped on the ground that double jeopardy had attached. The US Constitution's Fifth Amendment prohibits a defendant from being tried twice for the same exact offense. Sánchez Valle argued that he had been tried and found guilty already under federal law, so he could not be tried again under Puerto Rican law. The trial court agreed and dropped the charges against him.

The government of Puerto Rico, however, disagreed. The Double Jeopardy Clause allows for two prosecutions for the same offense if the prosecutions stem from two separate sovereigns. This is where the Puerto Rico prosecutors hung their case. They appealed the decision to the federal district court, arguing that Puerto Rico is, in fact, a separate sovereign for purposes of the dual sovereign exception to the Double Jeopardy Clause. This is the question that ultimately wound up in front of the Supreme Court: Is Puerto Rico a separate sovereign with the ability to prosecute Sánchez Valle under its own statutes despite his guilt in the federal case? Were Puerto Rico one of the fifty states, the answer to this question would have been an emphatic yes. However, this dispute butted right up against the lasting doubts created by the ELA in the mid-twentieth century. In this case, 115 years after *Downes*, the Supreme Court once again found itself asking, "What exactly is Puerto Rico in relationship to the United States?"

Ironically, and in a circular sort of way, the fact that the question persists more than a century after *Downes* is indeed the fault of what the decision established about the relationship in the first place. In 1901, the Court punted on giving a definitive answer about what Puerto Rico was. The Court has been kicking the question down the road for more than a century. June 2016 would be no different. *Sánchez Valle* offered the Court the possibility of giving a decisive answer; instead, the Court once again hedged its decision to not give the archipelago more sovereignty than Congress wanted it to have.

During the oral arguments in the case, the justices were visibly flummoxed by what to do with Puerto Rico. With the exception of the lone Puerto Rican voice on the Court, Justice Sonia Sotomayor, the justices were clearly uncomfortable with Puerto Rico's argument that the creation of the ELA and its adoption of a constitution had endowed Puerto Rico with some sort of sovereignty. Likewise, the justices were uncomfortable explicitly reaffirming Puerto Rico's lack of autonomy and colonial status. A demonstrably frustrated Justice Stephen Breyer asked Puerto Rico's attorney, "Well, what is it? That is, look. If we simply write an opinion and it says, Puerto Rico is sovereign, that has enormous implications. . . . The insular cases are totally changed in their applications. . . . The political implications, I'll just stay away from. On the other hand, if we write an opinion that says it's just a territory, that has tremendous implications. . . . How did we tell the UN it wasn't a colony? Why are we not reporting on this colony every year? So, either way, between those two, the implications in law and in politics and everything else are overwhelming."[19]

In this statement Breyer encapsulates the difficulty the Court faced in *Sánchez Valle*, a seemingly straightforward case about criminal prosecution. Puerto Rico's ambiguous relationship with the United States once again intruded into an arena that seemed fairly settled. Even to resolve the question of who can and who cannot be prosecuted for criminal offenses, the archipelago's precarious condition had to be addressed. The Court did not want to overturn the *Downes* decision and its sister Insular Cases but also did not want to state explicitly that Puerto Rico is a US colony without the sovereignty to prosecute criminal matters.

Ultimately, the Court concluded that, in the matter before it, "sovereignty . . . [did] not bear its ordinary meaning." Instead, the Court wrote, "the inquiry does not turn, as the term 'sovereignty' *sometimes suggests*, on the degree to which the second entity is autonomous from the first or sets its own political course. Rather, the issue is *only* whether the prosecutorial powers of the two jurisdictions have independent origins—or, said conversely, whether those powers derive from the same 'ultimate source'" (emphasis added).[20] The Court stated, "The Commonwealth's power to enact and enforce criminal laws proceeds from the island's Constitution as 'ordained' and 'established' by the people. However, Congress conferred the authority to create the island Constitution, which in turn confers authority to bring criminal charges."[21] The Court recognized that Puerto Rico today has a "distinctive, indeed exceptional, status as a self-governing commonwealth." Nevertheless, it is not sovereign for purposes of the dual sovereign exception because it lacks the "inherent sovereignty" that both states of the union and Indian Nations possess. Instead, the archipelago's power to prosecute criminals ultimately stems from Congress and a delegation of congressional power.

In short, because Congress gave Puerto Rico the ability to enact its own constitution, the powers conferred by that document were a delegation of Congress's plenary power over the archipelago. The effect of this finding was to definitively dispel the notion that Puerto Rico had received a special sort of sovereignty, or indeed any sovereignty at all, with the creation of the ELA. Instead, what Puerto Rico received in 1952 was Congress's permission to play at governance, even while Congress reserved the ability to override the colony. In fact, if Puerto Rico's power to perform a most basic governmental function—the prosecution of crime—derives from Congress, then it stands to reason that in fact there is no local facet over which Congress does not also have power, thus leaving the Constitution of Puerto Rico and its purported local autonomy wholly without meaning.

Act III—June 13, 2016: Puerto Rico v.
Franklin California Tax-Free Trust, et al.

A few days after the *Sánchez Valle* decision came down, the Court made its ruling in its second case involving Puerto Rico that term. In *Puerto Rico v. Franklin California Tax-Free Trust, et al.*, the Court went further in affirming the illusory nature of the archipelago's local autonomy.[22] The case stemmed from the government's passage of the Puerto Rico Recovery Act, a bankruptcy law that would have allowed several of the archipelago's municipal entities, including the beleaguered Puerto Rico Electric Power Authority (PREPA), to restructure their debts without the consent of the debt holders—the banks and hedge funds that had lent billions to Puerto Rico. Not surprisingly, those banks and hedge funds sued, claiming that the Recovery Act was barred by federal bankruptcy laws.

The overarching question for the justices was whether Puerto Rico could enact its own bankruptcy laws or whether the federal law preempted it from doing so. To answer this question, the justices had to determine whether Puerto Rico is defined as a state under the bankruptcy code. Chapter 9 of the code preempts states from writing bankruptcy laws that allow indebted municipalities to restructure their debt. However, it does allow municipalities to file for federal bankruptcy with the authorization of the state. For example, to use a well-known case, the state of Michigan could not have written its own state law allowing Detroit to file for bankruptcy; however, Detroit could file for federal bankruptcy if Michigan authorized the municipality to do so. In other words, the state defines who is a debtor and thus who can restructure debt under federal law.

Chapter 9 of the federal Bankruptcy Code defines Puerto Rico as a state for purposes of the code, "*except* for the purposes of defining who may be a debtor under Chapter 9." When the banks sued Puerto Rico for passing the Recovery Act, the territory argued that because Puerto Rico was not a state for the purpose of defining which entities were "debtors," it followed that Puerto Rico was not considered a state at all under Chapter 9 and thus could enact its own bankruptcy laws. The Court disagreed and found that Puerto Rico's municipal entities could not qualify as Chapter 9 debtors and thus could not file for federal bankruptcy, because Puerto Rico doesn't have the power to designate the entities as "debtors." Yet at the same time Puerto Rico remains a state for the other purposes related to Chapter 9, which also means it cannot write its own bankruptcy laws. The Court stated that "it is up to Congress, not Puerto Rico, to decide when the government-owned companies could seek relief."[23]

Confusing, I know. Bankruptcy law is nothing if not opaque, but the provisions that referenced Puerto Rico were not only circular but also nonsensical. The Court's reasoning left the territory in a legal conundrum, the end result of which was the further erosion of Puerto Rico's purported local autonomy and ability to self-govern—two of the hallmarks of the ELA. The Court insisted that Puerto Rico is not a state for the most beneficial parts of Chapter 9, the provision that allows a state to designate who may seek relief in federal bankruptcy; but it is a state for the more restrictive part of the legislation, the prohibition on states passing their own debt-restructuring laws. As a result of this reasoning, once again the archipelago cannot engage in a most basic governmental function: the organization of its economic affairs. This conclusion seemed so irrational to Justice Ruth Bader Ginsburg that while the banks' lawyer made the argument before the justices, she interrupted him and demanded, "Why would Congress put Puerto Rico in this never-never land? That is, it can't use federal bankruptcy law and it can't use a Puerto Rican substitute. . . . Why in the world? What explains Congress wanting to put Puerto Rico in this anomalous position?"[24]

To answer Justice Ginsburg's question, we need only look back to the Supreme Court's own decision in *Downes v. Bidwell*, wherein the Court first placed Puerto Rico in the anomalous position in which it continues to find itself. In 1901, it was the Supreme Court that established the notion of the unincorporated territory and designated Puerto Rico as such an entity under Congress's plenary power. This relationship is what allows Congress to pick and choose which provisions of the federal law will apply to Puerto Rico and how they will be applied. It is this status that allows Congress to exclude the territory and to carve out exceptions for it whenever Congress so chooses. And it's the *Downes* decision that continues to be the organizing principle that undergirds Puerto Rico's colonial relationship with the United States.

*Act IV—June 30, 2016: Puerto Rico Oversight,
Management, and Economic Stability Act*

The final blow to the so-called sovereignty that Puerto Rican lawyers and politicians claimed to have obtained in the early 1950s came on June 30, 2016, when Congress passed PROMESA. The law was an effort to address the most pressing issues in Puerto Rico's debt crisis. García Padilla's 2015 declaration that Puerto Rico's debts were unpayable spurred negotiations for legislation to address the crisis which had been ongoing since that fall. On June 9, in a rare show of unity, the House passed the bipartisan bill for PROMESA and sent it to the Senate for passage. Two days later, President Barack Obama's weekly address to the public focused on Puerto Rico's debt crisis. He commended the House for passing PROMESA and urged the Senate to act quickly.

Obama began the address by affirming that Puerto Ricans are "American citizens just like people in Maine or Oklahoma or New Mexico."[25] As with any discussion about Puerto Rico, the fact of US citizenship had to first be established to explain to mainland Americans why they should care about what happened in the colony. Much as Miranda did in his performance on John Oliver's show, Obama also invoked the poor conditions that Puerto Ricans were living under and the sacrifices they'd had to make to merely survive. Here, again, a call for sympathy for the poor inhabitants of the territory was first necessary to justify what might come next. When describing PROMESA, Obama, speaking directly to the concerns raised in the attack ads, first emphatically proclaimed that the bill "won't cost federal taxpayers a dime." Even in assuaging the fears of federal taxpayers, Obama affirmed Puerto Rico's difference. Had he not just stated that Puerto Ricans are US citizens? Why then was it necessary to differentiate between federal taxpayers and territory residents? These small proclamations of difference are what made the attack ads so effective in the first place. They elided the fact that Puerto Ricans pay taxes in a host of ways and asserted that, though they may be US citizens, their citizenship is, in fact, different.

"[This bill] doesn't include special interest bail outs and it gives Puerto Rico the ability to restructure its debts," the president continued. So, what did it contain? According to Obama, PROMESA would establish "a temporary system of oversight to help implement needed reforms and ensure transparency." He then addressed the concerns raised by people such as Senator Bob Menendez of New Jersey that the bill's oversight mechanism was undemocratic and did not allow Puerto Ricans enough say in the process: "I know that some folks in Puerto Rico are concerned about this kind of oversight but I've always insisted that any solution to this crisis has to respect the democratic rights of the people of Puerto Rico." Indeed, many folks in Puerto Rico were concerned about what oversight would mean for the territory, and with good reason. Despite the very real concern that the bill was undemocratic and fundamentally colonial, PROMESA passed the Senate with bipartisan approval, and Obama signed it into law on June 30.

The "temporary system of oversight" turned out to be the most reviled part of PROMESA: the Financial Oversight and Management Board (FOMB)—or the Junta, as it is called in Puerto Rico—which was put in charge of overseeing the territory's debts.[26] The term "Junta," of course, points back to the dictatorial governments that oversaw many Latin American and Caribbean countries in the twentieth century, often with the support of the United States. Thus, when Puerto Ricans referred to the board as "la Junta," they were quickly connecting this latest colonial entity with the repressive, US-backed neocolonial regimes in place all over the hemisphere in the previous century.

The Junta consists of seven members recommended by Congress and appointed by the president to serve for three-year terms. The members are not accountable to the people of Puerto Rico, nor do they have to have any specialized knowledge about Puerto Rico, and only one member need be a resident of Puerto Rico or have a business in the territory.[27] The members can only be removed by the president for cause. Puerto Rico's governor is an ex officio, nonvoting eighth member. The temporary nature of the board is also yet to be seen. At the time of writing, the board has been in place for eight years and will remain in place until Puerto Rico achieves a balanced budget consistently over four years.

The Junta has broad powers and little accountability. It is in charge of approving budgets and fiscal plans, it can veto debt issuances, and it can determine which projects get funded and which do not. It has the power to hold hearings and to subpoena people and information it deems necessary to meeting its mandate under PROMESA. It also has the power to review and approve any legislation enacted in Puerto Rico for compliance with the directives of the Junta vis-à-vis the fiscal plan. In other words, if a law does not meet with the Junta's approval, the legislature must amend it to comply with the directives of the Junta. If the legislation as amended still does not comply, the Junta has the power to bar enforcement of the legislation altogether. Put simply, the Junta, which consists of seven US-appointed individuals, has the power to override the will of the people of Puerto Rico and its representatives.

Perhaps the most expansive power that the Junta has is the ability to designate a territory or territorial instrumentality as a "covered entity." A "covered entity" then falls under the purview of the board, and it has authority to make decisions with respect to the finances of that entity. In other words, the board, in its sole discretion, has the power to decide precisely what it has power over. On September 30, 2016, the board designated the Commonwealth of Puerto Rico as a covered entity, thereby taking full control over the territory's fiscal affairs.

PROMESA has other unpopular provisions, such as those that allow lowering the minimum wage for certain individuals to a miserly $4.25 an hour, an outrageously low rate that amounts to poverty for those who would receive it. Most insulting to the people of Puerto Rico is the provision of PROMESA that requires Puerto Rico, and thus Puerto Ricans, to pay for the operations of the Junta. In other words, Puerto Ricans, already living under severe forms of austerity, are being forced to pay for the unelected, undemocratic board that decides their economic future. In effect, Puerto Ricans are paying for their own colonization.

Once passed, PROMESA gave Puerto Rico and its creditors a year to negotiate a restructuring agreement. Over the following months, contentious negotiations took place amid a backdrop of protest in the territory. Puerto Ricans, outraged by the imposition of the Junta and by its interest in placating Puerto Rico's creditors rather than considering the future of Puerto Ricans, took to the streets en masse over the subsequent year. On May 3, 2017, the Junta availed itself of the one tool that PROMESA offered the territory: restructuring through bankruptcy. Ironically, this is the very tool that the Puerto Rican government had petitioned Congress for before the passage of PROMESA. Title III of PROMESA contains a form of bankruptcy that mirrors Chapter 9 of the Federal Bankruptcy Code, which, as discussed earlier, applies to municipalities. "The 'Title III' process, as it's called in PROMESA, allows Puerto Rico to address all of its debts at once, in a comprehensive process. It's essentially a bankruptcy process custom-built for Puerto Rico's debt crisis."[28] The Junta alone can initiate the bankruptcy process, and it alone can approve a final bankruptcy exit plan. As the largest-ever municipal bankruptcy the United States had ever seen, and the first in a US territory, Puerto Rico once again found itself in uncharted waters.

With the passage of PROMESA and the Supreme Court's decisions in June 2016, Puerto Ricans immediately understood that the form of "local democracy" that they had purportedly been exercising for more than sixty years was no more. The events of that June had immediate effects on their lives—spurring residents to take to the streets in protest. Perhaps the most visible protest and sign of Puerto Rican's exhaustion and discontent came during the elections of November 2, 2016. While stateside residents were agonizing over who would become our next president, Puerto Ricans demonstrated their understanding of the limitations of colonialism by declining to participate in the territory's elections. Voter turnout was at a record low. In a territory that has historically had some of the highest voter turnout rates in the region, usually in the 75 percent range, only 55 percent of registered voters turned up to cast votes.[29] The rhetoric at the time of the election and the discussion among voters pointed to the fact that Puerto Ricans understood that their votes would have little effect in the face of the Junta's power. Why go through the charade of democracy if in the end colonialism rules the day? Why express a desire if the Junta had the power to ignore it or override it?

Act V—June 1, 2020: Financial Oversight and
Management Board v. Aurelius Investment, LLC

Four years after the Supreme Court's June 2016 decisions, another legal case with the potential to overturn *Downes* made its way before the Court.[30]

Financial Oversight and Management Board for Puerto Rico v. Aurelius Investment, LLC, challenged the constitutionality of the Junta and the Title III bankruptcy proceeding it enacted. *Aurelius* was a peculiar legal matter that brought together disparate parties to argue for the unconstitutionality of the Junta, even while their underlying financial interests were radically at odds.

Aurelius Investment, LLC, part of Aurelius Capital Group, is a hedge fund known for its cutthroat approach to recovering debt payments. The fund's founder, Mark Brodsky, a seasoned corporate lawyer, came to prominence for his work with Elliot Management Corporation, which famously, or perhaps infamously, sued the government of Argentina during its financial crisis.[31] The strategies Brodsky and Elliot Group employed in Argentina—inundating an indebted entity with lawsuits in US and international courts, refusing to accept a debt restructuring, essentially wearing the indebted entity down until it agreed to the fund's terms—have generally become the blueprint for hedge funds acquiring sovereign debt. However, while most hedge funds targeted private corporations, Aurelius became known for targeting indebted nations and "bullying" them in court.[32]

In the year after PROMESA was passed, the Junta went about evaluating Puerto Rico's debt and deciding how to service it. The Junta determined that general obligation debt, like that owned by Aurelius, should be paid out at thirty-five cents for every dollar. In all likelihood, Aurelius paid even less than that to acquire Puerto Rico bonds. However, Aurelius wanted to be paid the full value of the bonds. This is where hedge funds that specialize in distressed debt, like Puerto Rico's and Argentina's before it, make their money. When the Junta enacted the Title III process for Puerto Rico and several of its governmental entities, it became less likely that Aurelius would receive the full payout.

A debt restructuring by its nature is meant to move the order of payment around to ensure that essential services and funds, such as police departments, medical services, and government pensions, are paid first. In a simple proceeding, a judge evaluates the debts of an entity versus its assets and determines who should be paid first and how much. Puerto Rico's bankruptcy is exceedingly complicated and unprecedented.[33] The hierarchy of bond holders is muddled, and available funds are limited. Generally, hedge funds gamble when they invest in sovereign debt because they are usually at the back of the line for payout in a restructuring. However, because of the Puerto Rico Constitution's provision that requires general obligation debt be paid first, Aurelius believed that it and the other hedge funds should be at the front of the line for payment.

In the months before the Junta filed for Title III in May 2017, Aurelius had been pressuring it and the Puerto Rican government to cut funding for "unessential" services such as public television, the Institute of Puerto Rican Culture, and other arts organizations, as well as discretionary funds used to provide aid after natural disasters.[34] These funds, Aurelius argued, should be used to pay bond holders. Title III proceedings froze these individual discussions and moved the debt payment negotiations into bankruptcy court. This, of course, threatened the percentage of payout Aurelius might receive from Puerto Rico as well as the type of pressure it could assert over the negotiations.

On August 7, 2017, Aurelius filed a lawsuit arguing that the Junta was an unconstitutional entity and thus did not have the authority to enact Title III. The seven members of the Junta, Aurelius argued, had not gone through the proper appointment procedure established by Article II of the US Constitution. Article II, Section 2 requires the president to "nominate" all officers of the United States and then with the "advice and consent" of Congress to appoint the officers.[35] Aurelius argued that the Junta members had not undergone confirmation by Congress and thus were not properly acting as officers of the United States. The Junta, then, did not have authority to begin bankruptcy proceedings or to restructure debt agreements.

During its first year in operation, the Junta had also taken aim at public salaries and pensions. For years, the territory's government had been borrowing to pay its obligations to retired Puerto Ricans. At roughly $1,200 a month, pensioners were already receiving meager payments. However, the board decided that a further cut of 8 percent was necessary in order to meet the territory's overall debt burden. Not surprisingly, this move angered Puerto Rican workers and retirees who were already surviving on tight fixed incomes. Numerous public worker unions, such as the Asociación de Maestros de Puerto Rico, the Puerto Rico teacher's union, and the Unión de Trabajadores de la Industria Eléctrica y Riego (UTIER), the union of the Puerto Rico Electric Power Authority (PREPA), immediately began to protest the Junta and rallied public support against the pension cuts.[36]

As discussed earlier, PREPA was one of the most indebted and beleaguered public utilities in Puerto Rico. Like other entities of the Puerto Rican government, PREPA too had fallen into a pattern of borrowing to fund itself at a time when its customer base and revenue were shrinking. When *Aurelius* was filed, PREPA was responsible for $9 billion of the colony's debt, about one-eighth of Puerto Rico's total debt burden, much of it in worker pensions.[37] "The departure of . . . businesses in the 1990's and 2000's, government and political party interference with decision making, irresponsible energy use to benefit for-profit subsidies . . . ineffective rate structure maintenance, and a lack of commitment to public engagement all have led to PREPA's teetering existence."[38] PREPA was an immediate target for reform, and the Junta quickly set about creating a privatization plan for the utility. As a result, on August 7, 2017, UTIER also sued the Junta, adopting the same claims as Aurelius: that the Junta was unconstitutional because it violated the Appointments Clause of the US Constitution.[39]

As is customary when multiple legal disputes raise the same underlying question, the two case were consolidated as they made their way through the federal courts. And so it was that UTIER, whose goal was to keep employee paychecks and pensions intact, and Aurelius, whose goal was the reduction of those same pensions so that Puerto Rico would pay the full price of its bonds, found themselves arguing on the same side. Both entities asserted that the Junta was unconstitutional and that all the work it had done over the previous year should be invalidated.

The question that made its way to the Supreme Court was whether the members of the Junta were "officers of the United States," who had to undergo confirmation, or "officers of a territorial government," who did not. Among the arguments made by the Junta and the US government were that Congress had plenary power, as decided in *Downes*, to make any necessary laws for the territories. Furthermore, relying on the Insular Cases, the Junta and the US government argued that the Constitution's Article II didn't even apply to Puerto Rico, so the question was moot. The First Circuit Court of Appeals decided that Article II did apply to Puerto Rico and that the members of the Junta were officers of the United States and had been acting extraconstitutionally. However, the appeals court declined to invalidate the work the Junta had performed in the years before. Instead, the appeals court found that the Junta members were "de facto officers," whose decisions could not be undone. The First Circuit's judgment would have allowed for the Junta's members to be confirmed by Congress after the fact, because to invalidate members' work would have been unfair and posed an unnecessary burden on everyone involved in Puerto Rico's debt negotiations.

When the Supreme Court agreed to review the dispute, Puerto Ricans in the colony and outside believed that *Aurelius* posed the best possibility for the Court to overturn *Downes* and the other Insular Cases. As a result, the case attracted more than a dozen amicus briefs. Some came from legal scholars and civil rights groups, such as the American Civil Liberties Union, who argued that the Insular Cases were not applicable to the matter because

Article II extended to Puerto Rico and that the cases' meaning should not be expanded. Several groups, including a roll call of elected Puerto Rican officials and a group of former judges from Puerto Rico and other US territories, argued that the Insular Cases should be overturned as a matter of course. Still others chimed in to opine about why the judgment of the lower court should or should not be affirmed.

Even though, in the lower courts, the Insular Cases and *Downes* were raised as legal justification for the constitutionality of the Junta, those arguments were not included in the briefs before the Supreme Court. Instead, the lawyers for the Junta and the US government conceded that Article II did apply to Puerto Rico; so they focused their arguments on the definition of who was "an officer of the US." This was important because it gave the Court a means to avoid addressing the Insular Cases and *Downes*. If a party to a legal dispute does not raise an issue or an argument in its brief, then the Court is not compelled to make a decision as to that issue.

At oral arguments on October 15, 2019, UTIER's lawyer, Jessica Mendez-Colberg, nonetheless tried to bring the issue of the Insular Cases before the Court. She opened her statements by immediately invoking the cases and asking that they be overturned. At the outset, in reference to the territorial incorporation doctrine, she stated that the Court "should reject classifications grounded in ideas of alien races and savage people."[40] She continued, "it is a matter of overruling the insular cases, and the Doctrine of Territorial Incorporation, it is a matter of constitutional and [sic] law, but also a matter of who the United States is as a nation . . . In this case, the First Circuit stated correctly that the insular cases hover like a dark cloud over this case."

At this point, Justice Stephen Breyer interrupted Mendez-Colberg. Breyer first acknowledged that the Insular Cases were indeed "a dark cloud," then he dismissed their relevance entirely because, as the First Circuit Court of Appeals had decided, and the lawyers for the Junta had conceded, Articles I and II of the Constitution did indeed apply to Puerto Rico. So, the only issue before the Court was whether the members of the Junta were local Puerto Rican officers or officers of the United States. According to Justice Breyer, that determination could be made without considering the Insular Cases.

Again, Mendez-Colberg attempted to take the discussion back to the Insular Cases and the inequity they created for Puerto Rico and Puerto Ricans. She stressed that the powers given to the members of the Junta far exceeded the powers held by local Puerto Rican officials, and thus the members should be seen as officers of the United States. She then returned to the Insular Cases, only to be interrupted again, this time by Chief Justice John Roberts.

"As Justice Breyer has pointed out, none of the other parties rely on the insular cases in any way. So, it would be very unusual for us to address them in this case, wouldn't it?" Roberts asked her.

Understanding that the justices did not want to engage her arguments about the Insular Cases, a visibly frustrated Mendez-Colberg responded, "Well, your Honor, they relied on the insular cases since the beginning of the proceedings. . . . Now, it is very convenient for the other parties to rely on the insular cases in the lower courts where there is no authority to overrule those cases, but then when we come before this Court to say that they are not relevant." Here Mendez-Colberg highlighted the legal maneuvering that the opposing parties had used in the case, first arguing in the lower courts, which were powerless to overturn them, that the Insular Cases precluded the application of the Appointments Clause at all, then conceding that the Appointments Clause did indeed apply, but that the members of the Junta were not federal officers. Again, Roberts questioned the need to discuss the cases at all, given that they were no longer in dispute.

Pivoting, Mendez-Colberg took a different approach. She argued that despite Roberts's protestation that it would be unusual for the Court to address the Insular Cases when they were irrelevant to the dispute at hand, he had, in fact, done that very thing in the Court's prior session. In the case of *Trump v. Hawai'i*, the Muslim travel ban case, Roberts had acknowledged that the infamous case of *Korematsu v. US*, the Japanese internment camp case, "had nothing to do," with the issues presented in *Trump*. Nonetheless, he wrote in the opinion, "*Korematsu* was gravely wrong the day it was decided, has been overruled in the court of history, and—to be clear—'has no place in law under the Constitution.'"[41] In this statement, Roberts was seen to have effectively overturned the much-reviled *Korematsu* decision, even while he upheld Trump's travel ban. Supreme Court observers and lawyers in Puerto Rico had found hope in the Court's willingness to overturn *Korematsu*, even while finding that it wasn't relevant. Surely, *Downes* and the Insular Cases would receive the same treatment.

Mendez-Colberg pointed to the Court's own actions in *Trump v. Hawai'i*, while also stressing that the opposing parties had, indeed, relied heavily on the Insular Cases in the lower courts. "Last term, this Court went ahead and overruled the *Korematsu* case. In the *Trump vs. Hawai'i* case, the Court said that [*Korematsu*] had nothing to do with [*Trump v. Hawai'i*]. But still it was a morally repugnant doctrine that was purely on the basis of race, and, therefore, it was overruled. The same here with the insular cases. And I cannot stress enough that the parties have relied on the insular cases in this case.

That is why it's the perfect opportunity to address them." Once again, Mendez-Colberg was interrupted in her attempts to push the Court to even discuss the Insular Cases. This time, the justices followed a line of questioning about the nature of the duties of the board versus duties of local Puerto Rican officials. With this discussion, Mendez-Colberg's time expired, and she was left unable to fully make her arguments about the Insular Cases.

This was a disappointing turn of events for those who had hoped that the Court would roundly reject the racism inherent in the Insular Cases as it had in *Korematsu*. Not surprisingly, when the Court's opinion was issued, it did nothing to overturn *Downes* or the other Insular Cases. Instead, the Court found that the Appointments Clause of the Constitution did apply in Puerto Rico, and, as a result, "we need not consider the request by some of the parties that we overrule the much-criticized 'Insular Cases' and their progeny. Those cases did not reach this issue, and whatever their continued validity we will not extend them in these cases."[42] Here, again, the Supreme Court, when presented with the opportunity to overturn *Downes* and state emphatically that the Insular Cases' foundation in racism gave them "no place in law under the Constitution," declined to do so, even while it questioned their "continued validity." Instead, the Court acknowledged that the "dark cloud" of those decisions hangs over Puerto Rico but determined that it wasn't necessary to remove the cloud. Puerto Rico continues to live underneath that cloud and with the consequences of those decisions.

In the end, and to the surprise of very few people, the Court held that the Junta officers were not federal officials but instead were local Puerto Rican officers. As a result, they did not need to undergo confirmation by Congress, and their actions in filing for Title III bankruptcy were not unconstitutional. And so Aurelius lost, which was in the interest of the people of Puerto Rico, who would not be forced to pay the hedge fund the full face value of the bonds through more austerity. However, UTIER also lost, which meant that the Junta could proceed with the proposed cuts to public pensions—and so Puerto Rican workers and retirees lost as well.

Conclusion

Puerto Rico is living intense moments of political and societal reorientation that are forcing a reconsideration of the archipelago's governance. However, undergirding all of this upheaval are the *Downes* decision and Puerto Rico's long-standing colonial relationship with the United States, which, despite Puerto Ricans' demands, continues to limit the everyday possibilities of the territory and its people, as well as Puerto Rico's political future. This colonial status has left Puerto Rico susceptible to a repeating and overlapping history of crisis that has been made worse by debt, environmental disasters, and a global pandemic.

The events of the past decade in Puerto Rico have revealed the face of twenty-first-century colonialism in the US territory, and it looks much as it always has. Underneath the many actions taken by the US government and the Supreme Court over the past century is *Downes v. Bidwell*. That quaintly racist legal decision from the early twentieth century continues to be the guiding principle in the United States–Puerto Rico relationship. *Downes* is where the Court first declared Congress's plenary power over Puerto Rico. It is where the unincorporated territory was first created and where Congress was first given the power to keep Puerto Rico in that status indefinitely. *Downes* is also where Puerto Rico's exclusion was first sanctioned and justified on the basis of race. While the justices of the Supreme Court might argue that the Insular Cases are irrelevant in certain disputes relating to Puerto Rico, I would argue that they sit at the center of *every* dispute regarding Puerto Rico and the United States. This fact has been made grimly clear in the past decade, when *Downes* and all that it created have been used to justify the most recent iteration of colonial systems put into place in Puerto Rico.

Conclusion
(or *Rather* Seguimos Luchando . . .)

The earthquakes began in late December 2019, while people were still in the midst of their holiday celebrations, and continued into the new year—hundreds of quakes, though not all of them large enough to be felt aboveground. The biggest hit at night, driving people from their homes in terror. Then came the tsunami warning, and people held their breaths and hoped it would not come. The quakes have persisted underground ever since—thousands of earthquakes, shaking and destabilizing the ground underneath people's feet. An earthquake swarm, scientists called it. The big ones—those that were felt aboveground, those that caused fissures and cracks to appear on the walls of buildings and in the sidewalks and city streets, those that led to the collapse of several homes and historic buildings—terrorized people so much that they feared sleeping in their homes, in their own beds. Instead, hundreds of people gathered in the parking lots of stadiums and schools and in parks, forming makeshift camps where they slept in tents and in their cars in the safety of the open air without the fear of a ceiling collapsing on them in the middle of the night.

Thus began 2020 in the cities and towns of Puerto Rico's Caribbean region. The residents of the south and southwestern zones, many of whom were still not fully recovered from the devastation wrought by the hurricanes two years earlier, now faced another crisis. Mutual aid networks that had been created in the days and months following the 2017 hurricanes once again activated to deliver aid to the people of the southern coast. Recovery from this natural disaster, like the hurricanes before it, would also be complicated by the already razor-thin margins on which people lived and the crushing austerity imposed on them by the Puerto Rico government and the Junta.

The quakes continued to be felt for months even as people slowly tried to return to something like normalcy, to school, work, and the quotidian. Some buildings were permanently closed due to dangerous and irreparable structural damage, others because the damage was too costly to be repaired. Puerto Ricans now had to learn to live with this new added layer of disaster, all of which had been exacerbated by the crushing weight of the debt crisis.

Then, in March, a global pandemic began, and the world entered a new phase of life. For folks in Puerto Rico, the COVID-19 crisis brought further

pain and stress to what was already a difficult situation. For years, long before the pandemic began, Puerto Rico's medical and health infrastructure had
been in decline. Hundreds of doctors and medical professionals had left the
archipelago in the preceding years in search of economic stability. Following the devastation of Hurricane Maria, more departed, leaving many clin-
ics and hospitals understaffed and eventually leading to the closure of dozens
of medical centers. Entire communities were left without a medical facility,
and many Puerto Ricans were forced to travel to the San Juan area to receive
specialized care—a costly and difficult trip for many elderly and impoverished residents of the archipelago.

As a result of this health infrastructure breakdown and due to reduced
government funding for medical care, the archipelago's medical facilities
were already underfunded, understaffed, and lacking up-to-date technology
when the pandemic began. Thus, COVID-19 posed a particularly acute threat
to the archipelago's residents, which is an aged population including many
individuals suffering from the preexisting conditions that made the virus particularly dangerous. To protect the archipelago's fragile health care system
from being overwhelmed, the Puerto Rican government implemented some
of the strictest lockdown measures in the United States—imposing nightly
curfews, limiting which days individuals could do their shopping and run er-
rands, closing all nonessential businesses and all schools. The government
even went so far as to close beaches and ports. Furthermore, the archipelago was among the first in the United States to implement a mask mandate,
and the Puerto Rican government sent daily text messages to the populace
reminding it of the curfew and rules.[1]

The people of Puerto Rico initially supported these measures because they
understood the unique danger that COVID-19 posed for the territory. The
requirements were necessary. All around the Caribbean region, Puerto
Rico's neighbors were closing their borders to visitors and imposing strict
quarantine requirements for residents who traveled home from abroad during this period. But Puerto Rico, because of its status as a US territory, was
not able to follow the lead of other Caribbean nations. Instead, it implemented strict rules and hoped to dissuade travelers.

As the months wore on, stir-crazy US mainlanders began to feel the itch
to travel, to seek escape and distraction from the monotony of pandemic life.
With Europe and the rest of the Caribbean closed to them, US tourists instead turned to Puerto Rico. As Luis Muñoz Marín was known to say, Puerto
Rico offered them the best of both worlds. It was a Caribbean destination
that felt foreign but did not require a passport, and because it is a US terri-

tory, Puerto Rico could not prohibit interstate travelers from visiting. As a result, thousands of US American tourists flocked to Puerto Rico.

They arrived in search of freedom and release. They arrived ready to frolic and party. They arrived, like many US Americans before them, with their paternalism, chauvinism, and colonial mindsets firmly in place. These tourists saw Puerto Rico as a playground where they could do whatever they desired. And so, they flouted Puerto Rico's strict protocols.[2] They gathered in large groups, refused to wear masks, ignored the curfew, got into fights with local residents, and generally created chaos, in particular in the streets of Viejo San Juan. One resident was quoted as saying, "They were behaving as if no one else existed in Old San Juan. I don't have a problem with people trying to have a good time, but they have to be respectful. We're still living in the middle of a pandemic, and people can't come here and act as if the virus doesn't exist. . . . They have a sense of entitlement and apathy I don't understand."[3] Unsurprisingly, Puerto Rican residents began to grow frustrated with living under strict restrictions while they watched tourists act as though the rules did not apply to them.

Against this background of earthquakes and pandemic, the operations of government and the Junta continued to churn along. The archipelago continued to experience regular blackouts as the aged and crippled power grid underwent a contentious privatization. Hearings were held in Congress to discuss the need to decolonize Puerto Rico. The House Democrats introduced bills calling for a plebiscite and self-determination. Puerto Ricans continued to protest the Junta, austerity, government corruption, and neglect.

On March 15, 2022, Puerto Rico officially exited bankruptcy proceedings. The debt restructuring plan approved by Judge Laura Taylor Swain, of New York, "reduced claims against Puerto Rico's government from $33 billion to just over $7.4 billion, with 7 cents of every taxpayer dollar going to debt service, compared with 25 cents previously."[4] The plan also set aside money to fund state worker pensions and attempted to limit cuts that affected Puerto Rican retirees. While the plan could have been far worse, placing more of a burden on the people of Puerto Rico, for many Puerto Ricans the debt restructuring plan is nonetheless unsustainable and unjust.[5] The plan itself notes that Puerto Rico currently has sufficient resources to meet debt payments only through 2034. Furthermore, opponents have also noted that the territory government does not have the finances required to meet debt service payments. Ultimately, the plan still lays the burden on the people of the territory to pay billions of dollars that many see as unlawful. Adding insult to injury, the people of Puerto Rico must also bear the costs incurred in the legal proceedings, which have been estimated as exceeding one billion dollars.[6] "The cost of the bankruptcy has been paid with public funds belonging to the government of Puerto Rico, paid by taxpayers in Puerto Rico," Governor Pedro Pierluisi said on October 21, 2021. "All the federal government has done in this, is to provide Puerto Rico with a debt-restructuring mechanism." Again, Puerto Ricans are forced to pay for their own colonization.

On June 30, 2023, the Junta approved Puerto Rico's budget for fiscal year 2023. Officials for the government of Puerto Rico claimed the 2023 budget marked the territory's third approved budget and that, as a result, the Junta could wrap up its work as early as the next year following adoption of the 2024 budget plan. However, the Junta countered that the two previous budgets had not yet undergone auditing, and it continues to work "to help the island meet the requirements to gain access to, and the trust, of credit markets."[7] Thus, the Junta claimed it is premature to "forecast when its role would end given ongoing work with Puerto Rico's government." Despite what appears to be progress toward meeting PROMESA's onerous financial requirements, the Junta nevertheless stands to be in place for many years to come.

Meanwhile, the Insular Cases continue to gain broader attention. With the debt and the Junta still important topics of conversation and sources of tension, the Insular Cases have had a bit of a renaissance. A growing number of discussions about Puerto Rico's debt and way forward mention the place of the Insular Cases in the territory's dynamic with Congress. Recently, more and more scholarship has taken up questions stemming from the cases, and several prominent law journals have dedicated entire issues to the "law of the territories."[8] Furthermore, the Court has been forced to directly contend with the cases' legacies.

On April 21, 2022, the Supreme Court decided another dispute about Puerto Rico's relationship with the United States. The case of *US v. Vaello Madero* concerned government-provided Supplemental Security Income, or SSI.[9] José Vaello Madero began receiving SSI benefits after an accident left him unable to work while living in New York. These payments were directly deposited into his bank account. About a year later, he moved to Puerto Rico, where he continued to receive SSI benefits for several years. Upon reaching the age of sixty-two, Vaello Madero applied for Social Security benefits. His application alerted the Social Security Administration that he was no longer living in New York, and within two months it stopped his SSI benefits. The Social Security Administration also sued Vaello Madero for $28,000 in restitution for payments he had received while residing in Puerto Rico and ineligible for the benefit. Vaello Madero argued that excluding US citizens who reside in Puerto Rico from access to SSI benefits violated the equal protection guarantees of the Fifth Amendment.

Both the federal District Court and the First Circuit Court of Appeals agreed with Vaello Madero that denying the US citizens residing in Puerto Rico SSI benefits solely because they live in Puerto Rico is a violation of equal protection, which requires that similarly situated individuals be treated the same. The Supreme Court disagreed, finding that Congress can exclude Puerto Rico if it has a rational basis for that exclusion. In this case, the fact that Puerto Ricans in the territory do not pay federal income, gift, estate, or excise taxes was enough of a rational basis for Congress to choose to exclude the territory.

For those of us who study and pay attention to Supreme Court decisions related to Puerto Rico, the opinion was not at all surprising. As we have seen, it is historically consistent for the Court to affirm Congress's power to exclude Puerto Rico. It was also not surprising that Justice Sotomayor would stand alone in her dissent from the Court's decision. What was surprising was the concurring opinion written by the conservative justice, Neil Gorsuch, who had famously been Donald Trump's first appointee to the Court. Gorsuch concurred with the decision of the Court because he said that no party had asked the Court to overrule the Insular Cases in order to resolve the dispute; however, he took the Court to task for its continued reliance on the cases and their failure to overturn them and correct a constitutional wrong.

"The Insular Cases have no foundation in the Constitution," he wrote, "and rest instead on racial stereotypes. They deserve no place in our law."[10] His scathing concurrence condemned the Court for its continual reliance on what is in essence a legal fiction—the distinction between an incorporated and an unincorporated territory—categories that Gorsuch claimed do not exist in the US Constitution. "With the passage of time, this Court has come to admit its discomfort with the Insular Cases," Gorsuch continued, "but instead of confronting their errors directly, this Court has devised a workaround. Employing the specious logic of the Insular Cases, the Court has proceeded to declare 'fundamental' . . . more and more of the Constitution's guarantees. That solution is no solution . . . and the fictions of the Insular Cases on which this workaround depends are just that."[11]

For Gorsuch the "flaws in the Insular Cases are as fundamental as they are shameful," and though the "Insular Cases can claim support in academic work of the period, ugly racial stereotypes, and the theories of social Darwinists . . . they have no home in our Constitution."[12] Gorsuch declared that the illogical conclusions that the Insular Cases have led the Court to, and here I am reminded of Ruth Bader Ginsberg's frustrations during oral arguments for *Franklin California Trust*, had led to an "implausible and embarrassing state of affairs."[13]

He roundly rejected the idea that the Insular Cases can or should remain valid law, even while the Court has tried to limit their applicability or declined to expand their reach in recent cases. These mealy-mouthed limitations do nothing to undo a constitutional wrong, according to Gorsuch; instead, they prolong the injustice and inequity perpetrated in the Insular Cases. The point that Gorsuch sought to emphasize is that the status of unincorporated territory that Puerto Rico bears was founded on racist ideas; thus, the ability to exclude Puerto Rico in various contexts is born from racism. As a result, that racism undergirds Congress's repeated reliance on Puerto Rico's status as an unincorporated territory to exclude it from benefits and protections, such as SSI and federal bankruptcy, and to treat it differently than it treats the states.

Though Neil Gorsuch and I undoubtedly disagree on most things, we do agree on the source of Puerto Ricans' exclusion and resulting continued inequalities. While I do not believe that simply overturing the Insular Cases will be a panacea for all the challenges that Puerto Rico faces, recognizing that its colonial status and its history of exploitation and subjugation are intrinsically tied with the racism of those decisions and rejecting that logic as legally valid are important first steps. That the undoing of more than a century of colonial structures will not be easy is a given, but that they *must* be undone is also a given. For the millions of Puerto Ricans living under this latest iteration of colonial onslaught, the time is long overdue.

Notes

Introduction

1. Trías Monge, *Puerto Rico*.

2. A poll conducted by the group Morning Consult shortly after the passage of Hurricane Maria revealed that nearly 50 percent of US Americans did not know that Puerto Ricans were US citizens. See Kyle Dropp and Brendan Nyhan, "Nearly Half of Americans Don't Know Puerto Ricans Are Fellow Citizens," *New York Times*, September 26, 2017.

3. Sotheby's International Realty, "Puerto Rico Tax Incentives."

4. Chloe Berger, "Puerto Rico Is Becoming the New Florida for the Ultrawealthy and Remote Workers," *Fortune*, May 23, 2023.

5. Fidel Martinez, "Latinx Files: Will Puerto Rico Stop Being for Puerto Ricans Soon?," *Los Angeles Times*, January 13, 2022.

Chapter One

1. *The Insular Cases*.

2. For many years there has been debate among scholars as to the periodization of the Insular Cases. Some have argued that only the group of cases decided in 1901 should be considered within the group (Juan Torruella, José Trías Monge); others have argued that later cases from the 1920s and even into the 1970s should be considered part of this group. Recently, there are those who have argued for inclusion of several contemporary cases relating to Puerto Rico's territorial status to be included in the canon of *Insular Cases* (Emanuelli). The crux of the arguments for which decisions to include rests with considering when and how the Supreme Court has sought to define and delineate the relationship between the United States and the insular territories, which, despite the passage of over a century, continues to be a source of ambiguity.

3. Go, *American Empire and the Politics of Meaning*; Román, *Citizenship and Its Exclusions*; Love, *Race Over Empire*.

4. See generally Beisner, *Twelve against Empire*; Welch, *Imperialists vs. Anti-Imperialists*.

5. Carl Schurz, "American Imperialism," *The Convocation Address Delivered on Occasion of the 27th Convocation of the University of Chicago* (January 4, 1899), in Greene, *American Imperialism in 1898*, 77–84.

6. Speech of Representative James Slayden (June 7, 1907), *Congressional Record*, US House of Representatives, 61st Congress, 1st Session, 2919.

7. Gobat, "Invention of Latin America,"1345–75.

8. See generally Duffy Burnett and Marshall, *Foreign in a Domestic Sense*; Sparrow, *Insular Cases*; Neuman and Brown-Nagin, *Reconsidering the Insular Cases*.

9. Downes v. Bidwell, 182 U.S. 244 (1901).

10. For works that engage these questions, see generally Gómez, *Manifest Destinies*; Haney-Lopez, *White by Law*; Chang, "Whitewashing Precedent"; Kurashige, *Two Faces of Exclusion*.

11. I use "American" as a shorthand for the United States, even while I acknowledge that "America" encompasses the entirety of the hemisphere and that other parts of the world make no distinction between North and South America.

12. Jiménez, "Puerto Rico under the Colonial Gaze"; Fusté, "Repeating Islands of Debt"; Atiles, "State of Exception as Economic Policy."

13. For a fuller discussion on the political debates at the time, see Rivera Ramos, *Legal Construction of Identity*; Beisner, *Twelve against Empire*; Román, *Other American Colonies*; Weston, *Racism in US Imperialism*; Fernandez, *Disenchanted Island*; Kennedy, "The Racial Overtones of Imperialism as a Campaign Issue, 1900."

14. Balzac v. Porto Rico, 258 U.S. 298, 306 (1922).

15. *Balzac*, 306.

16. Erman, "Accomplices to Abbot Lawrence Lowell," 106.

17. Erman, *Almost Citizens*, 27–46; Duffy Burnett and Marshall, "Between the Foreign and the Domestic," 5; McGreevy, *Borderline Citizens*, 33–35.

18. Erman, "Accomplices to Abbot Lawrence Lowell," 105.

19. Soltero, *Latinos and American Law*, 21.

20. Padilla-Babilonia, "Sovereignty and Dependence in the American Empire."

21. Román, *Other American Colonies*.

22. MacLennan, *Sovereign Sugar*.

23. Poblete, *Islanders in the Empire*.

24. *Downes*, 287.

25. Skaggs, *Great Guano Rush*.

26. *United States Guano Islands Act*, 48 United States Code § 1411–19.

27. *United States Guano Islands Act*.

28. 48 United States Code § 1412.

29. Duffy Burnett, "The Edges of Empire," 780.

30. 48 United States Code § 1419.

31. Jones v. United States, 37 U.S. 202 (1890).

32. Nichols, "Navassa," 505–10.

33. Pan American Union, "Guano Islands of Peru," 12; Duffy Burnett, "Edges of Empire," 788.

34. Duffy Burnett, "Edges of Empire," 789.

35. Duffy Burnett, "Edges of Empire," 789

36. Duffy Burnett, "Edges of Empire," 789.

37. Duffy Burnett, "Edges of Empire," 789.

38. Duffy Burnett, "Edges of Empire," 790.

39. Duffy Burnett, "Edges of Empire," 790

40. Nichols, "Navassa," 509.

41. Duffy Burnett, "Edges of Empire," 791.

42. Duffy Burnett, "Edges of Empire," 791.

43. *Jones*, 212.

44. "The Navassa Rioters," *New York Times*, May 19, 1891.

45. Agamben, *Homo Sacer*.

46. *Downes*, 277.

47. *Downes*, 251.

48. *Downes*, 286.

49. *Downes*, 283.

50. *Downes*, 282

51. *Downes*, 283.

52. *Downes*, 280.

53. *Downes*, 305.

54. *Downes*, 342.

55. Duffy Burnett, "Edges of Empire," 795.

56. Smith, "Bitter Roots of Puerto Rican Citizenship."

57. Findlay, *Imposing Decency*; Briggs, *Reproducing Empire*.

58. González v. Williams, 192 U.S. 1 (1904).

59. *González*, 192.

60. Perez, "Citizenship Denied"; Smith, "Insular Cases, Differentiated Citizenship."

61. Cabranes, *Citizenship and the American Empire*; Aleinikoff, *Semblances of Sovereignty*.

62. Aleinikoff, *Semblances of Sovereignty*; Benítez Nazario, Orria, and Ortega, *Ciudanía y Exclusión en Puerto Rico*; Bosque Pérez and Colón Morera, *Puerto Rico under Colonial Rule*.

63. Balzac v. People of Porto Rico, 258 U.S. 298 (1922).

64. Meléndez Badillo, *Lettered Barriada*, 60–62.

65. Ortiz Santini, *Balsac vs. el Pueblo de Puerto Rico*; Soltero, *Latinos and American Law*, 25.

66. Constitution of the United States, Amendment VI: "In all criminal prosecutions, the accused shall enjoy the right to a speedy and public trial, by an impartial jury of the state and district wherein the crime shall have been committed."

67. Soltero, *Latinos and American Law*, 25.

68. El Pueblo de Puerto Rico v. Balzac, 28 D.P.R. 150 (1920).

69. Dorr v. United States, 195 U.S. 138 (1904).

70. *Balzac*, 305.

71. *Balzac*, 305.

72. *Balzac*, 306.

73. *Balzac*, 308.

74. *Balzac*, 308.

75. *Balzac*, 309.

76. *Balzac*, 310

77. *Balzac*, 311.

78. Sparrow, *Insular Cases*, 205.

79. Go, *American Empire and the Politics of Meaning*; McCoy and Scarano, *Colonial Crucible*.

80. Speech of Representative James Slayden.

Chapter Two

1. See generally Blackhawk, *Rediscovery of America*; Riley, "History of Native American Lands and the Supreme Court"; Jones, *Birthright Citizens*; Ramey Berry, *Price for Their Pound of Flesh*; Graber, *Dred Scott*.

2. Román, *Citizenship and Its Exclusions*, 87.

3. Maggie Blackhawk, "The Indian Law That Helps Build Walls," *New York Times*, May 26, 2019.

4. Blackhawk, "Federal Indian Law as Paradigm," 1795.

5. Johnson v. M'Intosh, 21 U.S 543, 572 (1823).

6. Riley, "History of Native American Lands and the Supreme Court," 371.

7. Robertson, "Judicial Conquest of Native America," 29.

8. Robertson, "Judicial Conquest of Native America," 29.

9. 25 United States Code § 177 — "Purchases or grants of lands from Indians."

10. Watson, *Buying America from the Indians*, xiii.

11. Riley, "History of Native American Lands and the Supreme Court," 371.

12. Banner, *How the Indians Lost Their Lands*, 179.

13. Banner, *How the Indians Lost Their Lands*, 179.

14. Robertson, "Judicial Conquest of Native America," 31–35; Riley, "History of Native American Lands and the Supreme Court," 372.

15. Robertson, "Judicial Conquest of Native America," 31–35.

16. Robertson, "Judicial Conquest of Native America," 31–35.

17. Letter from Edward Ingersoll to John Hill Brinton, February 20, 1823, cited in Robertson, "Judicial Conquest of Native America," 51.

18. *Johnson*, 572.

19. Cleveland, "Powers Inherent in Sovereignty," 32.

20. Cleveland, "Powers Inherent in Sovereignty," 30.

21. *Johnson*, 587.

22. Cleveland, "Powers Inherent in Sovereignty," 34.

23. Pommersheim, *Broken Landscape*, 90.

24. *Johnson*, 590.

25. *Johnson*, 589.

26. *Johnson*, 590.

27. Cleveland, "Powers Inherent in Sovereignty," 32.

28. Blackhawk, "Federal Indian Law as Paradigm," 1818.

29. Blackhawk, "Federal Indian Law as Paradigm," 1819.

30. Blackhawk, "Federal Indian Law as Paradigm," 1819.

31. Banner, *How the Indians Lost Their Lands*, 194.

32. Blackhawk, "Federal Indian Law as Paradigm," 1820.

33. Cited in Banner, *How the Indians Lost Their Lands*, 195.

34. Citer in Banner, *How the Indians Lost Their Lands*, 200.

35. Banner, *How the Indians Lost Their Lands*, 201.

36. Pommersheim, *Broken Landscape*, 102.

37. Cherokee Nation v. Georgia, 30 U.S. (5 Pet.) 1 (1831); Pommersheim, *Broken Landscape*, 102.

38. Strickland, "Tribal Struggle for Indian Sovereignty," 70.

39. Cleveland, "Powers Inherent in Sovereignty," 36.

40. Strickland, "Tribal Struggle for Indian Sovereignty," 71.

41. Cleveland, "Powers Inherent in Sovereignty," 36.

42. *Cherokee Nation*, 16.

43. *Cherokee Nation*, 17.

44. *Cherokee Nation*, 17.

45. *Cherokee Nation*, 17–18.

46. Cleveland, "Powers Inherent in Sovereignty," 39.

47. Strickland, "Tribal Struggle for Indian Sovereignty," 73.

48. Cited in Strickland, "Tribal Struggle for Indian Sovereignty," 74.

49. Cited in Strickland, "Tribal Struggle for Indian Sovereignty," 74.

50. Worcester v. Georgia, 31 U.S. (6 Pet.) 515 (1832).

51. Strickland, "Tribal Struggle for Indian Sovereignty," 74.

52. *Worcester*, 559.

53. Cleveland, "Powers Inherent in Sovereignty," 40.

54. Cleveland, "Powers Inherent in Sovereignty," 40.

55. *Worcester*, 561.

56. Banner, *How the Indians Lost Their Lands*, 222.

57. Cited in Strickland, "Tribal Struggle for Indian Sovereignty," 77.

58. Banner, *How the Indians Lost Their Lands*, 191.

59. *Worcester*, 559.

60. Pommersheim, *Broken Landscape*, 115.

61. Pommersheim, *Broken Landscape*, 115.

62. Román, *Citizenship and Its Exclusions*, 88.

63. Pommersheim, *Broken Landscape*, 105.

64. Downes v. Bidwell, 182 U.S. 244, 280 (1901).

65. Román, *Citizenship and Its Exclusions*, 91–92.

66. Wilkins, *American Indian Sovereignty*, 39.

67. Wilkins, *American Indian Sovereignty*, 39.

68. Wilkins, *American Indian Sovereignty*, 39.

69. Schlereth, *Quitting the Nation*.

70. Cited in Wilkins, *American Indian Sovereignty*, 40.

71. Wilkins, *American Indian Sovereignty*, 41.

72. United States v. Rogers, 45 U.S. 567, 571 (1846).

73. *Rogers*, 571.

74. Blackhawk, "Federal Indian Law as Paradigm," 1823.

75. *Rogers*, 572.

76. Wilkins, *American Indian Sovereignty*, 46.

77. Wilkins, *American Indian Sovereignty*, 46.

78. Blackhawk, "Indian Law That Helps Build Walls."

79. Blackhawk, "Indian Law That Helps Build Walls."

80. Dred Scott v. Sanford, 60 U.S. 393, 407 (1856).

81. *Dred Scott*, 407.

82. The following biographical and historical narrative is compiled from Graber, *Dred Scott*; Finkelman, *Dred Scott v. Sanford*; and Maltz, *Dred Scott and the Politics of Slavery*.

83. Graber, *Dred Scott*, 18–19.

84. *Dred Scott*, 397.

85. *Dred Scott*, 393–394.

86. Finkelman, *Dred Scott v. Sandford*, 25.

87. Finkelman, *Dred Scott v. Sandford*, 27.

88. Graber, *Dred Scott*, 19.

89. Graber, *Dred Scott*, 19.

90. Strader v. Graham, 10 U.S. 82 (1850).

91. Finkelman, *Dred Scott v. Sandford*, 31.

92. Finkelman, *Dred Scott v. Sandford*, 32.

93. Finkelman, *Dred Scott v. Sandford*, 34.

94. Finkelman, *Dred Scott v. Sandford*, 34.

95. *Dred Scott*, 405.

96. Kettner, *The Development of American Citizenship*.

97. *Dred Scott*, 403.

98. *Dred Scott*, 403.

99. *Dred Scott*, 404.

100. *Dred Scott*, 405.

101. Finkelman, *Dred Scott v. Sanford*, 36.

102. Article IV, Section 3, Paragraph 2 of the Constitution of the United States: "Congress shall have Power to dispose of and make all needful Rules and Regulations respecting the Territory or other Property belonging to the United States."

103. Finkelman, *Dred Scott v. Sanford*, 38.

104. Constitution of the United States, Article IV, Section 3, Paragraph 2.

105. *Dred Scott*, 449.

106. *Dred Scott*, 449.

107. *Dred Scott*, 450.

108. *Dred Scott*, 572–73.

109. *Dred Scott*, 572–73.

110. Finkelman, *Dred Scott*, 45.

111. Finkelman, *Dred Scott*, 46.

112. Arenson, "Dred Scott versus the Dred Scott Case," 26.

113. Arenson, "Dred Scott versus the Dred Scott Case," 28.

114. Hardy, "Dred Scott, John San(d)ford, and the Case for Collusion."

Chapter Three

1. Ashford, *A Soldier in Science*, 40.

2. Santana, Ramírez de Arellano, and Rigau Pérez, *A Sojourn in Tropical Medicine*.

3. Trujillo-Pagán, *Modern Colonization by Medical Intervention*; De Barros, Palmer, and Wright, *Health and Medicine in the Circum-Caribbean*.

4. Agricultural Research Service, "Tropical Crops and Germplasm Research."

5. Trujillo-Pagán, *Modern Colonization by Medical Intervention*; Trías Monge, *Puerto Rico*.

6. Ashford, *A Soldier in Science*; Briggs, *Reproducing Empire*; Hernández-Díaz, *Labor-Management Relations in Puerto Rico*.

7. Greene, *Canal Builders*; Findlay, *Imposing Decency*; Espinosa, "A Fever for Empire."

8. Ramírez de Arellano and Seipp, *Colonialism, Catholicism, and Contraception*, 7.

9. Ramírez de Arellano and Seipp, *Colonialism, Catholicism, and Contraception*, 7.

10. Schwartz, "Hurricane of San Ciriaco."

11. Ashford, *A Soldier in Science*, 42–45.

12. Ashford, *A Soldier in Science*, 42.

13. Ashford, *A Soldier in Science*, 42

14. Ashford, *A Soldier in Science*, 67.

15. Ashford, *A Soldier in Science*, 67.

16. "Hawkworm [sic] Offers Serious Problem," *The State* (Columbia, SC), March 21, 1920.

17. "Hawkworm [sic] Offers Serious Problem."

18. "Hawkworm [sic] Offers Serious Problem."

19. "Hawkworm [sic] Offers Serious Problem."

20. Briggs, *Reproducing Empire*, 40–48.

21. Briggs, *Reproducing Empire*, 46–73; Findlay, *Imposing Decency*, 167–201.

22. For a discussion of the American Plan, see Rosen, *Lost Sisterhood*, and Pivar, *Purity and Hygiene*.

23. Flores Ramos, "Virgins, Whores, and Martyrs."

24. Goodman, "Porto Rican Experiment," 185.

25. Goodman, "Porto Rican Experiment," 185.

26. Goodman, "Porto Rican Experiment," 187.

27. Goodman, "Porto Rican Experiment," 187.

28. Goodman, "Porto Rican Experiment," 187.

29. Findlay, *Imposing Decency*, 170.

30. Goodman, "Porto Rican Experiment," 189.

31. Flores Ramos, "Virgins, Whores and Martyrs," 93.

32. Flores Ramos, "Virgins, Whores and Martyrs," 94.

33. Flores Ramos, "Virgins, Whores and Martyrs," 97.

34. Flores Ramos, "Virgins, Whores and Martyrs," 97.

35. Cited in Findlay, *Imposing Decency*, 183.

36. Findlay, *Imposing Decency*, 183.

37. Findlay, *Imposing Decency*, 174.

38. Findlay, *Imposing Decency*, 185.

39. Findlay, *Imposing Decency*, 185.

40. Briggs, *Reproducing Empire*, 47.

41. Briggs, *Reproducing Empire*, 73.

42. Ramírez de Arellano and Seipp, *Colonialism, Catholicism, and Contraception*.

43. Del Moral, "Negotiating Colonialism," 139–41.

44. McGreevey, *Borderline Citizens*.

45. Greene, *Canal Builders*; Nodín Valdés, *Organized Agriculture and the Labor Movement*; Ortiz, *Puerto Rican Women and Work*.

46. Department of Labor, "To Increase Common Labor Supply with Porto Rican," *United States Employment Service Bulletin*, May 21, 1918.

47. Committee on Public Information, *Official U.S. Bulletin*, October 3, 1918.

48. Committee on Public Information, *Official U.S. Bulletin*.

49. National Archives and Record Administration (NARA), Record Group (RG) 350, Records of Bureau of Insular Affairs (BIA), Document No. 64, "Letter of Arthur Yager to Brigadier General Walcott, Jr. dated September 25, 1918."

50. RG 350, Records of BIA, Document No. 64.

51. RG 350, Records of BIA, Document Nos. 99, 99A.

52. RG 350, Records of BIA, Document Nos. 99, 99A.

53. RG 350, Records of BIA, Document No. 123, "Letter of Ramón Viña to Resident Commissioner dated October 7, 1918."

54. RG 350, Records of BIA, Document No. 123.

55. RG 350, Records of BIA, Document No. 123.

56. RG 350, Records of BIA, Document No. 124, "Sworn Statement of Rafael Marchán dated October 24, 1918."

57. RG 350, Records of BIA, Document No. 124.

58. RG 350, Records of BIA, Document Nos. 99–99A.

59. RG 350, Records of BIA, Document Nos. 99–99A.

60. RG 350, Records of BIA, Document Nos. 99–99A.

61. "10,000 Porto Ricans Found Jobs Here," *New York Times*, December 1, 1918.

62. "10,000 Porto Ricans Found Jobs Here."

63. NARA, RG 350, Records of BIA, Document No. 92, "Letter from Gavin Payne to Chief of Bureau of Insular Affairs dated December 5, 1918."

64. NARA, RG 350, Records of BIA, Document No. 92.

65. NARA, RG 350, Records of BIA, Document No. 92.

66. NARA, RG 350, Records of BIA, Document No. 92.

67. NARA, RG 350, Records of BIA, Document No. 92.

68. NARA, RG 350, Records of BIA, Document No. 92.

69. See generally Hernández-Díaz, *Labor-Management Relations in Puerto Rico*; Dietz, *Economic History of Puerto Rico*; Mathews, *Puerto Rican Politics and the New Deal*.

70. Jiménez and LeBrón, "Instruments of Colonialism."

71. Cabán, *Constructing a Colonial People*, 157.

72. Cabán, *Constructing a Colonial People*, 157.

73. Cabán, *Constructing a Colonial People*, 157.

74. Villanueva, "Criollo Bloc."

75. Cabán, *Constructing a Colonial People*, 155.

76. Bosque-Pérez, "Carpetas y persecución política," 53.

77. Bosque-Pérez, "Political Persecution," 16.

78. Bosque-Pérez, "Political Persecution," 16.

79. Martínez Valentín, *La presencia de la policia*, 30.

80. Martínez Valentín, *La presencia de la policia*, 156.

81. Capozzola, "United States Empire," 246.

82. Martínez Valentín, *La presencia de la policia*, 30.

83. Martínez Valentín, *La presencia de la policia*, 29–30.

84. Capozzola, "United States Empire," 248.

85. Estades-Font, "Critical Year of 1936," 55.

86. Estades-Font, "Critical Year of 1936," 55.

87. Bosque-Pérez, "Carpetas y persecución pólitica," 46–62.

88. Estades-Font, "Critical Year of 1936," 51.

89. Cabán, *Constructing a Colonial People*, 157.

90. Cabán, *Constructing a Colonial People*, 157.

91. Hernández-Díaz, *Labor-Management Relations in Puerto Rico*, 144.

92. Hernández-Díaz, *Labor-Management Relations in Puerto Rico*, 144.

93. *Oxford English Dictionary*, 2nd ed., 20 vols. Oxford: Oxford University Press, 1989. Continually updated at http://www.oed.com.

94. Wall, Saberi, and Jackson, *Destroy, Build, Secure*, 7.

95. Dietz, *Economic History of Puerto Rico*, 135.

96. Hernández-Díaz, *Labor-Management Relations in Puerto Rico*, 144.

97. Randall, *El pueblo no solo es testigo*, 23–25.

98. "Mayagüez Needleworkers Strike," *Porto Rico Progress* (San Juan), August 31, 1933.

99. "Mayagüez Needleworkers Strike."

100. "Mayagüez Needleworkers Strike."

101. NARA, RG 165, Records of the War Department General and Specific Staffs, Military Intelligence Division, Correspondence 1917–1941: Box No. 2843, File No. 10110-2662/77, "Estimate of the Subversive Situations as of December 31, 1933," January 10, 1934.

102. NARA, RG 165, Records of the War Department General and Specific Staffs, Military Intelligence Division, Correspondence 1917–1941, File No. 10110-2662/80, "Estimate of the Subversive Situations as of January 31, 1934," February 10, 1934.

103. Santiago-Valles, *"Subject People" and Colonial Discourses*, 189.

104. Santiago-Valles, *"Subject People" and Colonial Discourses*, 189.

105. Hernández-Díaz, *Labor-Management Relations in Puerto Rico*, 144.

106. Hernández-Díaz, *Labor-Management Relations in Puerto Rico*, 144.

107. Hernández-Díaz, *Labor-Management Relations in Puerto Rico*, 144.

108. Hernández-Díaz, *Labor-Management Relations in Puerto Rico*, 145.

109. Taller de Formación Política, *¡Huelga en la caña!*

110. Taller de Formación Política, *¡Huelga en la caña!*, 119.

111. Taller de Formación Política, *¡Huelga en la caña!*, 123.

112. NARA, RG 165, "Estimate of the Subversive Situations as of January 31, 1934."

113. Taller de Formación Política, *¡Huelga en la caña!*, 123.

114. Taller de Formación Política, *¡Huelga en la caña!*, 123.

115. Albizu Campos, "La esclavitud azucarera," *El Mundo* (San Juan), January 19, 1934, 2, 10.

116. Albizu Campos, "La esclavitud azucarera."

117. Taller de Formación Política, *¡Huelga en la caña!*, 125.

118. Taller de Formación Política, *¡Huelga en la caña!*, 132.

119. Taller de Formación Política, *¡Huelga en la caña!*, 132.

120. *El Mundo*, January 17, 1934, 1, 5.

121. *El Mundo*, 1, 5.

122. *El Día* (Ponce, PR), January 19, 1934, 5.

123. *El Día*, 5.

124. Taller de Formación Política, *¡Huelga en la caña!*, 153.

125. Taller de Formación Política, *¡Huelga en la caña!*, 153.

126. Taller de Formación Política, *¡Huelga en la caña!*, 165.

127. Taller de Formación Política, *¡Huelga en la caña!*, 178.

128. Dietz, *Economic History of Puerto Rico*, 164.

129. Santiago-Valles, *"Subject People" and Colonial Discourses*, 192.

Chapter Four

1. Morales, *Fantasy Island*, 45–48.

2. Morales, *Fantasy Island*.

3. Dietz, *Economic History of Puerto Rico*, 133.

4. Manuel Suarez, "Luis Munoz Marin Is Dead at 82," *New York Times*, May 1, 1980.

5. Ymayo Tartakoff, "Puerto Rico's Luis Muñoz Marín," 670; Vázquez, *El Jefe*.

6. Gatell, "Art of the Possible," 2.

7. Zapata Oliveras, *"Nuevos caminos hacia viejos objetivos,"* 31–37; Rivera, *El pensamiento politico*, v–vii; Rosario Natal, *Luis Muñoz Marín*, 155; Geigel Polanco, *La farsa del Estado Libre Asociado*.

8. Fundación Luis Muñoz Marín, Seccion III, Serie 1: Correspondencia, Cartapacio 13 (1952 [sic], 1922), Carta de Julio 4 de 1922 al Sr. E. Fernandez Vanga.

9. Fundación Luis Muñoz Marín, Seccion III, Serie 1: Correspondencia, Cartapacio 12 (1931), Carta publicada en *La Democracia* de Nov 11 de 1931 [published on November 12, 1931] al Gobernador Teodoro Roosevelt.

10. Ayala and Bernabe, *Puerto Rico in the American Century*, 151–52.

11. Ayala and Bernabe, *Puerto Rico in the American Century*, 111.

12. "Cable enviado por Muñoz Marín a Ruby S. [sic] Black, Washington, 13 de mayo de 1936," in Bothwell Gonzalez, *Puerto Rico: Cien años de lucha política*.

13. Rivera, *El pensamiento politico*, 1; Muñoz Marín, *Historia del Partido Popular Democrático*; Duprey Salgado, *Conversaciones en el bohio*.

14. Trías Monge, *Puerto Rico*, 101.

15. Mintz, *Worker in the Cane*, 128–30.

16. Maldonado, *Luis Muñoz Marín*, 191.

17. People of Puerto Rico v. Rubert Hermanos, Inc., 309 U.S. 543 (1940).

18. Tugwell, *Stricken Land*, 7–8.

19. Maldonado, *Boom and Bust*, 23.

20. Ayala and Bernabe, *Puerto Rico in the American Century*, 143.

21. Rivera, *El pensamiento político*, 9.

22. Maldonado, *Luis Muñoz Marín*, 268; Geigel Polanco, *La farsa del Estado Libre Asociado*, 7–15.

23. Trías Monge, *Puerto Rico*, 99–106.

24. Maldonado, *Boom and Bust*, 24.

25. Maldonado, *Luis Muñoz Marín*, 288; Goodsell, *Administration of a Revolution*, 1–31.

26. Trías Monge, *Puerto Rico*, 109.

27. Trías Monge, *Puerto Rico*, 109.

28. Trías Monge, *Puerto Rico*, 109.

29. Maldonado, *Luis Muñoz Marín*, 289; Velez Velez, *Jose Trías Monge*, 102.

30. Maldonado, *Luis Muñoz Marín*, 289.

31. Velez Velez, *Jose Trías Monge*, 101.

32. Trías Monge, *Como Fue*, 141.

33. Trías Monge, *Como Fue*, 145.

34. Cited in Maldonado, *Luis Muñoz Marín*, 295.

35. Public Law 600 available in *Documents on the Constitutional History of Puerto Rico*, 153.

36. Ayala and Bernabe, *Puerto Rico in the American Century*, 162.

37. Trías Monge, *Puerto Rico*, 113.

38. Trías Monge, *Puerto Rico*, 112.

39. Cited in Velez Velez, *Jose Trías Monge*, 103.

40. Geigel Polanco, *La farsa del Estado Libre Asociado*, 17–24.

41. Ayala and Bernabe, *Puerto Rico in the American Century*, 164.

42. Trías Monge, *Puerto Rico*, 114.

43. Trías Monge, *Puerto Rico*, 114.

44. Trías Monge, *Puerto Rico*, 117–18.

45. Trías Monge, *Puerto Rico*, 115.

46. Trías Monge, *Puerto Rico*, 115.

47. Zapata Oliveras, "Nuevos caminos hacia viejos objetivos," 381–83.

48. García Muñiz, "Puerto Rico in the United Nations," 58.

49. García Muñiz, "Puerto Rico in the United Nations," 59.

50. García Muñiz, "Puerto Rico in the United Nations," 67.

51. Cited in García Muñiz, "Puerto Rico in the United Nations," 76.

52. García Muñiz, "Puerto Rico in the United Nations," 77.

53. García Muñiz, "Puerto Rico in United Nations," 77.

54. Cited in García Muñiz, "Puerto Rico in the United Nations," 80.

55. Trías Monge, *Puerto Rico*, 123.

56. García Muñiz, "Puerto Rico in the United Nations," 85.

57. Aleinikoff, *Semblances of Sovereignty*, 75.

58. Duany, *Puerto Rican Nation on the Move*, 122–36.

59. Reid v. Covert, 354 U.S. 1 (1956). This case was about the legality of the use of military tribunals to criminally prosecute US citizen civilians residing in military bases abroad. The Insular Cases were invoked on appeal to argue that Article III and the Fifth and Sixth Amendments of the US Constitution did not apply to US citizens

abroad. The Court in *Reid* held that the Insular Cases did not apply and the protections of the Constitution did apply to US citizen civilians abroad.

60. Cited in Rosado, *Pedro Albizu Campos*, 350.

Chapter Five

1. "Despiden al ELA con una esquela," *Primera Hora* (Guaynabo, PR), July 24, 2016.

2. Blackhawk, "Federal Indian Law as Paradigm," 1805.

3. Marxuach, *Policy Brief: Tax Reform (Again)*.

4. Maldonado, *Boom and Bust*, 106–17.

5. De Onis, *Energy Islands*, 45–46.

6. Larry Rohter, "Trade Pact Threatens Puerto Rico's Economic Rise," *New York Times*, January 3, 1993.

7. Gonzalez, "Hurricane Colonialism."

8. Michael Corkery and Mary Williams Walsh, "Puerto Rico's Governor Says Island's Debts Are 'Not Payable'," *New York Times*, June 28, 2015.

9. Corkery and Walsh, "Puerto Rico's Governor Says."

10. "General obligation debt is secured by the full faith and credit of the local government issuing the debt. The municipality pledges its tax revenues unconditionally to pay the interest and principal on the debt as it matures. If the debt is in the form of a bond, the bond owners have a legal claim on all the general income of the jurisdiction if a default occurs." Municipal Resources and Service Center, "Types of Municipal Debt."

11. See, for example, Andrés Velasco, "The Greece of the Caribbean?," *World Economic Forum*, January 29, 2016; Gary O'Donoghue, "Puerto Rico: the Greece of the Caribbean?," *BBC News*, July 6, 2015.

12. Center for Individual Freedom, "Washington Is Trying to Pull a Fast One."

13. Center for Individual Freedom, "Small Investors Like Teresa."

14. Michelle Wilde Anderson, "Let the US Treasury Rescue Puerto Rico," *New York Times*, December 6, 2015; Express News Editorial Board, "Congress Must Rescue Puerto Rico," *San Antonio Express News*, April 17, 2016; Ari Paul, "The Cure for Puerto Rico Is Independence," *Al Jazeera America*, July 13, 2015.

15. Editorial Board, "Don't Abandon Puerto Rico," *New York Times*, December 26, 2015; Editorial Board, "Congress Needs to Throw Puerto Rico a Lifeline," *New York Times*, March 12, 2016.

16. Oliver, "Puerto Rico."

17. Nick Brown and Daniel Bases, "Puerto Rico Declares Moratorium on Government Development Banks's Debt," *Reuters*, May 1, 2016.

18. Puerto Rico v. Sánchez Valle, 36 S. Ct. 1863 (2016).

19. Oral arguments, *Sánchez Valle* (January 13, 2016), 17.

20. *Sánchez Valle*, 1870.

21. *Sánchez Valle*, 1874.

22. Puerto Rico v. Franklin-California Tax Free Trust, et al., 136 S. Ct. 1938 (2016).

23. *Franklin-California Tax Free Trust*, 1938.

24. Oral argument, *Franklin-California Tax Free Trust* (March 22, 2016), 41.

25. Obama, "Weekly Address."

26. Puerto Rico Oversight, Management, and Economic Stability Act, 48 United States Code § 2101.

27. At the time of writing, the members of the FOMB are David A. Skeel Jr., Andrew G. Biggs, Arthur J. González, John E. Nixon, Betty A. Rosa, and Juan A. Sabater.

28. Camila Domonoske, "Puerto Rico Eyes Options as It Faces Debt Deadline—Again," *NPR*, May 1, 2017.

29. International Foundation for Electoral Systems, "Election Guide."

30. Financial Oversight and Management Board for Puerto Rico v. Aurelius Investment, LLC, 140 S. Ct. 1649 (2020).

31. Jesse Barron, "The Curious Case of Aurelius Capital v. Puerto Rico," *New York Times Magazine*, November 26, 2019.

32. Renae Merle, "How One Hedge Fund Made $2 Billion from Argentina's Economic Collapse," *Washington Post*, March 29, 2016.

33. Mary Williams Walsh, "Hedge Fund Sues to Have Puerto Rico's Bankruptcy Case Thrown Out," *New York Times*, August 7, 2017.

34. Barron, "Curious Case of Aurelius Capital."

35. Constitution of the United States, Article II, Section 2.

36. Daniel Rivera Vargas, "En líos la AEE con unionados y gerenciales," *Primera Hora*, May 18, 2017.

37. De Onis, *Energy Islands*, 48.

38. De Onis, *Energy Islands*, 48.

39. Metro PR Staff, "UTIER impone demanda contra la Junta," *Metro Puerto Rico* (San Juan), August 7, 2017.

40. Oral arguments, *Aurelius* (October 15, 2019), 81.

41. Trump, President of the United States, et al. v. Hawai'i, et al., 138 S. Ct. 2392 (2018).

42. *Aurelius*, 1665.

Conclusion

1. Nicole Acevedo, "Puerto Rico Enacted Strict Covid Measures. It Paid Off, and It's a Lesson for the Mainland," *NBC News*, March 15, 2021.

2. Nicole Acevedo, "'Chaotic Situation': Puerto Ricans Indignant at Tourists Breaking Covid Mandates," *NBC News*, March 20, 2021.

3. Acevedo, "'Chaotic Situation.'"

4. Associated Press Staff, "Puerto Rico Formally Exits Bankruptcy Following Largest Public Debt Restructuring," *NBC News*, March 15, 2022.

5. Power 4 Puerto Rico, "Power 4 Puerto Rico Denounces Approval."

6. Nicole Acevedo and Gabe Gutierrez, "Will Puerto Rico's Debt Restructuring Deal End the Largest Bankruptcy in US History?," *NBC News*, October 29, 2021.

7. "Federal Board Approves $12.7 Billion Budget for Puerto Rico as Island Shakes Off Bankruptcy," *Associated Press*, June 30, 2023.

8. See for example, *Harvard Law Review* 130, no. 6 (April 2017) and *Yale Law Journal* 131, no. 8 (June 2022).

9. United States vs. Vaello Madero, 142 S. Ct. 1539 (2022).

10. *Vaello Madero*, 1552.

11. *Vaello Madero*, 1555.

12. *Vaello Madero*, 1554.

13. *Vaello Madero*, 1556.

Bibliography

Primary Sources

Archival Collections

Fundación Luis Muñoz Marín, San Juan
    Fondo: Correspondencia
    Fondo: Artículos, Editoriales, Manifiestos
    Fondo: Gobierno Federal, Correspondencia
National Archives and Record Administration (NARA), College Park, MD
    Record Group (RG) 165: Records of the War Department General and Specific
        Staff, Military Intelligence Division, Correspondence 1917–41
Universidad de Puerto Rico, Rio Piedras
    Colección Puertorriqueña
    Periódicos

Government Documents and Reports

Congressional Record, 1907.
Constitution of the United States
Documents on the Constitutional History of Puerto Rico, 2nd ed. Washington, D.C.:
    Office of the Commonwealth of Puerto Rico, 1964.
The Insular Cases: Comprising the Records, Briefs, and Arguments of Counsel in the Insular
    Cases of the October Term, 1900, in the Supreme Court of the United States,
    Washington, D.C.: Government Printing Office, 1901.
Official U.S. Bulletin, 1918.
Report of Brig. Gen. George W. Davis, U.S.V. on Civil Affairs of Porto Rico, 1899,
    Washington, D.C.: Government Printing Office, 1900.
United States Code

Periodicals

Al Jazeera America
    (New York, NY)
Associated Press
    (New York, NY)
BBC News (London, UK)
El Día (Ponce, PR)
El Mundo (San Juan, PR)
El Nuevo Día (San
    Juan, PR)

Fortune (New York, NY)
La Democracia
    (Ponce, PR)
Los Angeles Times
    (Los Angeles, CA)
Metro Puerto Rico (San
    Juan, PR)
National Public Radio
    (Washington, DC)

NBC News (New York, NY)
New York Times (New
    York, NY)
New York Times Magazine
    (New York, NY)
Primera Hora (Guaynabo,
    PR)
Porto Rico Progress (San
    Juan, PR)

Reuters (London, UK)
San Antonio Express News
   (San Antonio, TX)

The State (Columbia, SC)
Washington Post (Wash-
   ington, DC)

World Economic Forum
   (Cologny,
   Switzerland)

Books, Articles, and Pamphlets

Ashford, Bailey K. *A Soldier in Science: The Autobiography of Bailey K. Ashford*. New York: W. Morrow and Company, 1934.

Bothwell Gonzalez, Reece B. *Puerto Rico: Cien años de lucha política, Volumen II: Documentos varios, 1869–1936*. Rio Piedras: Editorial Universitaria, 1979.

Goodman, Herman. "The Porto Rican Experiment." *Social Hygiene* 5 (1919): 185–91.

Pan American Union. *The Guano Islands of Peru*. Washington, DC: Pan American Union, 1954.

Tugwell, Rexford Guy. *The Stricken Land: The Story of Puerto Rico*. New York: Doubleday & Company, 1947.

Secondary Sources

Articles and Book Chapters

Arenson, Adam. "Dred Scott versus the Dred Scott Case: The History and Memory of a Signal Moment in American Slavery, 1857–2007." In *The Dred Scott Case: Historical and Contemporary Perspectives on Race and Law*, edited by David Thomas Konig, Paul Finkelman, and Christopher Alan Bracey, 25–46. Athens: Ohio University Press, 2010.

Atiles, José. "State of Exception as Economic Policy: A Socio-Legal Analysis of the Puerto Rican Colonial Case." *Oñati Socio-legal Series* 8, no. 6 (2018): 819–44.

Blackhawk, Maggie. "Federal Indian Law as Paradigm within Public Law." *Harvard Law Review* 132, no. 7 (2019): 1787–877.

Bosque-Pérez, Ramón. "Carpetas y persecución política en Puerto Rico: La dimensión federal." In *Las Carpetas: Persecución política y derechos civiles en Puerto Rico*, edited by Ramón Bosque Pérez and José Javier Colón Morera, 37–90. Rio Piedras: CIPDC, 1997.

——. "Political Persecution against Puerto Rican Anti-colonial Activists in the Twentieth Century." In *Puerto Rico under Colonial Rule: Political Persecution and the Quest for Human Rights*, edited by Ramón Bosque-Pérez and José Javier Colón Morera, 13–48. Albany: State University of New York Press, 2006.

Capozzola, Christopher. "The United States Empire." In *Empires at War: 1911–1923*, edited by Robert Gerwarth and Erez Manela, 235–53. New York: Oxford University Press, 2014.

Chang, Robert S. "Whitewashing Precedent: From the Chinese Exclusion Case to *Korematsu* to the Muslim Travel Ban Cases." *Case Western Reserve Law Review* 68, no. 4 (2018): 1183–222.

Cleveland, Sarah H. "Powers Inherent in Sovereignty: Indians, Aliens, Territories, and the Nineteenth Century Origins of Plenary Power over Foreign Affairs." *Texas Law Review* 81, no. 1 (2002): 1–284.

del Moral, Solsirée. "Negotiating Colonialism: 'Race,' Class, and Education in Early-Twentieth-Century Puerto Rico." In *Colonial Crucible: Empire in the Making of the Modern American State*, edited by Alfred W. McCoy and Francisco A. Scarano, 135–44. Madison: University of Wisconsin Press, 2009.

Duffy Burnett, Christina. "The Edges of Empire and the Limits of Sovereignty: American Guano Islands." *American Quarterly* 57, no. 3 (2005): 779–803.

Duffy Burnett, Christina, and Burke Marshall. "Between the Foreign and the Domestic: The Doctrine of Territorial Incorporation, Invented and Reinvented." In *Foreign in a Domestic Sense: Puerto Rico, American Expansion, and the Constitution*, edited by Christina Duffy Burnett and Burke Marshall, 1–36. Durham, NC: Duke University Press, 2001.

Erman, Sam. "U.S. Territories Commentary Series: Accomplices of Abbott Lawrence Lowell." *Harvard Law Review* 131, no. 5 (2018): 105–15.

Espinosa, Mariola. "A Fever for Empire: US Disease Eradication in Cuba as Colonial Public Health." In *Colonial Crucible: Empire in the Making of the Modern American State*, edited by Alfred W. McCoy and Francisco A. Scarano, 288–96. Madison: University of Wisconsin Press, 2009.

Estades-Font, Maria E. "The Critical Year of 1936 through the Reports of the Military Intelligence Division." In *Puerto Rico under Colonial Rule: Political Persecution and the Quest for Human Rights*, edited by Ramón Bosque-Pérez and José Javier Colón Morera, 49–58. Albany: State University of New York Press, 2006.

Flores Ramos, Jose. "Virgins, Whores, and Martyrs: Sex-work in the Colony, 1898–1919." In *Puerto Rican Women's History: New Perspectives*, edited by Felix V. Matos Rodriguez and Linda C. Delgado, 83–104. New York: Routledge, 1998.

Fusté, José. "Repeating Islands of Debt: Historicizing the Transcolonial Relationality of Puerto Rico's Economic Crisis." *Radical History Review* 128 (2017): 91–119.

García Muñiz, Humberto. "Puerto Rico in the United Nations, 1952: An Appraisal." *Caribbean Studies* 16, no. 2 (1976): 44–91.

Gatell, Frank Otto. "The Art of the Possible: Luis Muñoz Rivera and the Puerto Rican Jones Bill." *The Americas* 17, no. 1 (1960): 1–20.

Gobat, Michel. "The Invention of Latin America: A Transnational History of Anti-imperialism, Democracy, and Race." *American Historical Review* 118, no. 5 (2013): 1345–75.

Hardy, David T. "Dred Scott, John San(d)ford, and the Case for Collusion." *Northern Kentucky Law Review* 41, no. 1 (2014): 1–39.

Jiménez, Mónica A. "Puerto Rico under the Colonial Gaze: Oppression, Resistance and the Myth of the Nationalist Enemy." *Latino Studies* 18, no. 1 (2020): 27–44.

Jiménez, Mónica A., and Marisol LeBrón. "Instruments of Colonialism: Historicizing Corruption and Abuse in the Puerto Rico Police." *CENTRO: Journal of the Center for Puerto Rican Studies* 34, no. 2 (2022): 51–74.

Kennedy, Philip. "The Racial Overtones of Imperialism as a Campaign Issue, 1900." In *Race and US Foreign Policy in the Ages of Territorial and Market Expansion, 1840–1900*, edited by Michael Krenn, 266–67. New York: Routledge, 2013.

Nichols, Roy F. "Navassa: A Forgotten Acquisition." *American Historical Review* 38, no. 3 (1933): 505–10.

Padilla-Babilonia, Alvin. "Sovereignty and Dependence in the American Empire: Indian Nations, Territories, and Overseas Colonies." *Duke Law Review*, forthcoming in 2024.

Perez, Lisa Maria. "Citizenship Denied: The Insular Cases and the Fourteenth Amendment." *Virginia Law Review* 94, no 4 (2008): 1028–81.

Riley, Angela R. "The History of Native American Lands and the Supreme Court." *Journal of Supreme Court History* 38 (2013): 369–85.

Robertson, Lindsay G. "The Judicial Conquest of Native America: The Story of Johnson v. M'Intosh." In *Indian Law Stories*, edited by Carole Goldberg, Kevin K. Washburn, and Philip P. Frickey, 29–60. New York: Foundation Press, 2011.

Schwartz, Stuart B. "The Hurricane of San Ciriaco: Disaster, Politics, Society in Puerto Rico, 1899–1901." *Hispanic American Historical Review* 72, no. 3 (1992): 303–34.

Smith, Rogers M. "The Bitter Roots of Puerto Rican Citizenship." In *Foreign in a Domestic Sense: Puerto Rico, American Expansion, and the Constitution*, edited by Christina Duffy Burnett and Burke Marshall, 1–36. Durham, NC: Duke University Press, 2001.

———. "The Insular Cases, Differentiated Citizenship, and Territorial Statuses in the Twenty-First Century." In *Reconsidering the Insular Cases: Past and Future*, edited by Gerald L. Neuman and Tomiko Brown-Nagin, 103–28. Cambridge, MA: Harvard University Press, 2015.

Strickland, Rennard. "The Tribal Struggle for Indian Sovereignty: The Story of the Cherokee Cases." In *Indian Law Stories*, edited by Carole Goldberg, Kevin K. Washburn, and Philip P. Frickey, 61–80. New York: Foundation Press, 2011.

Villanueva, Joaquín. "The Criollo Bloc: Corruption Narratives and the Reproduction of Colonial Elites in Puerto Rico, 1860–1917." *CENTRO: Journal of the Center for Puerto Rican Studies* 34, no. 2 (2022): 27–50.

Ymayo Tartakoff, Laura. "Puerto Rico's Luis Muñoz Marín: Poet, Politician, and Paradox." *Society* 51, no. 6 (2014): 670–78.

Books

Agamben, Giorgio. *Homo Sacer: Sovereign Power and Bare Life*. Translated by Daniel Heller-Roazen. Palo Alto, CA: Stanford University Press, 1998.

Aleinikoff, Thomas Alexander. *Semblances of Sovereignty: The Constitution, the State, and American Citizenship*. Cambridge, MA: Harvard University Press, 2002.

Ayala, Cesar and Rafael Bernabe. *Puerto Rico in the American Century: A History Since 1898*. Chapel Hill: The University of North Carolina Press, 2007.

Banner, Stuart. *How the Indians Lost Their Lands: Law and Power on the Frontier*. Cambridge, MA: Harvard University Press, 2007.

Beisner, Robert L. *Twelve against Empire: The Anti-Imperialists 1898–1900*. New York: McGraw Hill, 1968.

Benítez Nazario, Jorge, Astrid Santiago Orria, and Idsa Alegría Ortega, eds. *Ciudanía y Exclusión en Puerto Rico*. San Juan: Tal Cual, 2010.

Blackhawk, Ned. *The Rediscovery of America: Native Peoples and the Unmaking of U.S. History*. New Haven, CT: Yale University Press, 2023.

Bosque Pérez, Ramón, and José Javier Colón Morera, eds. *Puerto Rico under Colonial Rule: Political Persecution and the Quest for Human Rights*. Albany: State University of New York Press, 2006.

Briggs, Laura. *Reproducing Empire: Race, Sex, Science, and US Imperialism in Puerto Rico*. Berkeley: University of California Press, 2002.

Cabán, Pedro. *Constructing a Colonial People: Puerto Rico and the United States, 1898–1932*. New York: Routledge, 1999.

Cabranes, José A. *Citizenship and the American Empire: Notes on the Legislative History of the United States Citizenship of Puerto Ricans*. New Haven, CT: Yale University Press, 1979.

De Barros, Juanita, Steven Paul Palmer, and David Wright, eds. *Health and Medicine in the Circum-Caribbean, 1800–1968*. New York: Routledge, 2009.

De Onis, Catalina M. *Energy Islands: Metaphors of Power, Extractivism, and Justice in Puerto Rico*. Oakland: University of California Press, 2021.

Dietz, James L. *Economic History of Puerto Rico: Institutional Change and Capitalist Development*. Princeton, NJ: Princeton University Press, 1986.

Duany, Jorge. *The Puerto Rican Nation on the Move: Identities on the Island and in the United States*. Chapel Hill: The University of North Carolina Press, 2002.

Duffy Burnett, Christina, and Burke Marshall, eds. *Foreign in a Domestic Sense: Puerto Rico, American Expansion, and the Constitution*. Durham, NC: Duke University Press, 2001.

Duprey Salgado, Nestor R., ed. *Conversaciones en el bohio: Luis Muñoz Marín y Antonio Fernós Isern en sus propias palabras*. San Juan: Fundación Luis Muñoz Marín, 2006.

Emmanuelli Jiménez, Rolando. *Puerto Rico Oversight, Management, and Economic Stability Act "PROMESA"* (Compendios de Derecho Puertorriqueño no. 3). San Juan: Editorial Del Derecho y Del Revés, 2016.

Erman, Sam. *Almost Citizens: Puerto Rico, the US Constitution, and Empire*. Cambridge: Cambridge University Press, 2019.

Fernandez, Ronald. *The Disenchanted Island: Puerto Rico and the United States in the Twentieth Century*. New York: Praeger, 1992.

Findlay, Eileen Suárez. *Imposing Decency: The Politics of Sexuality and Race in Puerto Rico, 1870–1920*. Durham, NC: Duke University Press, 1999.

Finkelman, Paul. *Dred Scott v. Sanford: A Brief History with Documents*. New York: Bedford Books, 1997.

Geigel Polanco, Vicente. *La farsa del Estado Libre Asociado*. Rio Piedras, PR: Editorial Edil, 1972.

Go, Julian. *American Empire and the Politics of Meaning: Elite Political Cultures in the Philippines and Puerto Rico*. Durham, NC: Duke University Press, 2008.

Gómez, Laura E. *Manifest Destinies: The Making of the Mexican American Race*, 2nd ed. New York: New York University Press, 2018.

Goodsell, Charles T. *Administration of a Revolution: Executive Reform in Puerto Rico under Governor Tugwell, 1941–1946*. Cambridge: Harvard University Press, 1965.

Graber, Mark. *Dred Scott and the Problem of Constitutional Evil*. New York: Cambridge University Press, 2006.

Greene, Julie. *The Canal Builders: Making America's Empire at the Panama Canal*. New York: Penguin, 2009.

Greene, Theodore. *American Imperialism in 1898*. Boston: Heath, 1955.

Haney-Lopez, Ian. *White by Law: The Legal Construction of Race*, 10th anniversary ed. New York: New York University Press, 2006.

Hernández-Díaz, Arleen. *Labor-Management Relations in Puerto Rico during the Twentieth Century*. Gainesville: University Press of Florida, 2006.

Jones, Martha S. *Birthright Citizens: A History of Race and Rights in Antebellum America*. Cambridge: Cambridge University Press, 2018.

Kettner, James H. *The Development of American Citizenship*. Chapel Hill: The University of North Carolina Press, 2005.

Kurashige, Lon. *Two Faces of Exclusion: The Untold History of Anti-Asian Racism in the United States*. Chapel Hill: The University of North Carolina Press, 2016.

Love, Eric T. *Race Over Empire: Racism and US Imperialism, 1865–1900*. Chapel Hill: The University of North Carolina Press, 2004.

MacLennan, Carol A. *Sovereign Sugar: Industry and Environment in Hawai'i*. Honolulu: University of Hawai'i Press, 2014.

Maldonado, A.W. *Boom and Bust in Puerto Rico: How Politics Destroyed an Economic Miracle*. Notre Dame, IN: University of Notre Dame Press, 2021.

———. *Luis Muñoz Marín: Puerto Rico's Democratic Revolution*, Rio Piedras, PR: La Editorial Universidad de Puerto Rico, 2006.

Maltz, Earl. *Dred Scott and the Politics of Slavery*. Lawrence: University of Kansas, 2007.

Martínez Valentín, José E. *La presencia de la policia en la historia de Puerto Rico: 1898-1995*. Self-published, J. E. Martínez Valentín, 1995.

Mathews, Thomas. *Puerto Rican Politics and the New Deal*. Gainesville: University of Florida Press, 1960.

McCoy, Alfred W., and Francisco A. Scarano, eds. *Colonial Crucible: Empire in the Making of the Modern American State*. Madison: University of Wisconsin Press, 2009.

McGreevey, Robert C. *Borderline Citizens: The United States, Puerto Rico, and the Politics of Colonial Migration*. Ithaca, NY: Cornell University Press, 2018.

Meléndez Badillo, Jorell A. *The Lettered Barriada: Worker, Archival Power, and the Politics of Knowledge in Puerto Rico*. Durham, NC: Duke University Press, 2021.

Mintz, Sidney W. *Worker in the Cane: A Puerto Rican Life History*. New York: W. W. Norton & Company, 1974.

Morales, Ed. *Fantasy Island: Colonialism, Exploitation, and the Betrayal of Puerto Rico*. New York: Bold Type Books, 2019.

Muñoz Marín, Luis. *Historia del Partido Popular Democrático*. San Juan: Editorial El Batey, 1984.

Nodín Valdés, Dennis. *Organized Agriculture and the Labor Movement before the UFW: Puerto Rico, Hawai'i, California*. Austin: University of Texas Press, 2011.

Neuman, Gerald L., and Tomiko Brown-Nagin, eds. *Reconsidering the Insular Cases: Past and Future*. Cambridge, MA: Harvard University Press, 2015.

Ortiz, Altagracia, ed. *Puerto Rican Women and Work: Bridges in Transnational Labor*. Philadelphia: Temple University Press, 1996.

Ortiz Santini, Francisco. *Balsac vs. el Pueblo de Puerto Rico: Su historia; sus protagonistas*. Self-published, BookCreations, 2019.

Pivar, David J. *Purity and Hygiene: Women, Sex-work, and the "American Plan," 1900–1930*. Westport, CT: Greenwood Press, 2002.

Poblete, JoAnna. *Islanders in the Empire: Filipino and Puerto Rican Laborers in Hawai'i*. Champaign: University of Illinois Press, 2017.

Pommersheim, Frank. *Broken Landscape: Indians, Indian Tribes and the Constitution*. New York: Oxford University Press, 2009.

Ramey Berry, Daina. *The Price for Their Pound of Flesh: The Value of the Enslaved, from Womb to Grave, in the Building of a Nation*. Boston: Beacon Press, 2017.

Ramírez de Arellano, Annette B., and Conrad Seipp. *Colonialism, Catholicism, and Contraception: A History of Birth Control in Puerto Rico*. Chapel Hill: The University of North Carolina Press, 2011.

Randall, Margaret. *El pueblo no solo es testigo: La historia de Dominga*. Rio Piedras, PR: Ediciones Huracán, 1979.

Rivera, Jose A. *El pensamiento politico de Luis Muñoz Marín*. San Juan: Fundacíon Luis Muñoz Marín, 1996.

Rivera Ramos, Efrén. *The Legal Construction of Identity: The Judicial and Social Legacy of American Colonialism in Puerto Rico*. Washington, DC: American Psychological Association, 2001.

Román, Ediberto. *Citizenship and Its Exclusions: A Classical, Constitutional and Critical Race Critique*. New York: New York University Press, 2010.

———. *The Other American Colonies: An International and Constitutional Law Examination of the United States Nineteenth and Twentieth Century Island Conquests*. Durham, NC: Carolina Academic Press, 2006.

Rosado, Marisa. *Pedro Albizu Campos: Las llamas de la aurora, acercamiento a su biografía*. San Juan: Ediciones Puerto, 2008.

Rosario Natal, Carmelo. *Luis Muñoz Marín y la independencia de Puerto Rico, 1907–1946*. San Juan: Producciones Históricas, 1994.

Rosen, Ruth. *The Lost Sisterhood: Sex-work in America, 1900–1918*. Baltimore: Johns Hopkins University Press, 1982.

Sánchez Korrol, Virginia. *From Colonia to Community: The History of Puerto Ricans in New York City*. Berkeley: University of California Press, 1994.

Santana, Raúl Mayo, Annette B. Ramírez de Arellano, and José Gabriel Rigau Pérez, eds. *A Sojourn in Tropical Medicine: Francis W. O'Connor's Diary of a Porto Rican Trip, 1927*. San Juan: La Editorial, Universidad de Puerto Rico, 2008.

Santiago-Valles, Kelvin. *"Subject People" and Colonial Discourses: Economic Transformation and Social Disorder in Puerto Rico, 1898–1947*. Albany: State University of New York Press, 1994.

Schlereth, Eric. *Quitting the Nation: Emigrant Rights in North America, 1750–1870*. Chapel Hill: The University of North Carolina Press, 2024.

Skaggs, Jimmy M. *The Great Guano Rush: Entrepreneurs and American Overseas Expansion*. New York: St. Martin's Press, 1994.

Soltero, Carlos R. *Latinos and American Law: Landmark Supreme Court Cases*. Austin: University of Texas, 2006.

Sparrow, Bartholomew H. *The Insular Cases and the Emergence of American Empire*. Lawrence: University Press of Kansas, 2006.

Taller de Formación Política. *¡Huelga en la caña!: 1933–1934*. Rio Piedras, PR: Ediciones Huracán, 1982.

Torruella, Juan R. *The Supreme Court and Puerto Rico: The Doctrine of Separate and Unequal*. Río Piedras: University of Puerto Rico, 1985.

Trías Monge, José. *Como Fue: Memorias*. Rio Piedras: La Editorial, Universidad de Puerto Rico, 2005.

———. *Puerto Rico: Trails of the Oldest Colony in the World*. New Haven, CT: Yale University Press, 1997.

Trujillo-Pagán, Nicole E. *Modern Colonization by Medical Intervention: US Medicine in Puerto Rico*. Leiden, Netherlands: Brill, 2013.

Vázquez, Nieve de los Ángeles. *El Jefe: Populismo y corrupción en el Puerto Rico de 1898*. Self-published, Nieve de los Ángeles Vázquez, 2023.

Velez, Jorge E. *Jose Trías Monge: Estado Libre Ascociado y el reformismo jurídico colonial, 1950–2002*. Rio Piedras, PR: Publicaciones Gaviota, 2018.

Wall, Tyler, Parastou Saberi, and Will Jackson. *Destroy, Build, Secure: Readings on Pacification*. Ottawa: Red Quill Books, 2017.

Watson, Blake. *Buying America from the Indians: Johnson v. McIntosh and the History of Native Land Rights*. Norman: University of Oklahoma Press, 2012.

Welch, Richard E. *Imperialists vs. Anti-Imperialists: The Debate over Expansionism in the 1890's*. Primary Sources in American History. Itasca, IL: F.E. Peacock Publishers, 1972.

Weston, Rubin Francis. *Racism in U.S. Imperialism: The Influence of Racial Assumptions on American Foreign Policy, 1893–1946*. Columbia: University of South Carolina Press, 1972.

Wilkins, David E. *American Indian Sovereignty and the US Supreme Court: The Making of Justice*. Austin: University of Texas Press, 1997.

Zapata Oliveras, Carlos R. *"Nuevos caminos hacia viejos objetivos": Estados Unidos y el establecimiento del Estado Libre Asociado de Puerto Rico, 1945–1953*. Rio Piedras, PR: Editorial Edil, 1991.

Web-Based Sources

Agricultural Research Service. "Tropical Crops and Germplasm Research: Mayaguez, PR." US Department of Agriculture. Accessed August 8, 2023. https://www.ars .usda.gov/southeast-area/mayaguez-pr/tropical-crops-and-germplasm-research /docs/locations-history/.

Center for Individual Freedom. "Small Investors Like Teresa." Political ad, April 22, 2016. Internet Archive. https://archive.org/details/PolAd_Bankruptcy _Retirement_s9sgm.

———. "Washington Is Trying to Pull a Fast One." Political ad, April 13, 2016. Accessed November 2, 2023. https://politicaladarchive.org/ad/PolAd_Bankruptcy _Retirement_i87nk/

Gonzalez, Juan. "Hurricane Colonialism." Interview by Jeremy Scahill, *The Intercept*, September 19, 2018. https://theintercept.com/2018/09/19/hurricane-colonialism -the-economic-political-and-environmental-war-on-puerto-rico/.

International Foundation for Electoral Systems. "Election Guide: Commonwealth of Puerto Rico." Accessed August 8, 2023. https://www.electionguide.org/countries /id/175/.

Marxuach, Sergio M. *Policy Brief: Tax Reform (Again)*. San Juan: Center for a New Economy, April 2022. https://grupocne.org/wp-content/uploads/2022/04/2022.04 -Tax-Reform-Again.pdf.

Municipal Resources and Service Center. "Types of Municipal Debt." Accessed August 8, 2023. https://mrsc.org/explore-topics/finance/debt/types-of-municipal -debt.

Obama, Barack. "Weekly Address: Addressing Puerto Rico's Economic Crisis." June 11, 2016. YouTube video. https://youtu.be/l_rI1PGmkYc.

Oliver, John. *Last Week Tonight with John Oliver*, Season 3, Episode 10, "Puerto Rico." April 24, 2016. YouTube video (at 19:05). https://www.youtube.com/watch?v=Tt -mpuR_QHQ.

Power 4 Puerto Rico. "Power 4 Puerto Rico Denounces Approval of Unsustainable Debt Adjustment Plan." January 12, 2022. https://www.power4puertorico.com /statements/2022/1/19/power-4-puerto-rico-denounces-approval-of -unsustainable-debt-adjustment-plan.

Sotheby's International Realty. "Puerto Rico Tax Incentives." Accessed August 8, 2023. http://puertoricotaxincentives.com.

Index

capitalism, 3, 6, 11, 64–65, 79, 81,
83–86, 88–89, 93, 99, 112
Capó, Bobby, 12
Caribbean, the, 1, 4, 7, 22, 63, 66, 73,
99, 114, 125, 135–36
Chafee, Calvin, 58
Cherokee Nation, 41–46; *Cherokee Nation
v. Georgia*, 41–44; Cherokee Removal
Act, 41, 44; *United States v. Rogers*,
46–48; *Worcester v. Georgia*, 43–44, 46
Christianity, 38, 48; Catholicism, 29
circuit courts: Puerto Rico and, 31,
130–31, 139; in Dred Scott case, 53–54
citizenship: Black in US, 49–50, 52–55,
57–59; *Downes v. Bidwell* and, 18,
29–20; Guano Islands Act and, 21–22;
Indigenous in US, 39, 42–43, 45–47;
Jones-Shafroth Act and, 31–32, 100;
Jones v. United States and, 24;
PROMESA and, 124–25; Public Law
600 and, 103; Puerto Ricans and US,
15–16, 72, 90, 118–19, 151n59;
second-class, 30–31; Tydings-Piñero
bill and, 100–101; *US v. Vaello Madero*
and, 139
Civil Rights Act of 1964, 113
class: elites, 59, 69, 71, 73, 79–80, 83, 89,
96; middle, 69, 91, 98, 114; peasants,
63, 65, 67–68, 97; working, 30, 71, 75,
81, 93; wealthy Americans, 6–7. *See
also* poverty
coffee production, 3, 63, 81, 90
Cold War, 3, 99, 103, 106
colonialism: anticolonial rhetoric, 84,
86; and civilization rhetoric, 7, 16, 79,
103; commonwealth status and, 10,
91–93, 95, 101–2, 104–10; decolonization, 3, 10, 93, 98, 110, 137; extractive, 3–4, 10, 108; insular cases and, 3,
18, 35, 49; Missouri Compromise and,
56; settler, 8–9, 17, 20, 35–37, 41, 39,
47; twenty-first century, 4–5, 111–14,
116, 118–22, 124–27, 129–30, 133–34,
137–38, 140; and US experimentation,
64–65, 68–72, 78–81, 84, 88–89

commonwealth status, 105, 109, 111,
122, 126; Partido Popular
Democrático de Puerto Rico and, 111
compact language, 33, 103–4, 106,
108–10; bilateral, 102–3, 107
Congress, United States: and Dred Scott
case, 53, 55–57; and Guano Islands
Act, 21; House of Representatives, 18,
20, 41, 103, 124, 137; and Indigenous
tribes, 36–37, 41, 44–45, 48–49; and
insular cases, 18, 26–33; and
PROMESA, 11; and Puerto Rico as
commonwealth, 90, 92–94, 99, 101–5,
107–8, 110; and Puerto Rican
experimentation, 89; and twenty-first
Puerto Rican, 112, 116–25, 127,
129–30, 133–34, 137–40. *See also*
plenary power, US congressional
consent, Puerto Rican, 102, 104–5, 107;
mutual, 100–101
Constitution, Puerto Rican, 11, 99–108,
111, 116, 119; and Bill of Rights, 56
Constitution, United States: Amendment VI to, 143n65; Appointments
Clause of, 130, 132–33; Article I, 10,
131; Article II, 129–31; Article III, 42,
151n59; Bill of Rights, US, 20, 25–26,
31; Double Jeopardy Clause, 120; and
Dred Scott case, 49–50, 53–59; Fifth
Amendment, 56–57, 120–22, 128,
139, 151n59; Fourteenth Amendment,
29, 49, 59; insular cases and, 15,
17–21, 25–29, 31–33, 113, 132–33,
139–40; and Marshall Trilogy, 39–40,
42–45, 48; privileges of, 46, 50, 55, 58;
Sixth Amendment, 30–31, 33, 151n59;
Territories Clause of, 55–56; Thirteenth Amendment, 49, 59; unconstitutionality, 25, 19, 43–44, 55–56,
129–30, 133
Córdova Dávila, Félix, 75–76
corporations, 3, 10, 18, 59, 68, 83, 88,
91, 97, 114, 128; sugar, 81, 85
corruption, 5–6, 12, 96, 137
covered entity, Puerto Rico as, 126

Horton, Benjamin, 83, 86–87
Houston, Texas, 1–2
human rights, 93, 104–6
hunger, 27, 73, 82, 86–87
hurricanes, 5, 66, 101, 135; Irma, 4–5;
  Maria, 4–6, 136, 141n2; San Ciriaco,
  63, 66
hygiene, 63

Illinois, 37–38, 40, 50
Illinois Land Company, 37–38, 40
immigration, 29, 31, 70, 100; out-
  migration, 5
immunities, 46, 55, 58
imperialism, US, 15–16, 59, 64–65, 73,
  84; anti-imperialism, 16; imperial
  experiments, 8. See also empire, US
incorporation, territorial, 19, 28, 31–33,
  59, 103, 124, 131, 139–40; unincorporated territory, 3, 16, 20–21, 25, 28,
  30, 33, 56, 93, 104, 110, 134
independence, Puerto Rican, 84, 95–96,
  98–99, 104, 109–10; pro-
  independence activists, 80, 86, 96
independent nations, 39, 42–43, 48
Indiana, 37–38
Indigenous people. See Native tribes
industrialization, 91–93, 97–98, 108–9,
  114–15
inequality, 6, 22, 27, 30, 33–34, 37, 58,
  69, 87–88, 113, 131, 140; injustice, 57,
  72, 79, 113, 140
infrastructure, 97, 115, 136
Institute for Tropical Medicine, 65, 68
Insular Cases, 3, 8–9, 15, 17–21, 30, 109,
  121, 130–34, 138–40, 141n2
insular territories, 25–26, 28, 33, 45–46,
  49–50, 56, 73; Bureau of Insular
  Affairs, 74–75, 77; insular government, 82, 86; Insular Police, 65,
  79–81, 85–86, 88–89, 95–96

Japanese internment, 132
Johnson v. M'Intosh, 37–40, 45–46, 48
Jones v. United States, 22–24, 28

Jones-Shafroth Act, 29–32, 90, 100–101
Jones, Henry, 23–24
judicial system, 32, 45, 54, 71; judicial
  review, 21, 36, 48
Junta, the, 11, 125–33, 135, 137–38
jurisdiction, US, 22–24, 41–43, 46,
  51–55, 57, 110, 122
jury system, 30–33, 53; grand juries,
  25, 120

Kern, Howard L., 70–71
Key, George, 23–24
Korematsu v. US, 132–33

labor, 91–92, 98, 115; chauffeurs' union,
  83; construction workers, 73–74, 81,
  98; dockworkers, 82, 87; Federación
  Libre de Trabajadores (FLT), 30,
  83–87; hard, 43; labor camps, 70–72,
  74–77; migrant, 78; pensions, 7,
  114–16, 128–30, 133, 137; Puerto
  Rican in US, 1, 3, 30, 74–78; in Puerto
  Rico, 4, 22, 24, 65, 67–69, 71–76,
  80–88, 90–91, 94, 96–98, 115, 129,
  133; and riots, 22–23, 82–83; sex
  workers, 69–72; unemployment, 4–5,
  74, 78, 81–82; unions, 30, 71, 83, 86,
  129; US Department of, 74–75; wages,
  67, 74–75, 77, 82–84, 87–88, 98. See
  also strikes
land: Native tribes and, 36–41, 44, 48;
  Puerto Rican land reform, 96–98, 109
Latin America, 99, 103, 125
law: civil law, 32; civil marriages, 51;
  criminal, 30, 43, 56, 121–22, 151n59;
  divorce, 64–65; Elective Governor Act
  (Public Law 382), 98; international,
  39, 45, 128; legal codes, 45; legal
  genealogy, 8–9, 17, 36, 58; legal
  history, 9, 11, 24; legal precedents, 9,
  15–17, 32–33, 35–36, 45, 58; ley de la
  mordaza, 96; Public Law 382, 98;
  Public Law 600, 98–105, 110; Puerto
  Rico Arms Trafficking Act, 120; race
  and, 7–9, 113, 132, 134; statues, 29,

race (cont.)
    49; racial undesirables, 8–9, 17, 58; racialized logics, 8–10, 16–17, 50, 64, 68, 71, 112–13;. *See also* exclusion, racial; racism
racism: anti-Black, 9; Native people and, 36, 39, 49–50; racial undesirables, 8–9, 17, 25, 28, 58; "savage" rhetoric, 39–40, 131; segregation, 8, 16, 59, 93–94, 113; toward Puerto Ricans, 2–3, 8, 11, 16, 34, 73, 79, 93–94, 110, 113, 116, 118, 133–34, 139–40
recessions, 2, 114; Great Recession, 115–16
Reid v. Covert, 109, 151n59
Republican Party, US, 55, 57–58
retirees, 117, 129, 133, 137
rights: civil, 113, 130; *Downes v. Bidwell* and, 8, 23–27, 29–30, 32, 72, 78, 89; *Dred Scott v. Sandford* and, 49–50, 53, 55–56; human, 93, 105–6; natural, 26–27, 44–45, 78; Native tribes and, 39–47, 49; plenary power and, 11; property, 26–27, 40, 100; in Puerto Rico, 93, 99, 103, 105; rightlessness, 24; US Supreme Court and, 35, 37; of workers, 81, 86
Riggs, E. Francis, 95–96
Robbins Curtis, Benjamin, 57
Roberts, John, 131–32
Roby, Charles, 22–23
Rockefeller Foundation, 63, 67
Roosevelt, Theodore, Jr., 95
Ross, John, 22
Rosselló, Ricardo, 6, 11
rural areas, 67, 91–94, 96; laborers in, 90–93; peasants in, 67, 97

San Juan: COVID-19 in, 136–37; insular police in, 70, 74, 77, 82; protests in, 6, 111; Puerta de Tierra sector, 70, 111
Sanford, Irene, 51
Sanford, John, 51–52, 54, 58
Scott, Dred, 50–55, 57–58. See also *Dred Scott v. Sandford*

self-determination, 95, 100, 111, 137
self-governance, Puerto Rican, 92, 100–101, 105, 119, 122–23; non-self-governing territories, 104, 106–7
settler colonialism, 8–9, 17, 20, 35–37, 41, 39, 47
sex workers, 69–72
sexually transmitted infections, 69–72
slavery, 24–25, 35–36; abolition of, 35, 53–54, 57–58, 67–68, 70, 85, 113; free Blacks, 36, 50, 53–55, 57. See also *Dred Scott v. Sandford*
Slayden, James, 16
Smith, Edward, 23–24
social Darwinism, 7, 9, 17, 26, 139
social hygiene, 69, 72
Social Security, 138; Supplemental Security Income (SSI), 138–40
socialism, 71, 94–95, 98–99, 105–7; Partido Socialista (Socialist Party), 32, 83–86
Sotomayor, Sonia, 121, 139
sovereignty, Puerto Rican, 20; ELA and, 95, 98, 100–101, 103, 106, 108; insular cases and, 20, 22, 25, 28, 32; Marshall Trilogy and, 39–40, 42–45; separate sovereigns, 35; twenty-first century, 120–22, 124, 128
Soviet Union, 93, 106–7
Spain, 3, 18, 28, 32, 56, 65, 67–70, 94
Spanish language, 2, 29, 90, 117
state of exception, "American," 8, 17, 36, 49–50, 58; Puerto Rico as, 9, 17, 34, 58–59
statehood, Puerto Rican, 20–21, 33, 98–99, 104, 108–10, 111
Strader v. Graham, 53, 57
strikes: Insular Police and, 79, 81–87; violence during, 79–81, 83–84, 87–88
subsidies, 1, 114–15, 130
subversive activities, 80, 82
sugar industry, 3, 10, 65, 68, 78–85, 87–88, 91, 93; sugar strike of 1933–34, 82–83, 87

United States (cont.)
southern, 35, 41, 44, 53–55, 74–76; state violence by, 4, 24, 27, 35, 48, 58–59; United States Employment Service, 74, 78; United States–Puerto Rico relationship, 9–10, 32, 94, 101, 105, 110, 112, 114, 134; War Department, 74, 78. *See also* Congress, United States; Constitution, United States; empire, United States; federal government, United States; military, United States; Native tribes; Supreme Court, United States

United States v. Rogers, 36–37, 46

United States v. Vaello Madero, 138–39

utilities: creation of, 97; privatization of, 6, 130; Puerto Rico Electric Power Authority (PREPA), 122, 129–30; utility rates, 5, 117

Vaello Madero, José, 138–39

Viña, Ramón, 76

violence: toward strikers, 79–81, 83–84, 87–88; US state, 4, 24, 27, 35, 48, 58–59

Virgin Islands, US, 73, 106

voting: free Blacks and, 57; Puerto Ricans in US, 16, 29; in twentieth-century Puerto Rico, 96–97, 104; in twenty-first century Puerto Rico, 127

Wabash Land Company, 37–38, 40

wages, 67, 74–75, 77, 82–84, 87–88, 98

Walcott, Charles C., Jr, 74–75

War of 1898, 18, 26, 35; US acquisitions in, 16, 19–20, 33, 56, 64

war: Civil War, 49, 57, 59; Cold War, 3, 99, 103, 106; World War I, 29, 69–73, 77–78, 80; World War II, 5, 91, 93, 106

whiteness: *Downes v. Bidwell* and, 15–16, 20, 28; *Dred Scott v. Sandford* and, 27, 49–50; *Jones v. United States* and, 23; Native tribes and, 33, 36, 40–41, 43, 46–47; social Darwinism and, 7; white saviors, 69, 78

Wilkins, David E., 47

women, 69–72, 75, 82

Worcester v. Georgia, 43–44, 46

Worcester, Samuel, 43–44

workers. *See* labor

Yager, Arthur, 75, 77

www.ingramcontent.com/pod-product-compliance
Lightning Source LLC
Chambersburg PA
CBHW022236210325
23908CB00002B/66